Watercolour

MEETS

Hand lettering

A BOOK OF BLOGGER PROJECTS

Bunte Galerie
Geliebtes Chaos
Mädchenkunst
May & Berry

Contents

Backgrounds & Patterns

Leaves, Succulents & Cacti

Fantastic Beasts

Sweet Small Fruits

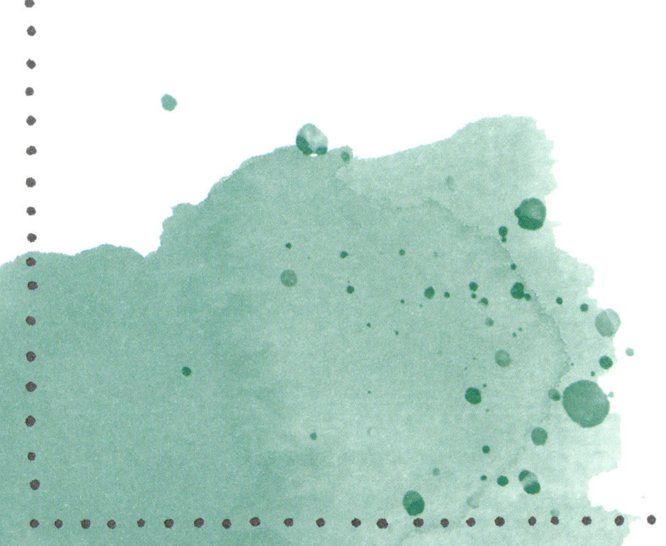

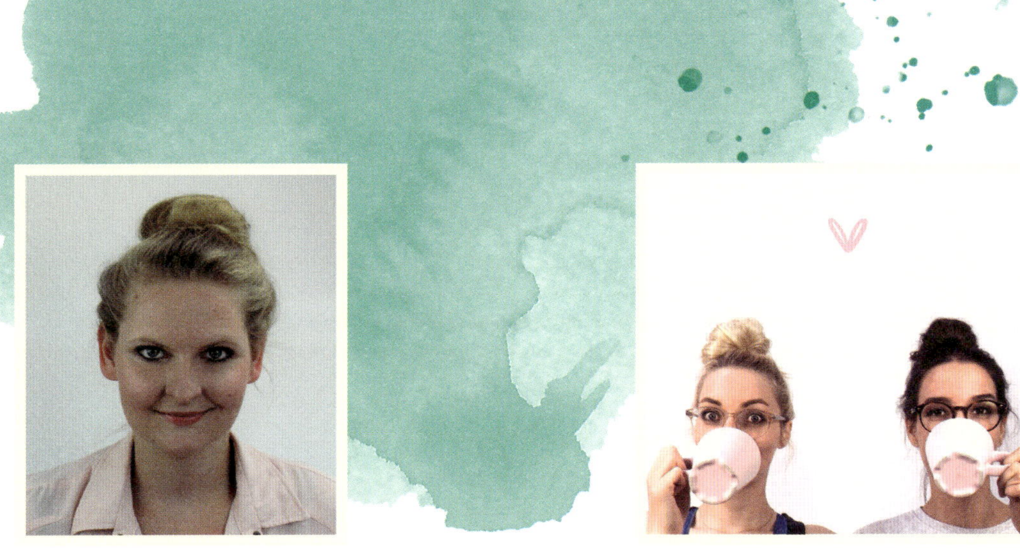

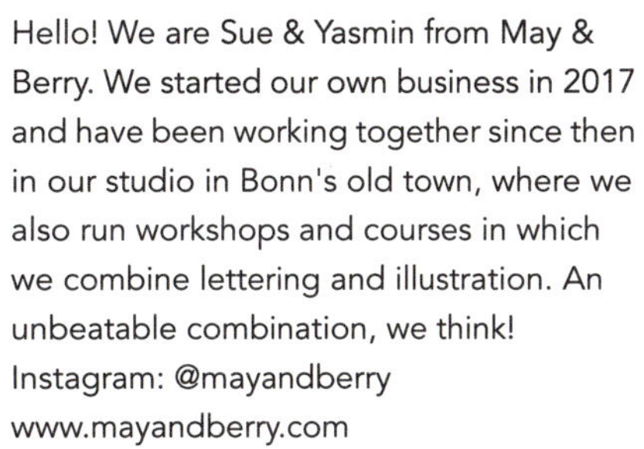

Hello, I am a Christin. I trained as a TV editor but now I'm self-employed. Creativity plays an important role in my life, so I'm happy to be able to combine my love of creative activity with journalism in my art blog Mädchenkunst and in many other projects. I discovered hand lettering about three years ago and today I am passionate about combining brush lettering with watercolour.
Instagram: @mädchenkunst
www.maedchenkunst.de
youtube.com/mädchenkunst

Hello! We are Sue & Yasmin from May & Berry. We started our own business in 2017 and have been working together since then in our studio in Bonn's old town, where we also run workshops and courses in which we combine lettering and illustration. An unbeatable combination, we think!
Instagram: @mayandberry
www.mayandberry.com

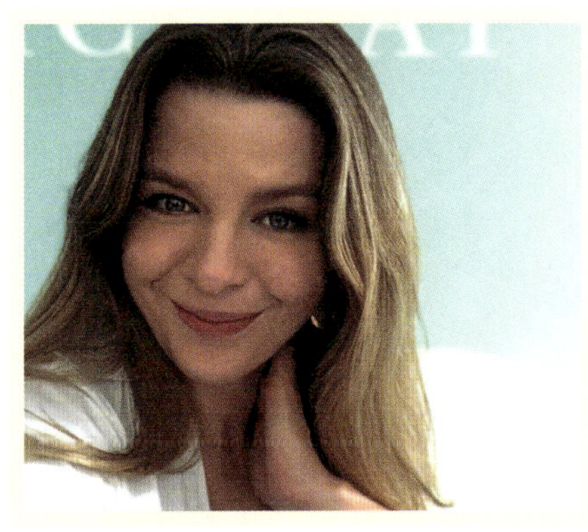

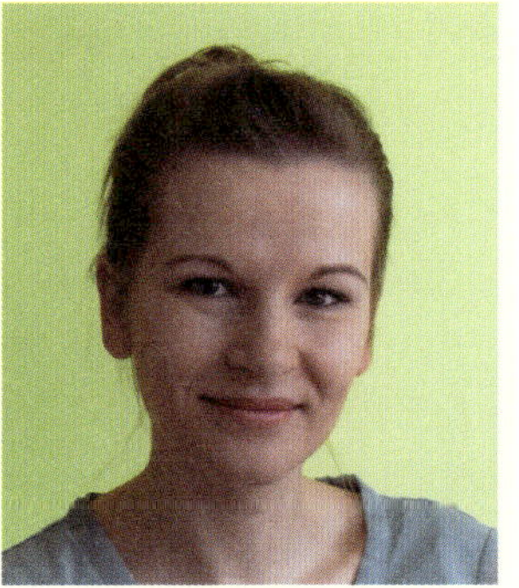

Hello dear ones! My name is Tanja and I live in the beautiful surroundings of Munich where the great lakes and mountains are always a reliable source of inspiration for my new designs. In 2017, I took the step into self-employment with my agency Nice Day Communications and the blog Geliebtes Chaos. Since then I have rediscovered my passion for watercolour paints and can't imagine a life without painting.
Instagram: @tanschiiibunny
@geliebtes_chaos
www.geliebtes-chaos.de

Hey, I'm Ludmila from Bunte Galerie. I like to work with diverse aspects of lettering, so that lettering and illustration have become inseparable for me. Beautifully painted letters already create a picture with their interplay of shape and colour. I love it if I can use the same colour shades when I combine my brush lettering with watercolour painting.
Instagram: @buntegalererie
www.bunte-galerie.de

What is Watercolour?

When you think of watercolour, your school days might come to mind: sitting in front of a paint box, wearing an old shirt of your dad's as a painting overall and trying to paint a family portrait with a thick bristle brush – the main thing was to use lots of colours!

But there is a lot more to watercolour. Unlike painting with acrylics, for example, it is not all about perfection. The water-soluble colours do what they want anyway. And that is exactly what is the attraction for me, which explains my passion for watercolour paints. I'm not interested in painting an accurate image from a photo. It's more about capturing a moment with just a few dabs of paint. It's about the essence of a design and the question of how much I can leave out without the image losing its shape. I find it inspirational to see how just a few brush strokes are needed for a flower to appear.

Nowadays, when perfectionism is part of everyday life, there can be nothing better than simply letting go and painting a unique small work of art without long deliberation.

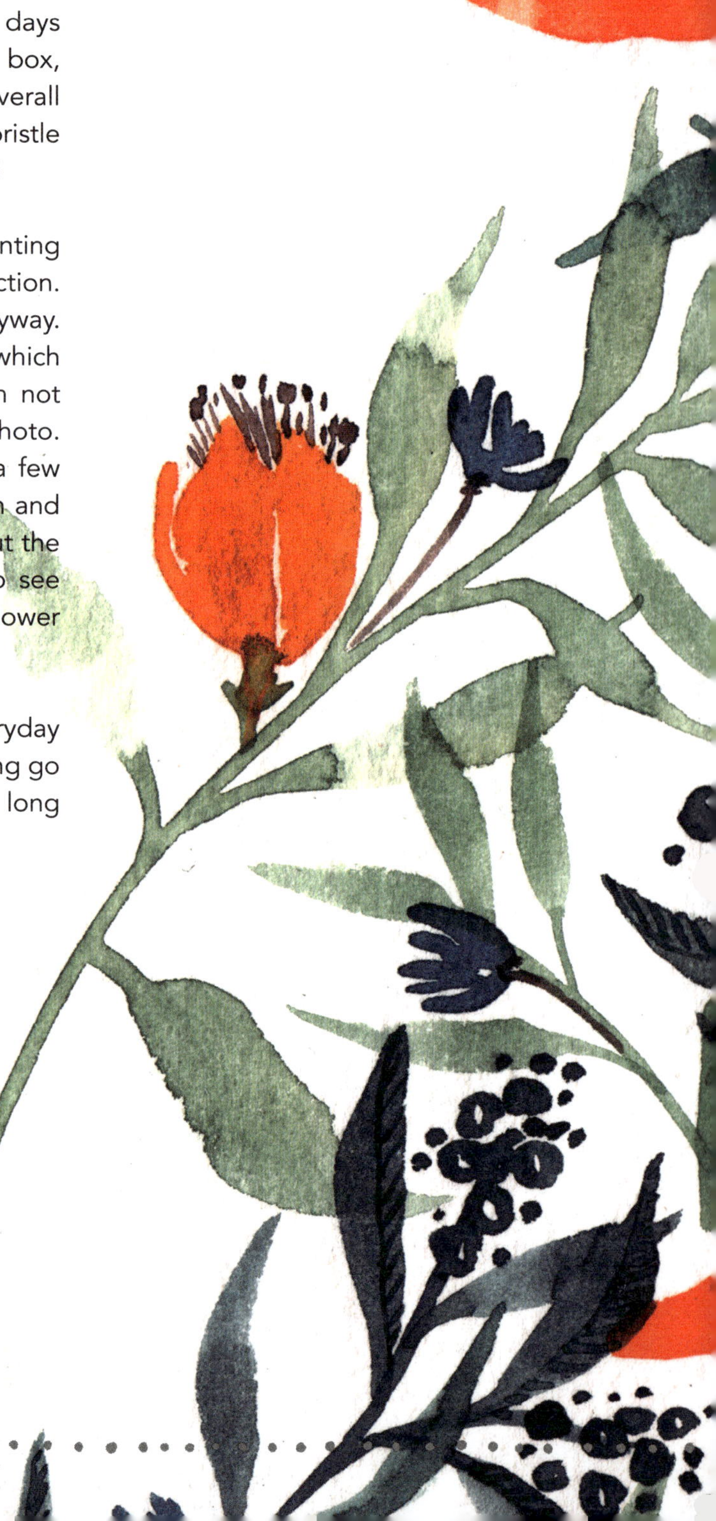

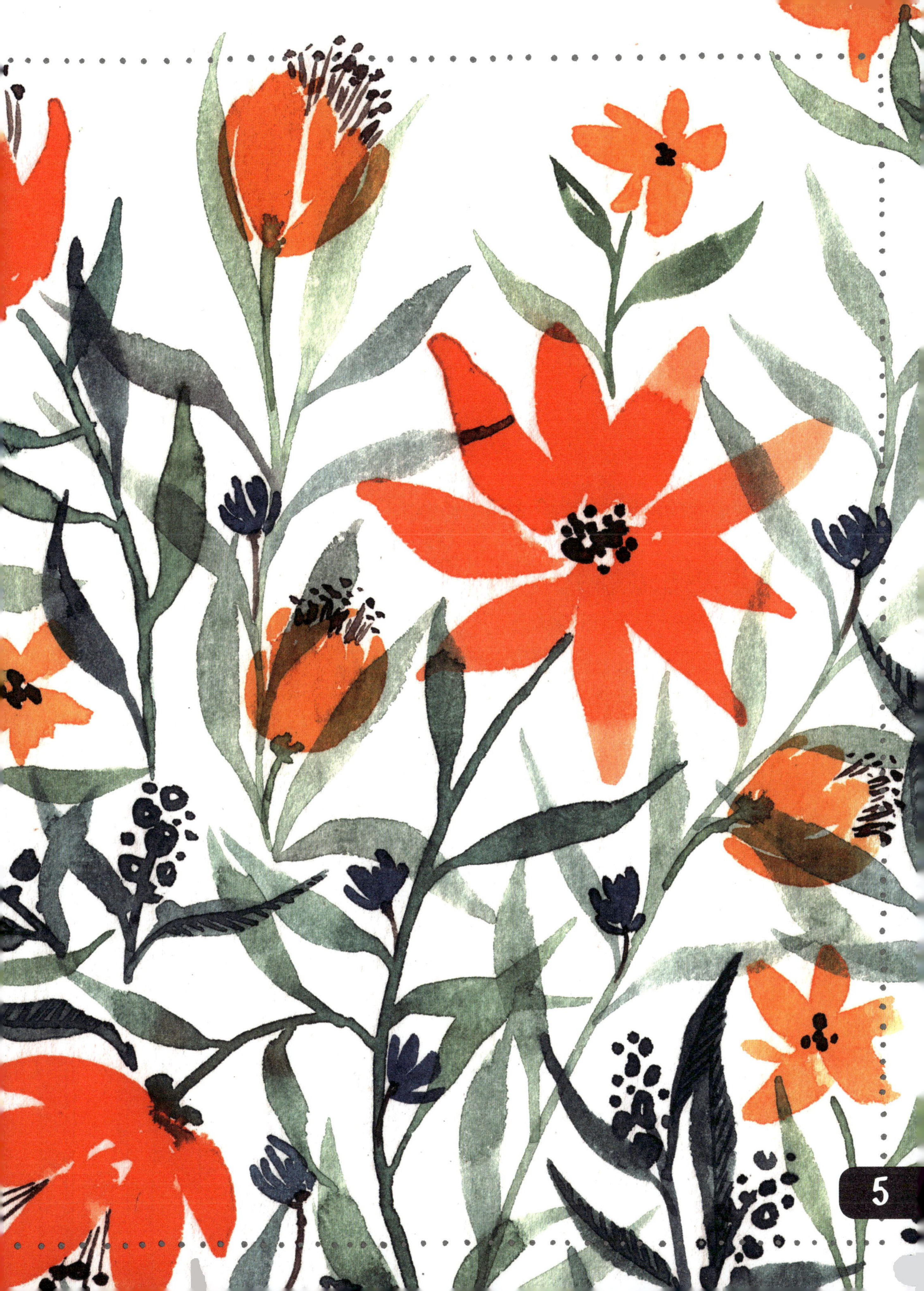

materials for Watercolour

You don't need much to paint watercolours.
The basic equipment includes:

- Pencil
- Rubber
- Round brush
- Wide or flat brush
- Watercolour paints
- Watercolour paper

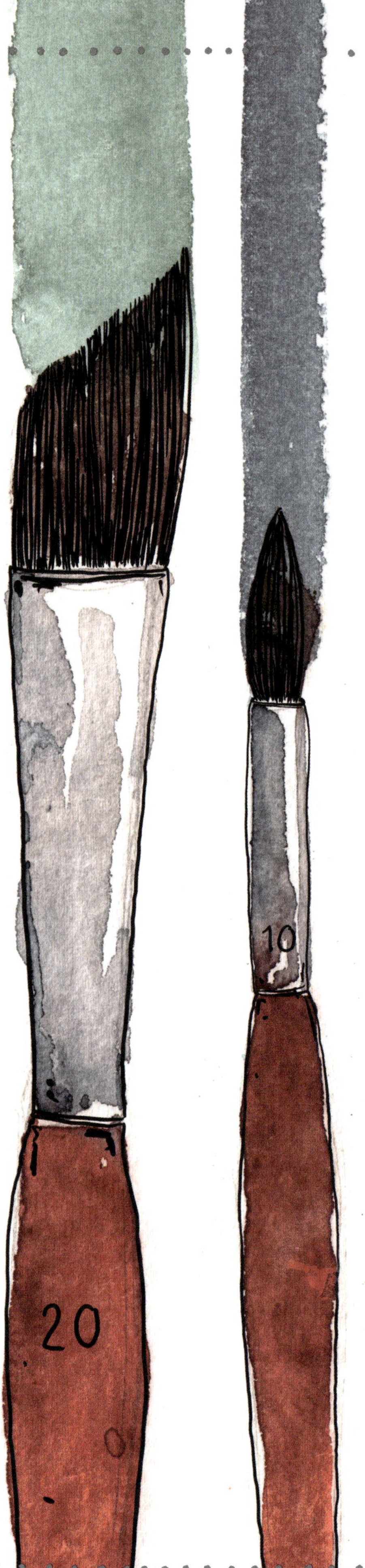

Brush: The question of which is the right brush is not easy to answer. The range on offer is infinite and prices differ greatly. The hair used in the brush has the greatest effect on price. You can choose between inexpensive synthetic hair or expensive animal hair, such as red sable. I would recommend buying two high quality round brushes instead of ten cheap ones. It is important that the brush fibres form a good tip - even a very thick brush can have a very fine tip if it's good quality. You can use it to draw both very thick and very thin lines. For example, I like to use the Da Vinci Cosmotop-Spin brushes in sizes 6 and 12. They are very soft and do not fray. In contrast to round brushes, wide or flat brushes are more suitable for larger areas such as backgrounds. A large wide brush is sufficient for your starter pack. You don't need much more to get started.

Pencil: When you are a beginner, sketching out is a great help. An HB pencil that is not too soft and not too hard is perfect. The lines become fine but are still clearly visible. They can also be erased without a trace. Always try not to press down too hard with a pencil, otherwise there will be grooves in the paper in which the paint will collect.

Paper: One type of watercolour paper is not like another. There are countless different varieties that can be broadly divided into rough, medium and fine. Every surface has its advantages. Very rough paper gives the illustration a special texture and makes the colour appear completely different from, for example, fine, smooth paper. This paper, in turn, is very suitable for working with brush pens that quickly fray on rough paper. Watercolour paper is 200 - 300gsm thicker than normal drawing paper, which is just 100 - 150gsm. One practical option is to buy watercolour paper in a block, which is usually glued all around. This keeps the paper in shape even if you use a lot of water. After drying, you can carefully remove the sheet of paper with a small knife. I like to use Hahnemühle paper; the selection is huge - from simple sketch pads and beautiful watercolour paper to handmade paper, you will find everything your heart desires.

TIP: **As you familiarize yourself with watercolour paints, it's fine to to start out with a cheaper paper.**

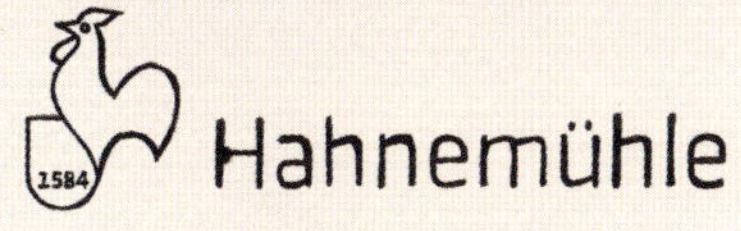

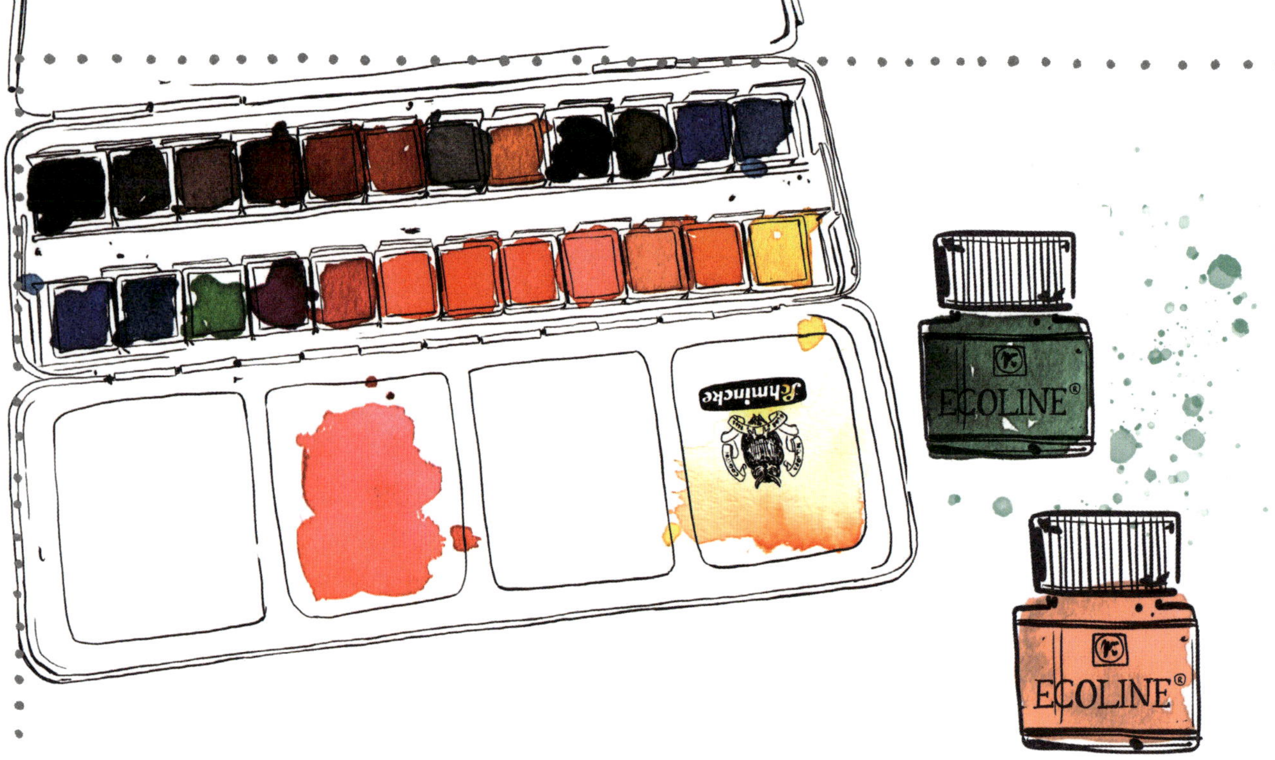

The Right Colours

The projects in this book have been completed using two different kinds of watercolour paint – Schmincke and Ecoline. Both types have their advantages, but it is a matter of taste which type of paint you choose to use.

Ecoline watercolours behave similarly to ink or airbrush colours. They come ready mixed with water, in small pots and they consist of artificial pigments, which is why they develop a strong luminosity. They are suitable for use on both watercolour paper and other grounds such as cardboard or drawing paper. Ecoline watercolours are not waterproof when dry, so you can dissolve your work with water when it is dry and then continue painting.

They are also perfect for hand lettering.

TIP: The watercolours and brush pens from Ecoline are compatible with each other – so you can dip a brush pen into a pot of paint and thus create gradients in your lettering.

Schmincke's watercolour paints are available in tubes and pans. I am a big fan of my watercolour box with built-in palette. It can be used very quickly and you can begin painting straight away. A small starter box with 12 pans in it is enough to get you started. You can mix many different shades from these basic colours.

MIXING COLOURS

Mixing up different colours is an important part of watercolour painting – after all, the choice of colours in an average watercolour box is limited. It takes a bit of time to get the hang of mixing new colours when you are a beginner. It's not always easy to estimate the correct amount of paint and a few colours can turn into a dirty grey or dark brown. Don't let this discourage you! Playing with the colours will help you get things right – after all, practice makes perfect.

In the beginning, you should never mix together more than two colours. Also, always use the lighter shade as a base. With watercolour paints, it is almost impossible to lighten a dark tone. So, for example, start with a yellow and gradually add more blue to get the shade of green you want. Take a little time to try out different ranges of colour. At some point you will intuitively mix the right amounts together.

TIP: **Natural-looking colours are particularly suitable for floral illustrations. When I'm painting a red flower with green leaves, I add a bit of green to the red and vice versa. As a result, the two colours appear more closely related and fit together perfectly.**

CREATE COLOUR CODES

Before you begin to paint, you can create a colour code. This helps you to test and determine the colour combinations for your illustration in advance and acts as a reminder when you come to start painting. To do this, draw several small squares on your sketch paper. Fill them with your two main colours then gradually add some different colours. You can see them side by side and get a better feeling of which colours work well together.

In another row of squares you can paint different shades of colour to see how light or dark the tones can get. Trying colours out in advance also helps you to lose your fear of the blank sheet of paper!

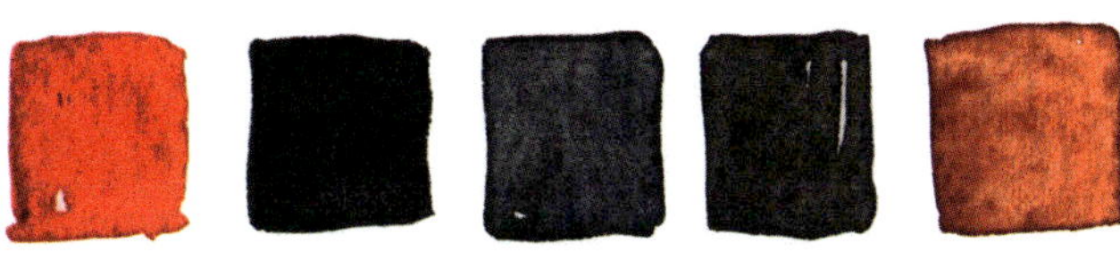

TIP: **An absolute must-have for my daily work is a piece of scrap paper on which I test out the paints and brushes I want to use. What is the intensity of the colour? How does it work on paper? Is there too much water on the brush or too little? How thin are the lines made with this brush?**
Use a scrap of paper like this as often as possible. It gives you a lot more certainty when using paints and brushes.

Playing with Transparency

A play between light and shadow can be seen in many famous paintings. And this isn't something that's difficult to achieve - there are many ways to add highlights or depth to a picture. A simple method with watercolour is to play with the transparency of the paint - in other words, with more or less transparent colour applications. You can give things that are supposed to appear inconspicuous a very delicate tint or you create space within the painting with different areas of opacity. If you look at the branches of leaves shown here, you can see what is meant: if you paint some leaves and a twig with a small amount of colour mixed with a lot of water, then the image will take a back seat. If you use a stronger shade - more colour mixed with less water - for the remaining leaves, then the whole branch starts to look much more three dimensional.

TIP: You can also observe this effect in nature. If you look into a landscape with mountains, for example, the mountains in the front appear a stronger colour than the ones behind. Try to be aware of your surroundings and you will be amazed at what you notice.

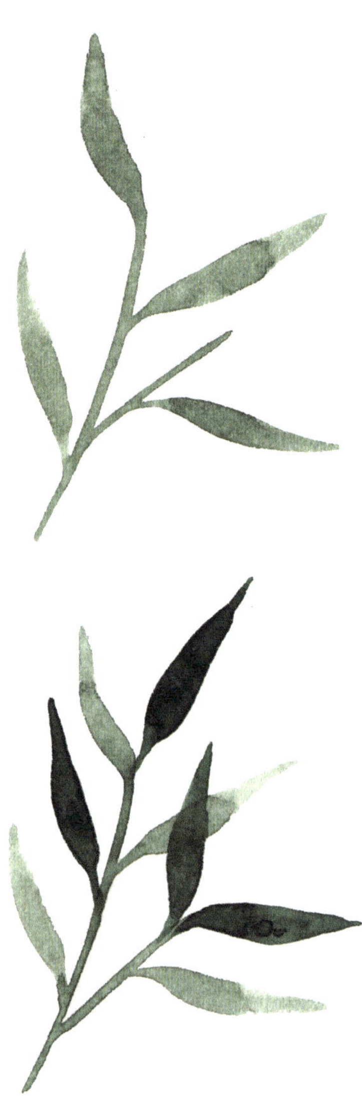

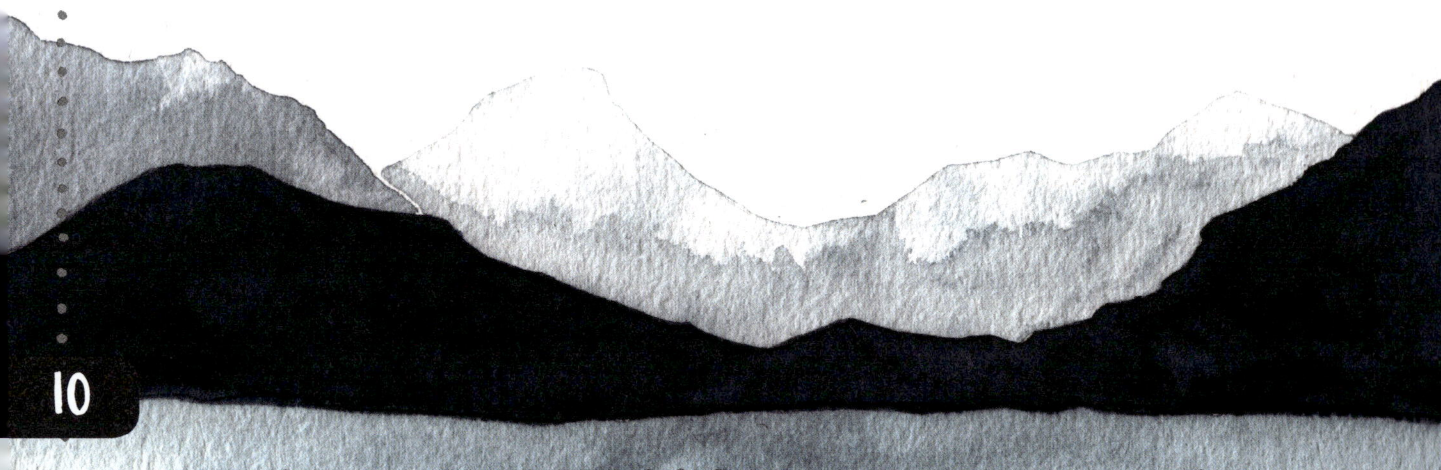

Embrace White Space

In many watercolour pictures, it is good to leave some areas unpainted These white patches give the illustration more structure and act like points of light. For example, you can use white spaces to separate the parts of a flower in such a way that the bloom can be recognized immediately, despite the abstract shapes.

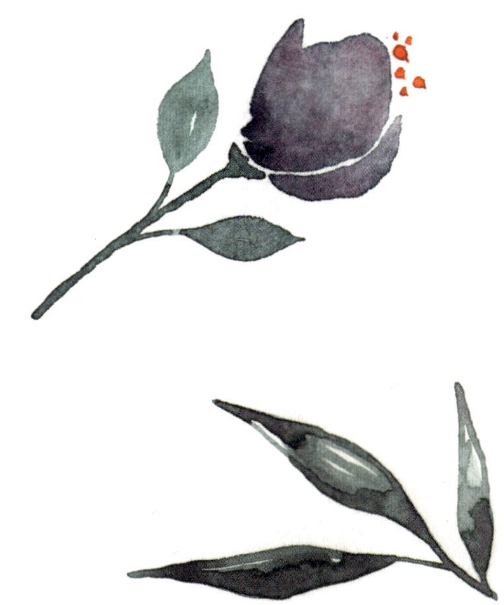

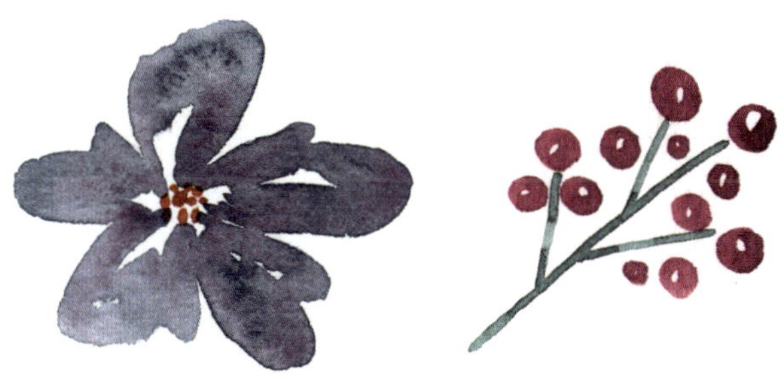

With a few white spots here and there, you also conjure up highlights in your picture, which make it appear much more vivid.

In watercolour, white spaces are created only by deliberately leaving paper unpainted. However, the difficulty, is that it is almost impossible to add white spots with watercolour paint afterwards.

In watercolour, layers of colour are added so that a picture is built up from light to dark, step by step. With the transparent shades of watercolour it is not possible to put a light colour over a dark one. It is different, for example, with acrylic painting. Here you simply reach for the tube of white paint when you want to add highlights.

Since we do not have this option with watercolour, any white areas must be decided upon before you begin and the paper left unpainted in advance. When you're a beginner it's quite difficult to know where to position points of light before you start painting but with plenty of practise you will get the hang of it.

The Colour Flow - Wash Drawing

One of the most fascinating things about watercolour paints is the way in which they flow into one another. It is hard to predict how the colour will develop on your paper - will it stay blue or yellow or will the colours mix completely? Depending on how much water is involved, you can get very different results.

There are two techniques in watercolour painting: wash drawing and glazing. Wash drawing is about letting colours develop freely. Several colours are applied to wet paper. The colours then flow into each other and form gradients. This technique can be used to great effect when painting leaves. A leaf is never a completely solid colour. Most of the time the leaf base is a little darker than the inner surface and in autumn yellow or red colours run through the leaf.

Start by painting a leaf on a sheet of damp watercolour paper in a very transparent tone, using lots of water and very little paint.

TIP: **When wash drawing, the moisture of the paper is very important. If it is too dry, the colours will not run together. If the brush is too wet, the water stays on the paper.**

Then pick up a bit more paint with the brush for a stronger colour and dab a little along the leaf base. The colour runs slowly along the leaf to the tip.

TIP: **Give the water time to disperse. The colours develop and combine further during drying.**

This technique also works the other way round. First paint the outline of a leaf with a strong colour. Again, it is important to find the right ratio of colour to water. Then wash out the brush and while still wet, brush it from the damp edges of the painted outline to the centre of the leaf. This creates a gradient that makes the leaf appear more three dimensional.

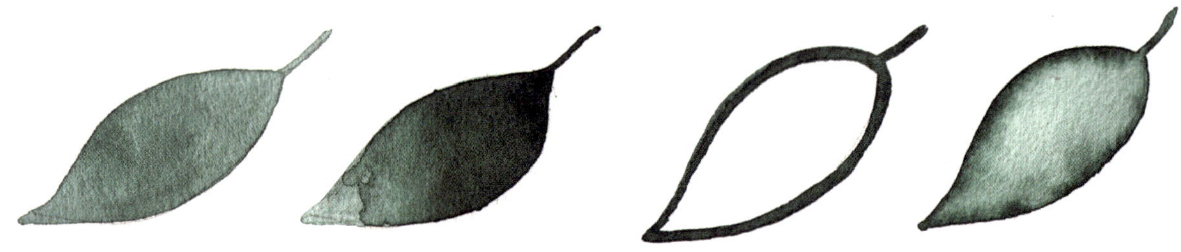

Layer by Layer - Glazing

The second important technique in watercolour painting is glazing. Areas of colour are allowed to dry and then a second, thinner layer of paint is placed over the top so the layer below still shows through. You can lay several layers of paint over each other - just make sure each layer is completely dry so that the colours do not flow into one another.

The different layers can create different colours and tones. For example, if a blue layer is painted over a red one, the area where the colours meet will be purple. If you overlap two areas of the same colour and transparency, the point where they meet will have a darker tone.

There are many ways to use this technique. You might, for example, want to paint a lush and colourful bouquet; by layering the flowers and leaves you can create a greater range of colours and tones and give your finished painting more depth.

Even a single flower looks much more three dimensional if made up of different layers of colour. A flower is always a little darker at the centre, because it doesn't get as much light as on the outer petals. So if you put one or two more layers in the middle of the flower, the image will be much more solid.

TIP: You can create space and depth in your paintings by using both glazing and washing. Ultimately, it is a matter of taste which technique you choose. Both ways need practice and experience – so concentrate on one technique at the beginning and gradually expand your skills. In the end, a combination of both techniques will make your illustrations more exciting.

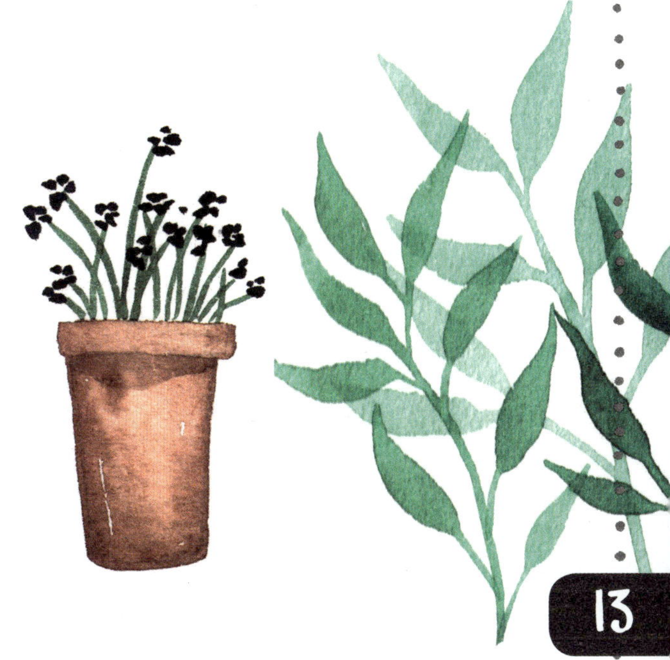

The Basics of Lettering – Anatomy of the Letters

Whether it's calligraphy, typography or hand lettering – it all starts with the letters. We know that there are upper- and lower-case letters, and that they can be bold, thin or italic. They can appear as coherent cursive characters or as individual block letters. They come in countless forms and styles, with each style saying something different. The art of writing has influenced us from an early age, even if we might not have noticed it. We see written things everywhere: on signs, on advertising posters, in books, on the computer – in fonts with a targeted message.

If you want to try your hand at lettering, you cannot avoid examining the structure of the letters.

If you compare the two lettering styles above you can see how the same word has a different sense if written in block capitals than in the curly cursive variant.

The great thing about hand lettering is that you can be very free with the design of the words. Unlike classic calligraphy, where you write between fixed guidelines, the letters can dance up and down. The only restriction is that you follow a horizontal line so that the lettering remains balanced and readable. You can easily imagine this line, although it is helpful at first to draw it in lightly with a pencil.

Faux Calligraphy

This simple hand-lettering technique is my absolute favourite because it allows you to mimic the style of calligraphy – so it is also known as fake calligraphy or faux calligraphy. When used correctly, you imitate the ink flow of a calligraphy pen. I usually use a black fine liner and/or a felt pen. Depending on how big the words should be, I choose a pen where the tip has a thickness of between 0.05mm and 0.8mm. Most of the time I choose 0.3mm.

For this technique, you first draw the 'skeleton' of a word with a pencil. Don't be discouraged if your drawing doesn't look too attractive at first.

When you are happy with your sketch, go over the pencil lines with a fine liner or felt pen, making sure that the lines are as smooth and clean as possible. Try to make your lines with a continuous stroke – when you do need to stop, wait until a new letter begins.

In the next step, you will double some of the lines. There is an important rule here: do this only on those lines that run downwards. Use a pencil to draw vertical guides to show where the double lines begin and where they end.
Finally, fill in the gaps between the double lines – this is much faster with a felt pen, but be careful not to draw over the edges.

As you can see, it's easy to convert a hand-drawn word into hand lettering. And the advantage of this technique is that you are free to determine how big the difference is between the thin and the thick lines.

Materials for Lettering

You don't need a lot of materials for hand lettering - your paper and writing medium is all that's required. The choice of paper and writing medium is, however, varied. You can use materials as diverse as pencils and ballpoint pens with printer paper as well as high-quality paper with brush pens and fine liners in a wide variety of colours and designs. Those who fall in love with hand lettering will soon be tempted by the many wonderful materials available from art suppliers! But when you begin, it's best to stick with the basics. You will be using the following materials when working with this book.

Paper You can never have enough notebooks and papers of all kinds for letterings. Simple printer paper is sufficient for quick designs. Tracing paper is excellent for working on designs without having to start over. Coated paper - which is nice and smooth and feels particularly soft - is ideal for using brush pens (their tips tend to fray quickly if not used with care). If you want to give away your lettering works, slightly thicker paper with a thickness of 250gsm to 300gsm is a good choice. We like to work with photo cardboard. This is available in a rough and smooth look and in many different colours. Kraft paper with a thickness of 300gsm is also one of our favourites. This brown paper brings out lettering to its best advantage – even in white - and has a very special look

Pencils A good HB pencil is sufficient for hand lettering. Just make sure that the tip is not completely sharp, otherwise it will scratch the paper and leave a traces, even when erased. The ideal pencil should fit comfortably in your hand, not smudge and be easy to erase. We like to use the pencils from Faber-Castell.

Rubber Your scribbles shouldn't leave any marks. That's why a good rubber is one of the most important materials. Inferior rubbers can smudge lines and, in the worst case, spoil the paper.

Ruler To ensure that your lettering is centred on the paper and follows a grid, you will need a ruler and possibly also a set square for diagonal lines. When you're a beginner, the preparatory work with the ruler will save you a lot of headaches – it's always a shame if you realize only after you've started that your lettering isn't in the middle.

Fine liners These are much better for hand lettering than ballpoint pens because their tips are finer and this ensures an even flow when writing. Fine liners are now part of everyday life; we use them mostly with tips the thickness of 0.4mm or 0.5mm. For hand-lettering enthusiasts, sizes between 0.05mm to 0.8mm and a large colour selection make fine liners very useful. Thin ones are ideal for details and delicate fonts. It's best to choose light-resistant and waterproof pens - these are ideal when combined with watercolour paints.

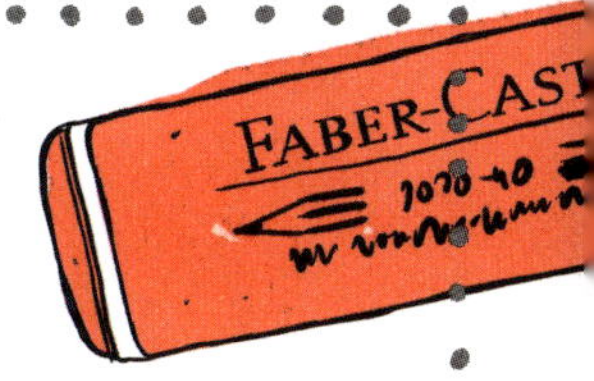

Felt pen, fibre-tip pen or marker What a fine liner can't do, a felt-tip pen can. These have an immovable tip, which distinguishes them from brush pens, and they are available in any size and colour. Felt-tip pens should also be waterproof when you are combining lettering and watercolour paints.

If you really get into doing hand lettering, then you will probably want to try these materials sooner or later.

Brush Pens If you enjoy hand lettering, then there is no way of avoiding brush pens. Ultimately, a brush pen is nothing more than a felt tip pen with a movable tip. This behaves like a brush because it gives way when pressed on. Using brush pens will take a lot of patience and effort when you're a beginner, but with a little practice you can conjure up great results in no time. The range of brush pens is now huge. They are available in countless colours, sizes and degrees of hardness, with rubber or fibre tips. In any case, there is something for everyone.

Brush Of course, brush lettering also works with a brush and paint. The technique is a bit more difficult than when writing with a brush pen, because brushes are usually much more flexible and difficult to control. Quality is particularly important here. Whether you are using natural or synthetic hair, the brush should not be frayed and must also be well maintained so that it keeps its shape for a long time. The brushes that we use in this book are ideal for both lettering and illustrations; we prefer to use Da Vinci brushes from the Cosmotop-Spin series.

Watercolour paint or Indian ink For inking or writing with a pen, conventional ink or watercolour paints are also ideal.

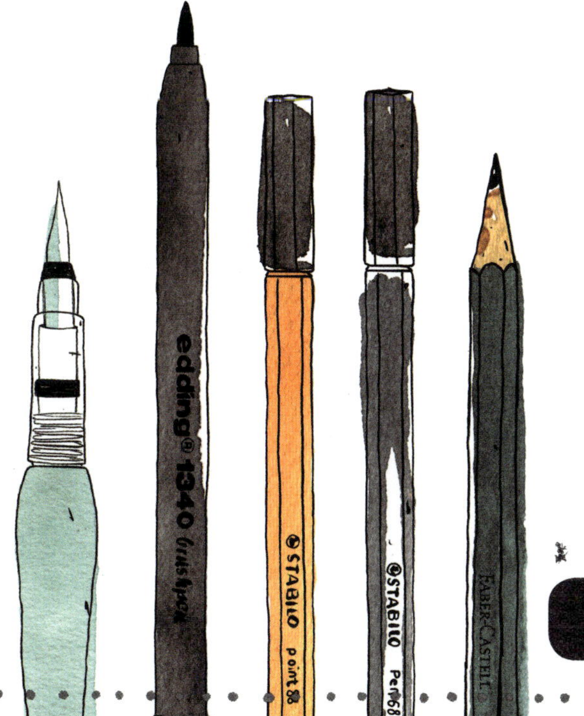

Lettering with Brush Pen

Brush pens (see also page 17) are probably the best-known medium for lovers of hand lettering. They are now available from almost every art shop or supplier. With a few skilful movements, hand lettering can be created in one go. The flexible tip of the brush pen gives way when writing and so a contrast between thin upward lines and the thicker downward ones is created automatically.

One thing is particularly important for this technique - practising! Writing with the brush pen requires a lot of patience. The head and hand have to get used to varying the pressure on the pen. At first, it is particularly difficult to master the thin lines that lead upwards. Do not be discouraged if they look shaky or not really thin at first.

Practise drawing thin, upward lines. For the thick lines, you have only to bend your wrist slightly so that the tip of the brush pen lies flatter on the paper.

When writing with the brush pen, also pay attention to when a new stroke begins. You can, of course, stop and put the pen down; you just have to know where is the best place to do this. It is best to stop after a line that runs up and down. The lower-case letter 'h' below, for example, is made up of two lines - it is best to pause at the end of the first stroke, before moving onto the second one.

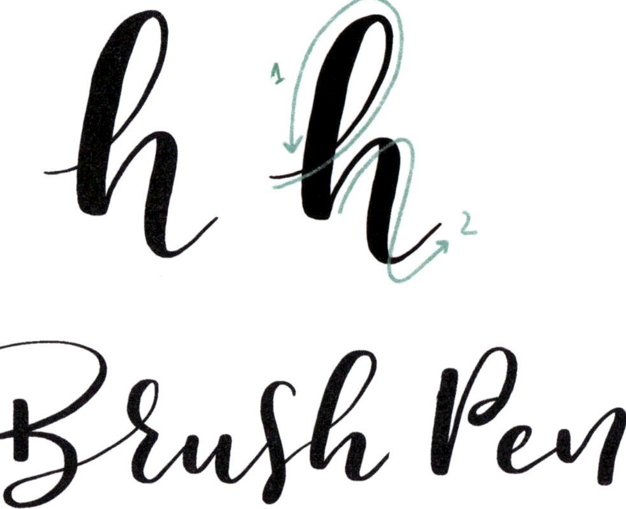

Why Does Lettering Go Well with Watercolour?

Hand lettering looks good on almost any surface. Whether it's paper, fabric, wood, a blackboard or even stone - the writing simply looks beautiful! The lettering can stand alone as a little gem, but it doesn't have to - illustrations can complement beautiful lettering wonderfully and bring it to life. They enhance the message without having to be particularly complex. With the right technique and a few tips and tricks, you can create the most beautiful lettering artworks!

This book is not only about lettering, but also about colour. Watercolour paints have a very special effect: this is also because it is not always possible to predict exactly what the colours will do. You can watch them run together and form new, random patterns.

Watercolour paints are very versatile and can be used as a background for lettering. They are usually diluted with plenty of water so that they run smoothly onto the paper. When the watercolour paper is dry, it can be written on.

A watercolour illustration will add impact to your lettering. The image not only decorates the writing, it can also support the message and improve the overall design.

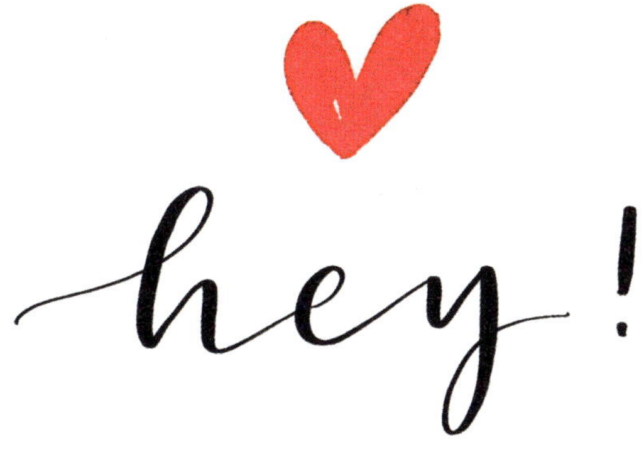

And not only that, watercolour paints are also ideal for lettering. You can use an imaginative play of colours and gradients to create beautiful lettering.

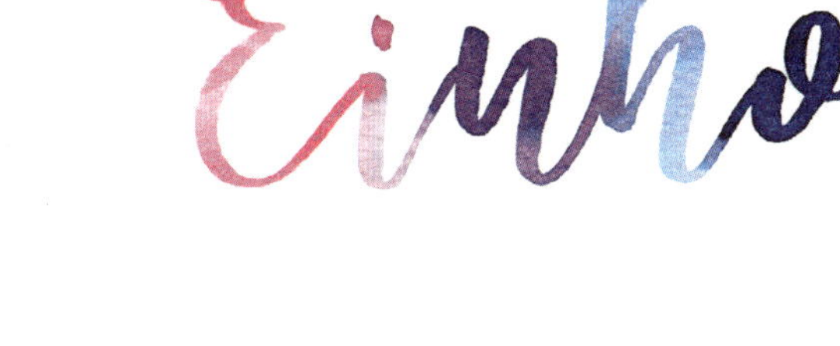

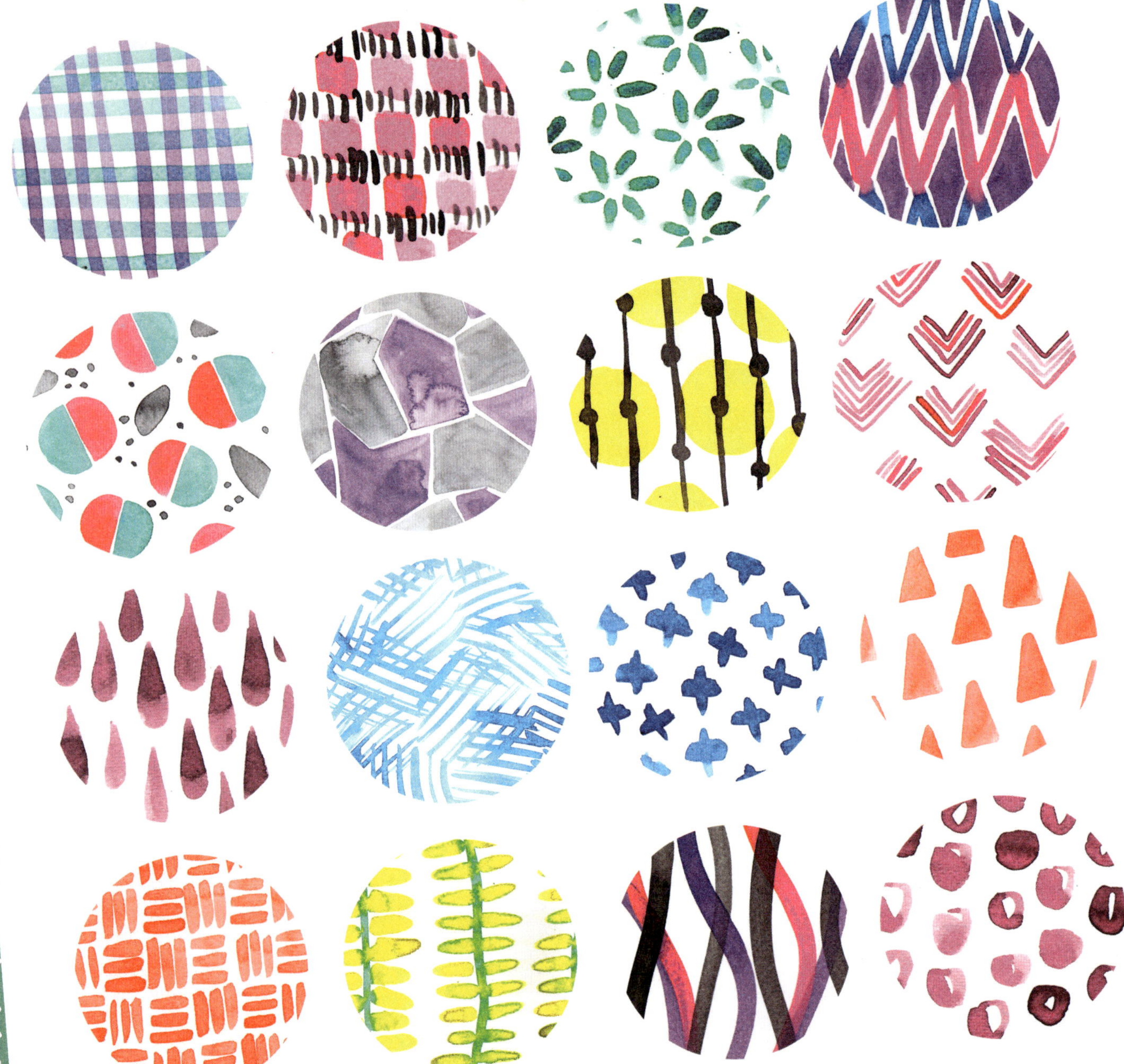

Backgrounds & Patterns

Are you worried that painting might be too difficult for you; that you might not be talented enough? Familiarize yourself with my projects, and you'll soon disagree! We'll get started by painting some watercolour backgrounds and patterns. If you're a beginner, then these are great warm-up exercises and a way to practise your brushwork skills.

We will move from simple motifs and techniques to more difficult ways of working. You will soon see how easy it is to create watercolour backgrounds that provide a great setting for your lettering. I will also show you how to spice things up with blobs, splashes and puddles. With the backgrounds made up of geometric patterns, you can practise your brushwork again. And when you are able to create even colour gradients, you will be getting closer to understanding the relationship between colour and water.

Once you have warmed up a bit, we will try some more difficult backgrounds, such as beautiful night skies and magical galaxies. Here you will get a chance to try out several techniques, combined in one painting. At the end of this chapter, I'll show you how you can paint floral watercolour illustrations that are like drawing with a pencil. Have fun!

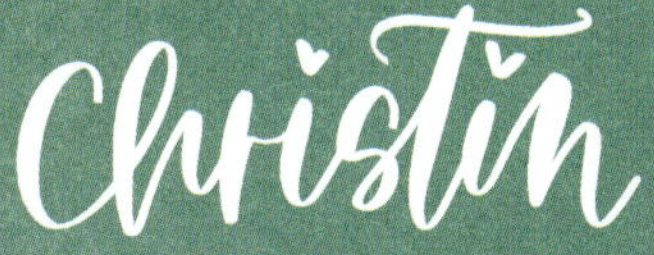

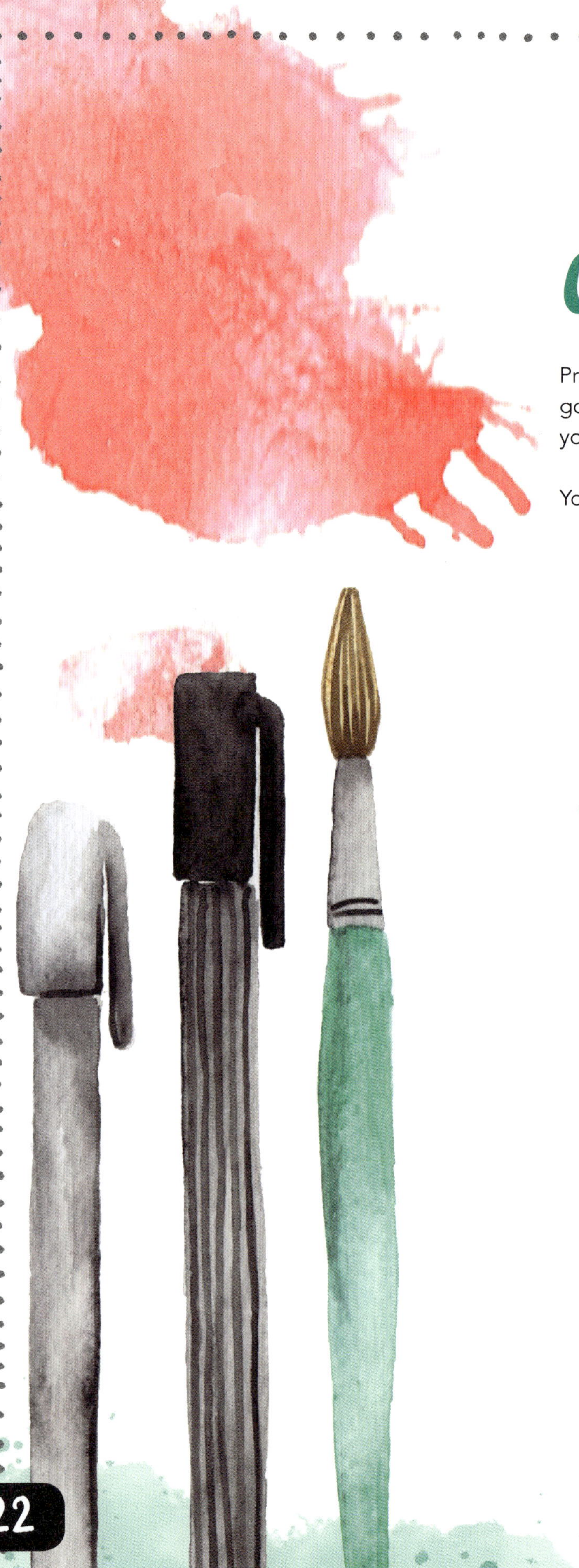

Get Started

Practice makes perfect as always, but nothing beats good preparation. Here you will find a list of materials you can use for the projects.

You will need:

- Matt watercolour paper
- Round brushes, sizes 2, 4, 6, 10
- Watercolour paint
- Palette
- Black fineliner
- Gouache or acrylic paint in white
- Masking fluid
- Removable adhesive tape
- Jar or glass of water

Let's Get Technical

COOL – BUT DIFFICULT

I love using wet-on-wet techniques that can create beautiful colour gradients on paper – you can work with simple shapes and still create real works of art. However, this method of working is also one of the most difficult watercolour techniques, because wet colour is very difficult to control.

Puddles can easily form on paper and the colour gradient won't look as uniform as you might like. On the following pages, I will show you some great practical examples to help you master the wet-on-wet technique.

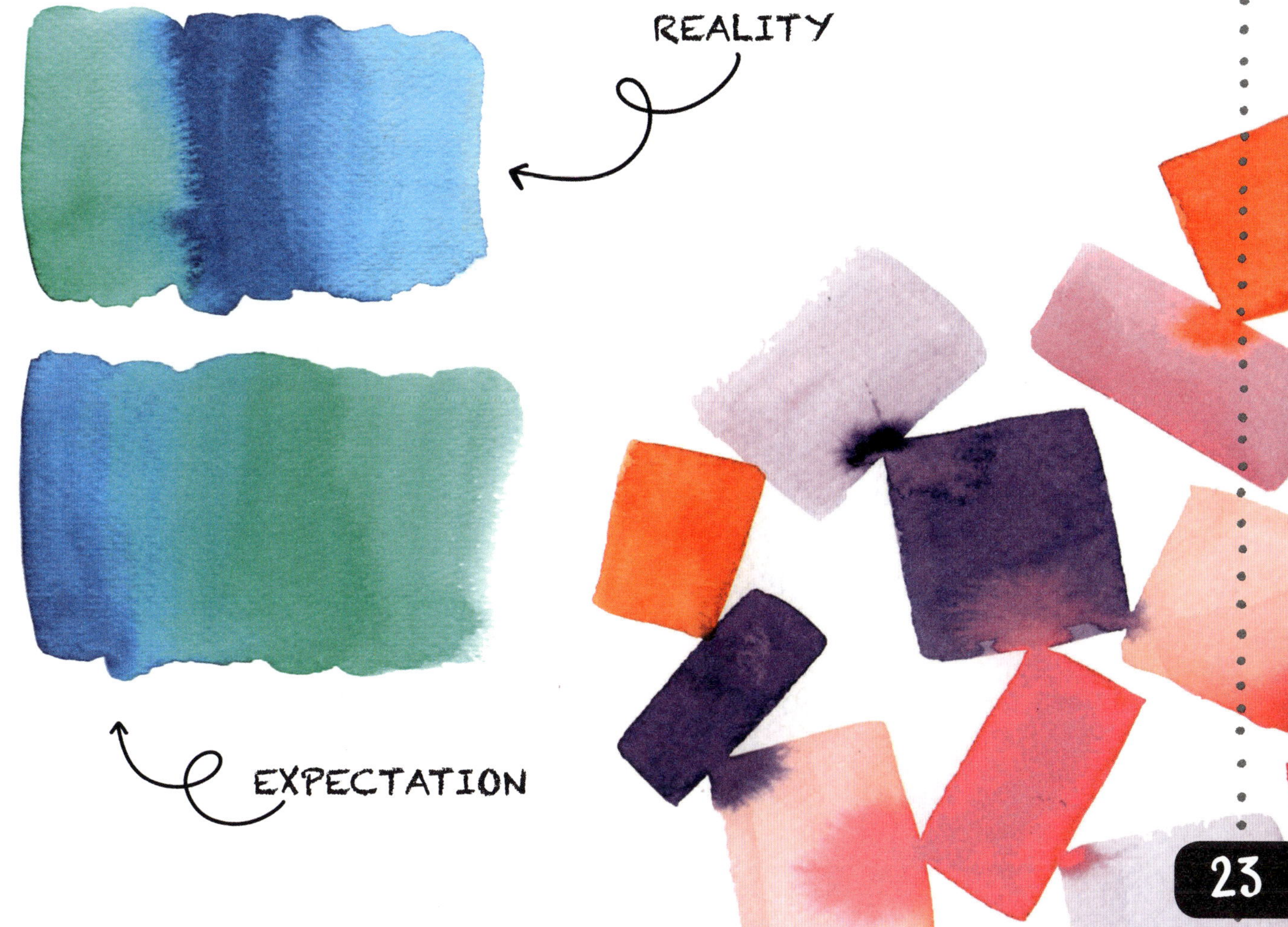

Let's Get Abstract

In this chapter, we will start with some simple motifs and work up to more difficult techniques. Painting with watercolour has so many different dimensions that if you try to master them all at once you may find it a bit overwhelming. For this very reason, we'll start out with some simple backgrounds that will allow us to practise some elementary techniques – brushwork and the relationship between paint and water.

CLASSIC WATERCOLOUR FLOW WITH STRIPES

1. Choose two different colours from your paints and mix them with plenty of water in separate chambers in your mixing palette.

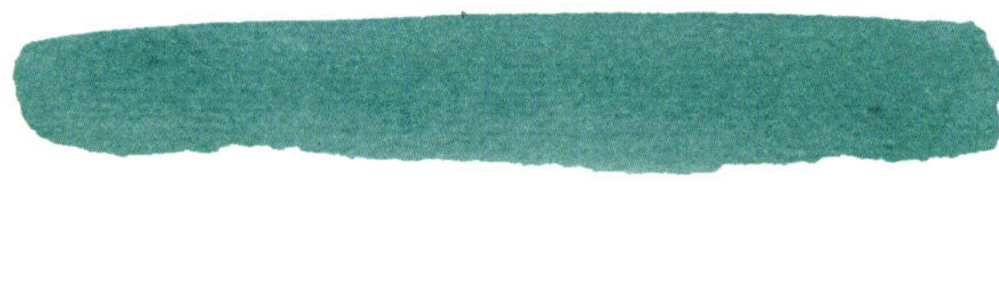

2. With a size 10 round brush and your first colour, start on the left side of your paper and draw a horizontal line with the full surface of the brush.

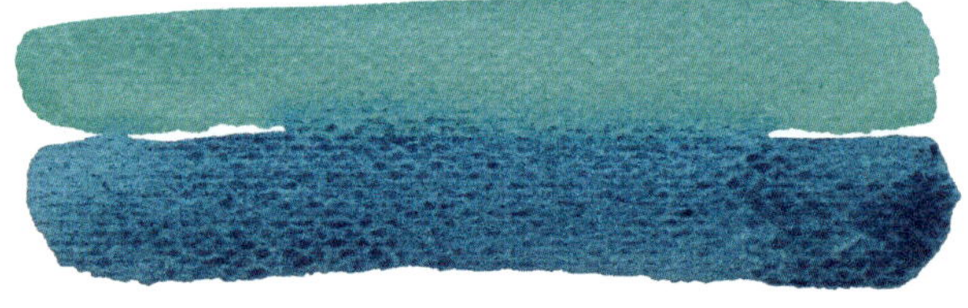

3. Paint a line in your second colour a small space below the first line. The lines may touch slightly at two or three places so that the colours merge into one another. This will probably happen automatically because brush strokes are rarely perfectly straight.

4. Continue to add stripes, alternating between the two colours, until you are happy with the result.

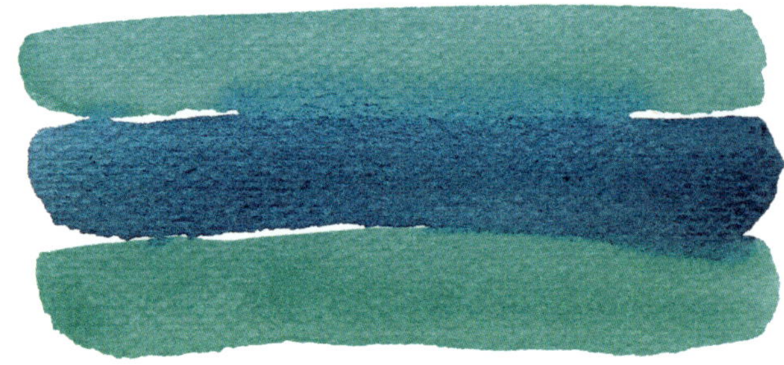

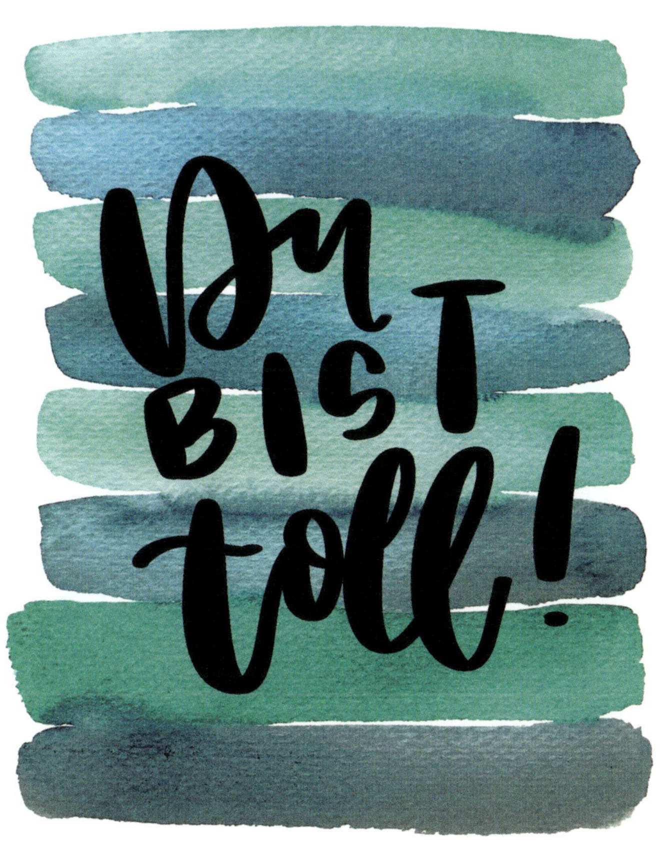

5 You should have created a cool, transparent background that can be an excellent base for some lettering.

TIP: **Make sure that your paint is mixed with a lot of water so the stripes can be painted evenly over the paper.**

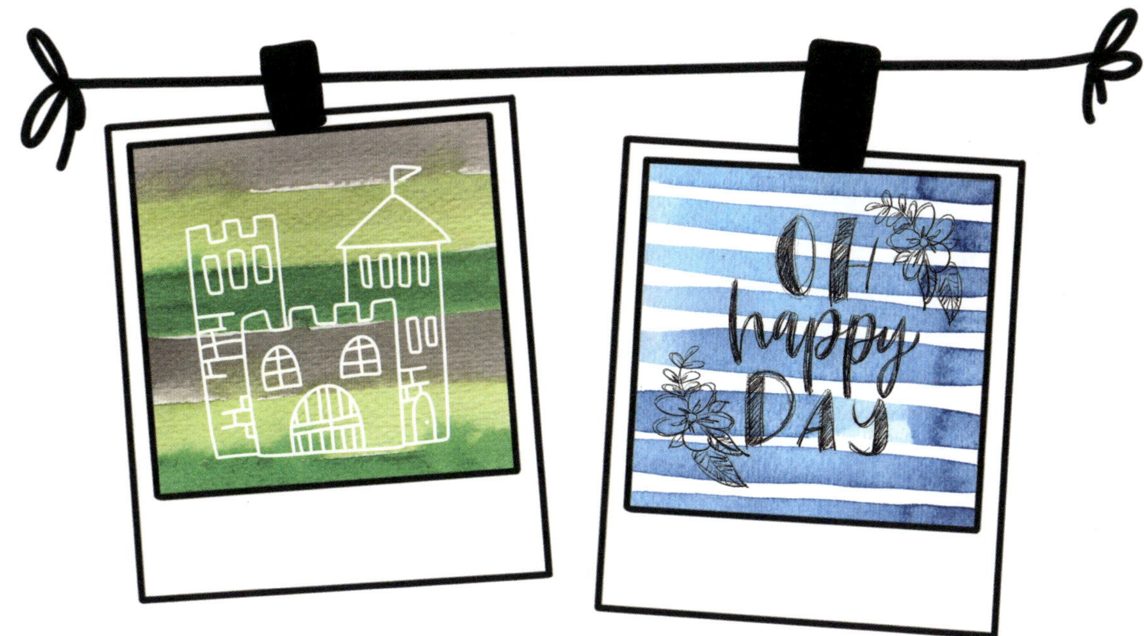

Watercolour Blobs

Creating splashes and blobs in watercolour can sometimes be harder than you think but with a few tricks, it's easy to create something that looks improvised.

Blobs are larger, random spots of colour that can give an illustration a charming, unfinished look.

HOW TO MAKE BLOBS

1. For large blobs, we also need a large round brush, for example, a size 10. Dip it in the paint of your choice. The brush tip should be covered generously with paint.

2. Now hold the brush about 10–15cm above the surface of your watercolour paper. Take a second, clean brush and use it to gently tap the first one.

3. The bigger the first brush is and the wetter the paint on it, the bigger the blobs will be.

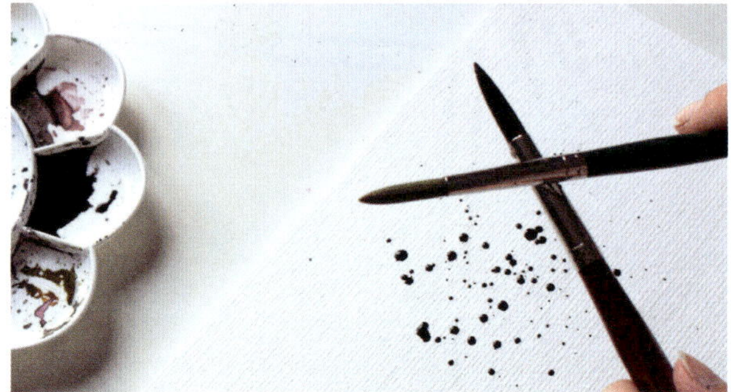

Speckles & Splashes

In principle, speckles and splashes are nothing more than smaller blobs. They can be annoying if they inadvertently spread out on your paper, but when used deliberately they can also loosen up your finished work. Here, we'll discover some of the tools that you can use to conjure up speckles and splashes.

METHOD # 1 FLAT BRUSH

Dip a flat brush in the colour of your choice and hold the brush 3–4cm above your paper. Now run your finger over the bristles of your brush so that the brush hairs are pushed apart and the paint splashes onto the surface of the paper.

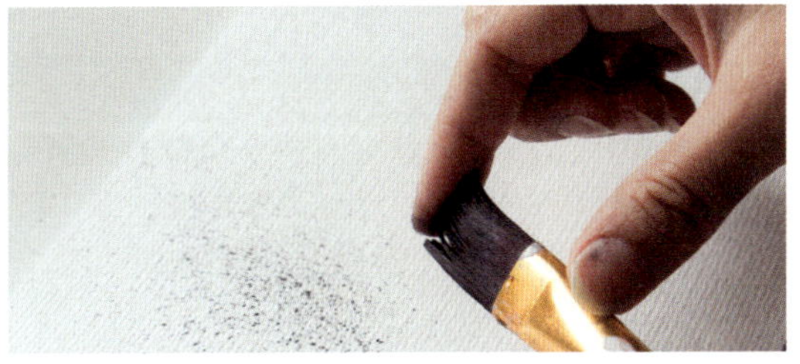

METHOD # 2 TOOTHBRUSH

Don't throw old toothbrushes away, you can use them to paint! First dip a toothbrush in some paint and then hold it diagonally over your paper at a distance of 2–4cm. Gently rub your finger over the bristles of the toothbrush to form many small splashes on the picture. I'm very keen on this method and like to use it when painting a starry sky.

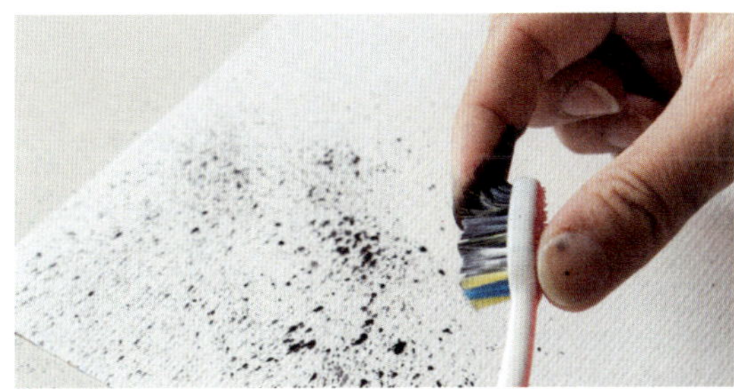

METHOD # 3 DRINKING STRAW

Place wet blobs of paint on your paper with the brush then use a drinking straw to blow on the wet blob, slightly at an angle to the paper. This makes the paint run over the paper. Blow in the direction you want the paint to run.

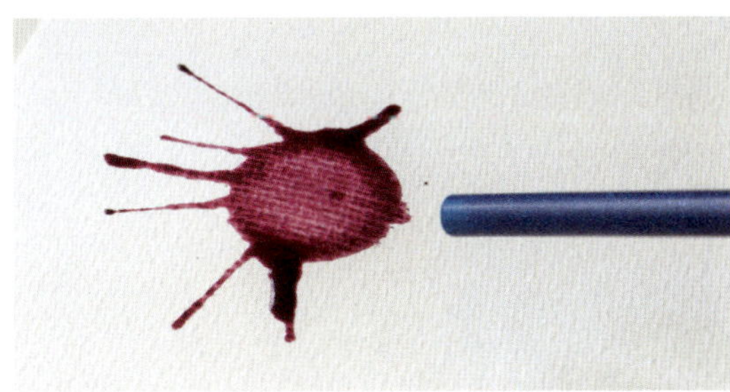

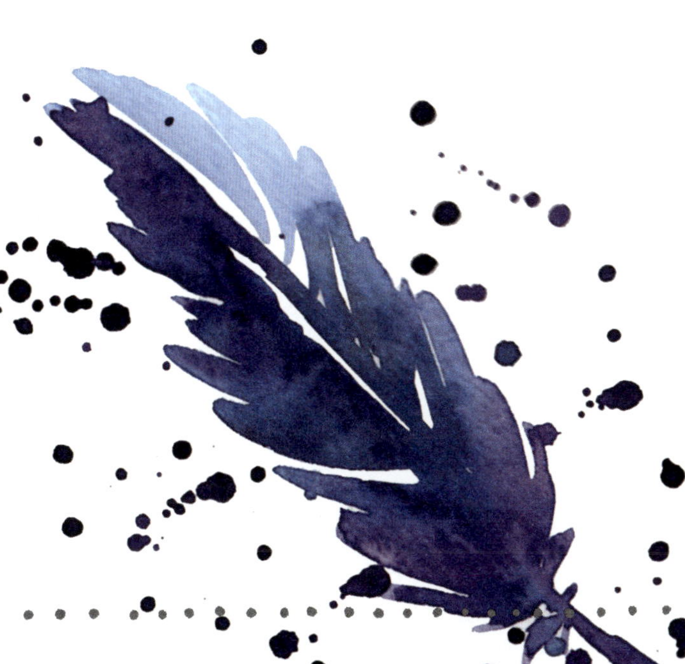

Watercolour Puddles

Beginners often want to start off by painting flowers or animals because these look good and are quite impressive. I understand; I wanted to do this too. However, sometimes you have to go back to the basics to make progress and practise painting skills. So I'm going to show you how to create backgrounds with puddles that, for example, can look very elegant and modern when combined with lettering.

Maybe you tried to paint an even background and you got something like the picture on the left, rather than the one on the right?

The paint in the picture on the left has formed puddles. This is what we call the phenomenon whereby the colour dries unevenly and coloured edges appear where the pigment has collected. Such puddles, if unwanted, can be quite annoying. But if you create them specifically, you can achieve wonderful effects.

So now I'm going to show you how to create some elegant backgrounds.

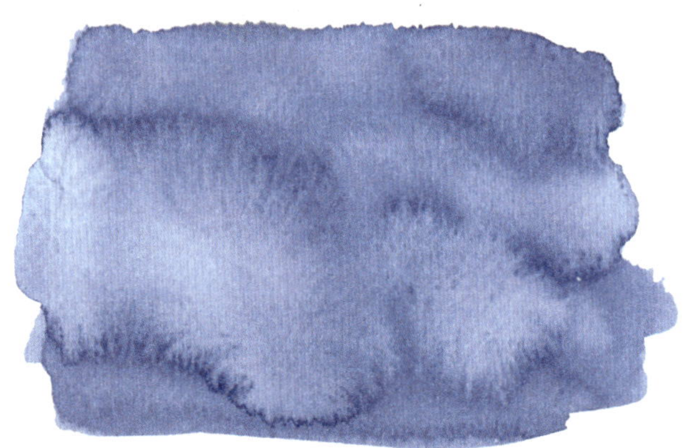 

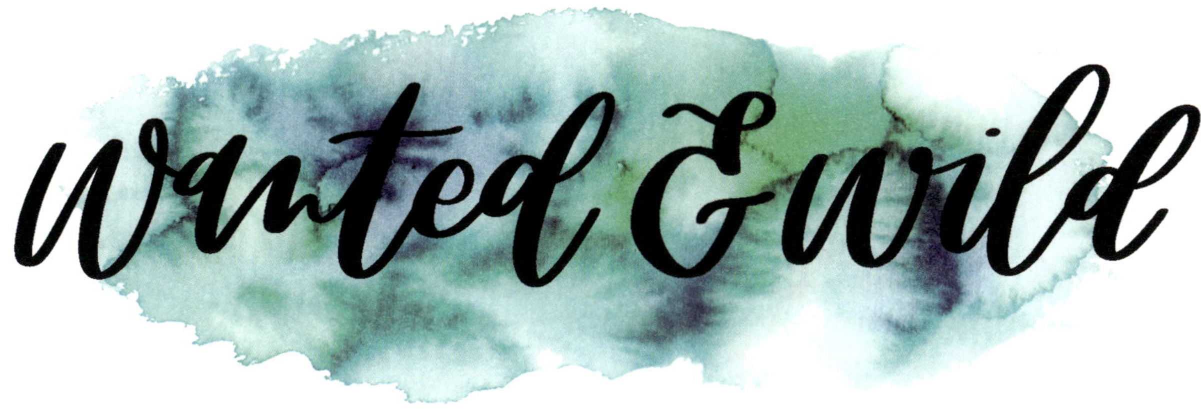

PAINTING PUDDLES FOR BEGINNERS

1. Paint an area of colour onto your watercolour paper. Don't choose too bright colour or you won't be able to see the different shades as well.

2. Leave the paint to dry slightly but not completely. If the colour is too wet, there will be a greater gradient of shade, but no puddle.

3. Now use a washed-out brush to put a full brush load of clear water on your painted area to create a puddle.

4. Move the water around a little. You can apply several brush loads of water to your paper if you like.

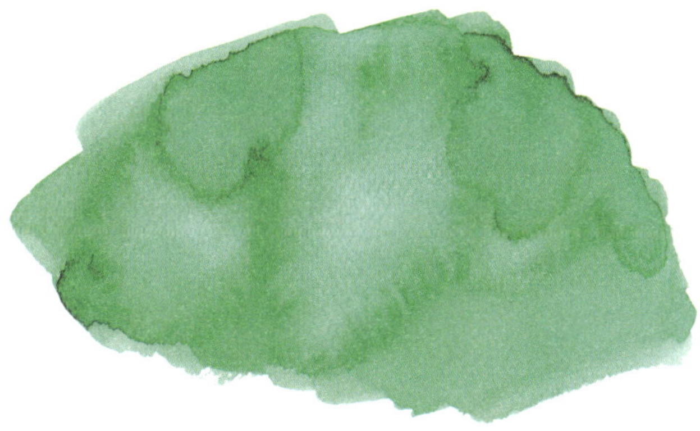

TIP: Instead of clear water, you could use a very thin dilution of a second paint colour to create a multicoloured puddle background. Just add some lettering for extra interest.

PAINTING PUDDLES - TAKING IT FURTHER

Here we combine some puddles with the glazing technique and get to grips with the different levels of transparency of watercolour paint.

1. For the first layer, start by mixing a very weak dilution of your chosed colour. Working from top to bottom on your paper, paint some wavy lines. After drying slightly, add clear water to the paint so that several puddles are created (see previous page). Let everything dry thoroughly.

2. Mix up a stronger shade of your colour and paint wavy lines a little below your first layer. Make some more puddles on this area.

3. Repeat the steps with two more shades of colour, each one stronger than the last. Don't forget to create puddles in every layer of paint.

4. A background like this can look very elegant when combined with creative lettering.

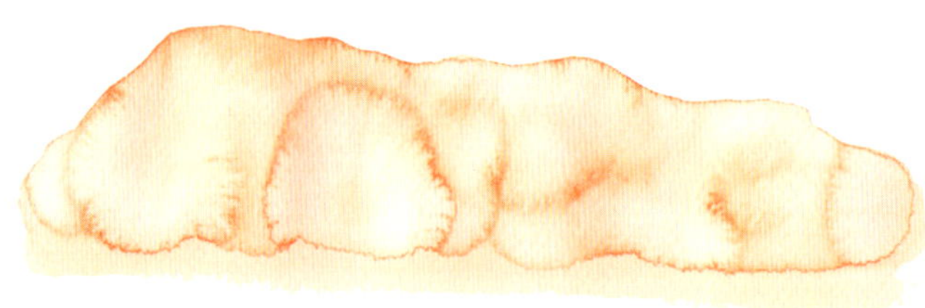

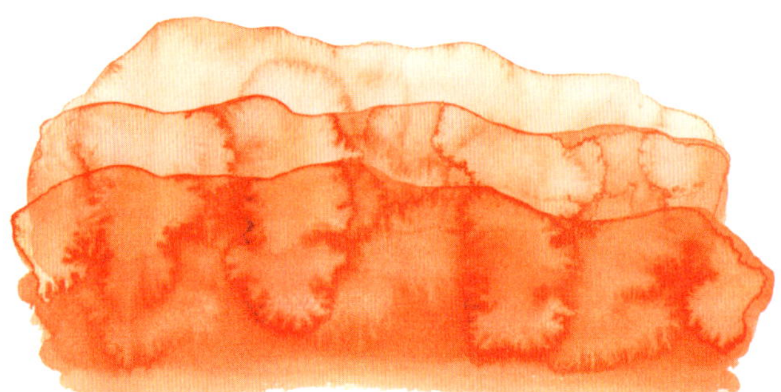

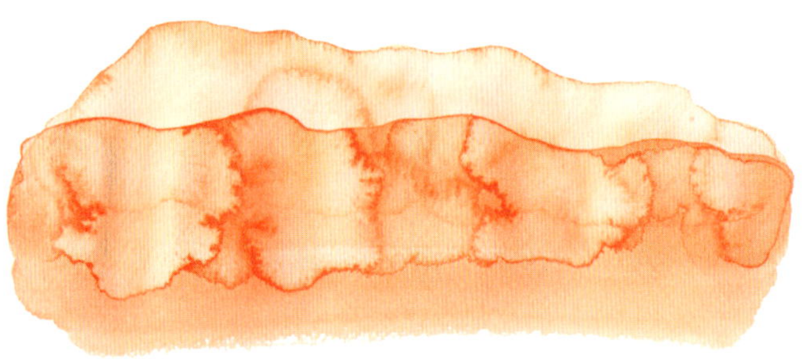

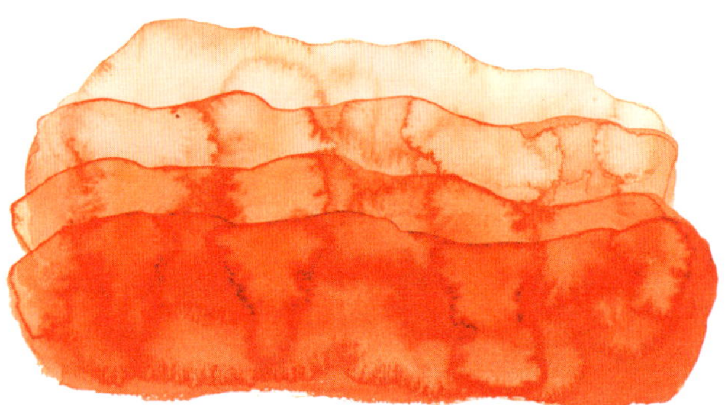

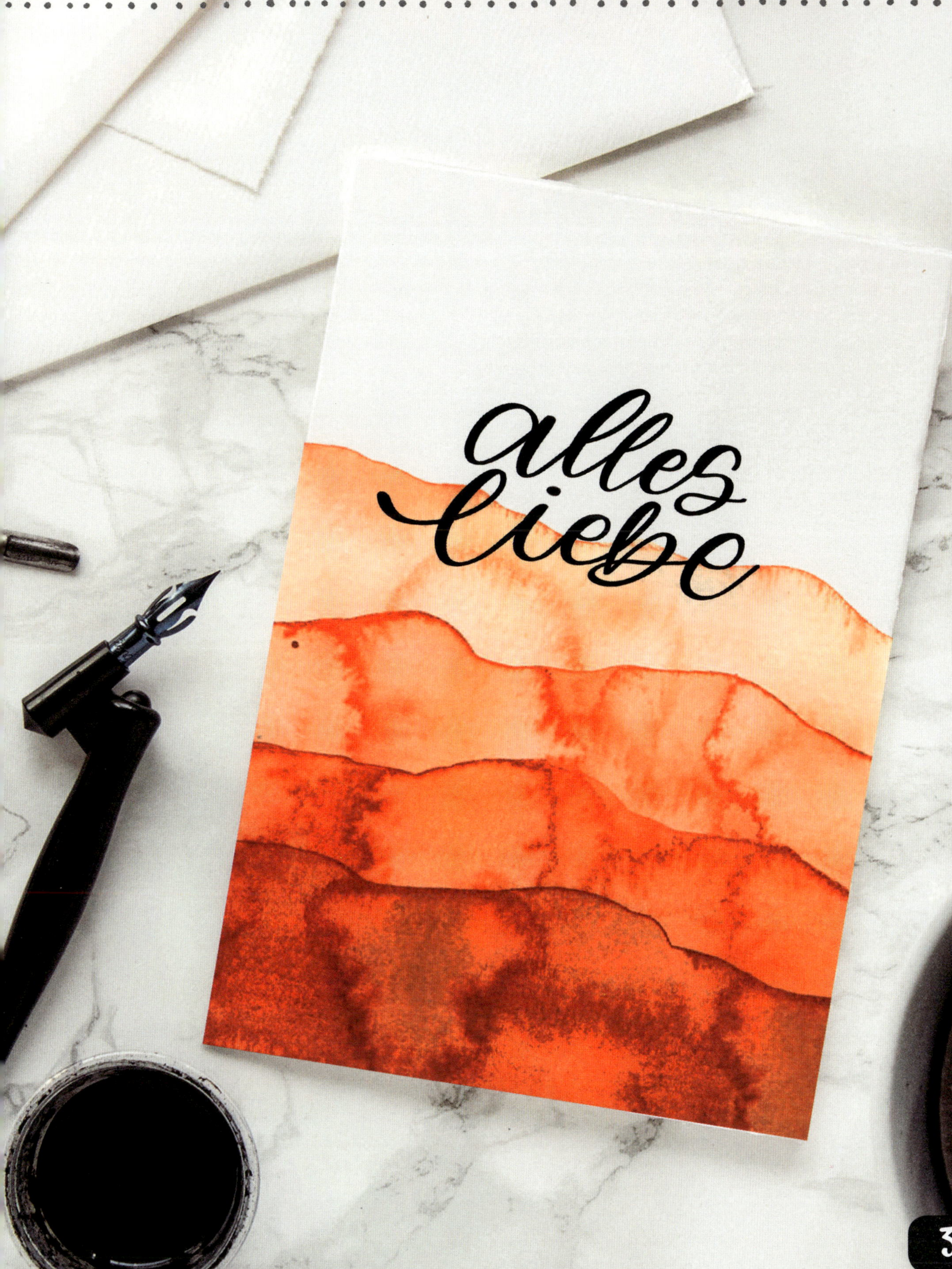
alles
liebe

Patterns from Basic Geometric Shapes

The exercises on the previous pages gave you a chance to experiment with colour. In the abstract projects that follow, you will be using significantly more brushwork to create some great patterns from simple shapes.

Start by choosing three colours. Put a little paint in one chamber of your palette and add just enough water to make it liquid. Put a small amount of paint in a separate chamber on the palette and mix in a bit more water so you have a thinner solution of paint. Repeat with the other two colours so you have six shades available – a thick and thin version of each colour. This project will alternate between the thick and thin paints so that the gradients in shade come into their own.

1. Using the thinner paint in one of your colours, paint a rectangle. Use enough paint so that the rectangle is shiny and damp, and doesn't dry out too quickly.

2. Using a thicker paint, paint another rectangle that touches the first one at one edge. Then paint another rectangle using the thinner paint that touches the second rectangle. The thicker (and darker) paint will run into the thinner (and lighter) paint and so create interesting gradients in shade. The thicker paint gives you a more opaque finish; the thinner paint will make a more transparent mark.

3. Continue adding rectangles in the same way, adjusting their sizes to fit in between the gaps. If you use only a little water as you paint, the colours won't run together much, so remember to paint wetly and quickly so the paints don't dry out.

4. Do you like the finished result? The interplay between the opaque and transparent rectangles creates a great contrast.

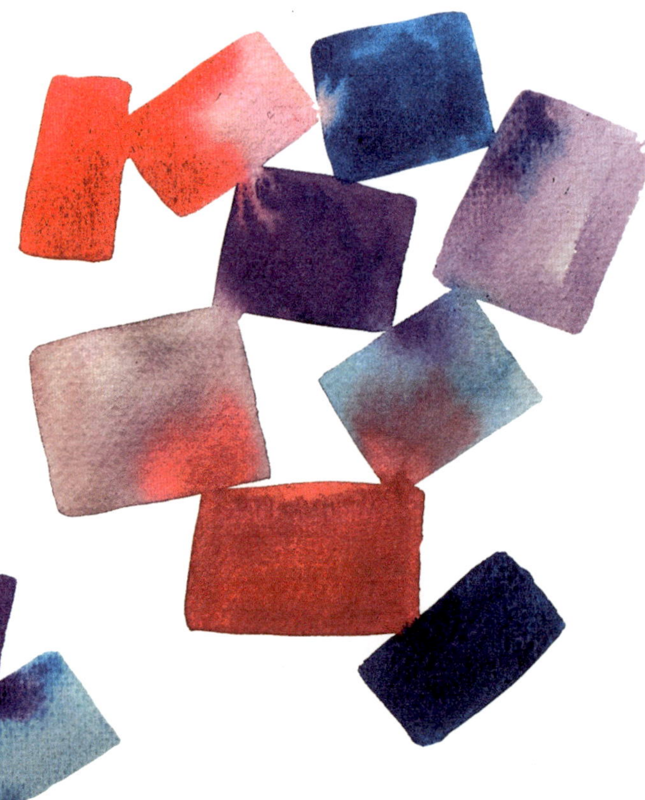

TRIANGLE PATTERN

A geometric pattern – that might sound a bit boring, but it is really fun in watercolour. If you use your favorite colour, the pattern can become a real work of art.

1 Start by painting a triangle with a size 4 round brush. First draw the outline of the shape with the tip of the brush. Paint the area then apply a another shade to the wet surface for a beautiful colour gradient. If you want, you can first draw the shape in pencil.

2 Draw more triangles next to each other on a baseline, with very little space in between and so the triangles interlock.

3 Paint two narrow lines under your triangles. Then paint a row of semicircles under these lines. Finally, outline the shapes of the semicircles with a set of three curving lines.

4 Under the pattern, paint a random selection of large and small circles to complete a great watercolour pattern based on just simple geometric shapes.

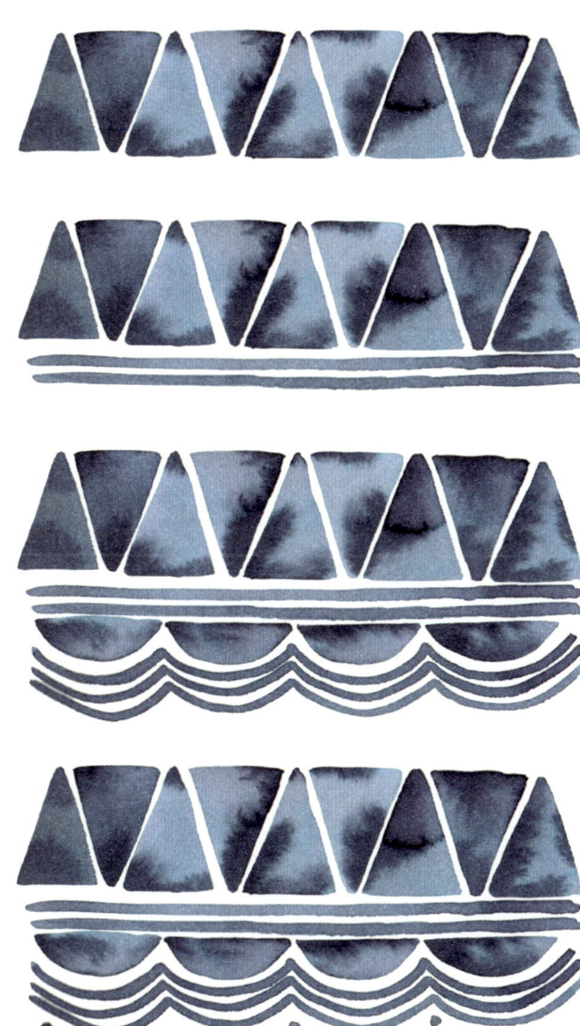

Wrapping Paper

Perhaps you are wondering how you might be able to use some of these watercolour patterns and backgrounds. I would like, therefore, to show you a cool DIY project that uses white wrapping paper rather than watercolour paper. You will see that you can get quite an effective finished look.

MATERIAL

- White wrapping paper
- Watercolour paint
- Round brush, size 6
- Jar or glass of water
- Pencil
- Ruler and scissors

1 Cut off as much white wrapping paper as you need for your gift. Spread it out in front of you and weigh it down at the edges so it doesn't curl up. Either get started straight away with a brush and paint, or carefully draw some triangles on the paper with a pencil and ruler or set square.

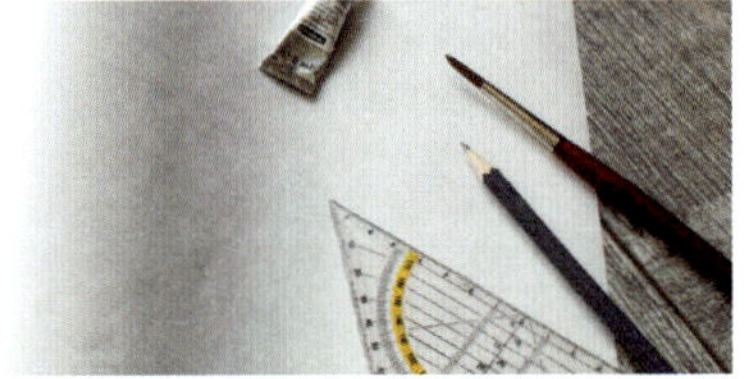

2 In my example, I used two different colours which I alternated between to paint the triangles. I left a small gap between the outer edges of all the triangles.

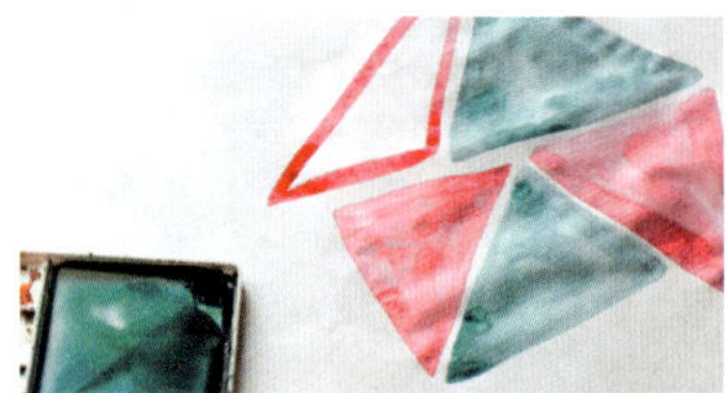

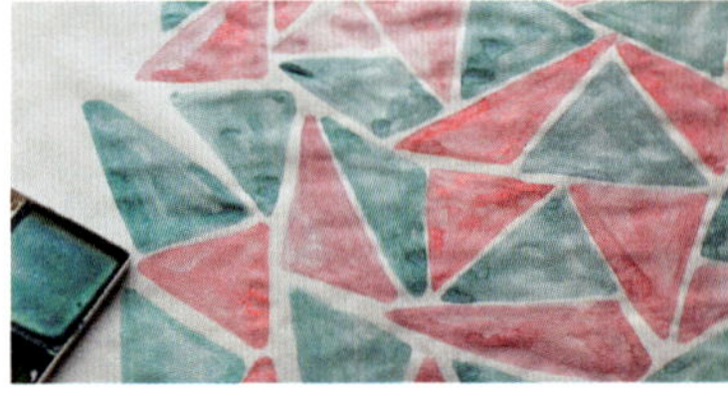

TIP: Wrapping paper is usually rather thin so you should work with less water to avoid both colour gradients or puddles. The paper will still wrinkle slightly, but personally I think this is a really great look. Whatever the finished result, such pretty, home-made gift packaging will be sure to bring a lot of joy to the recipient!

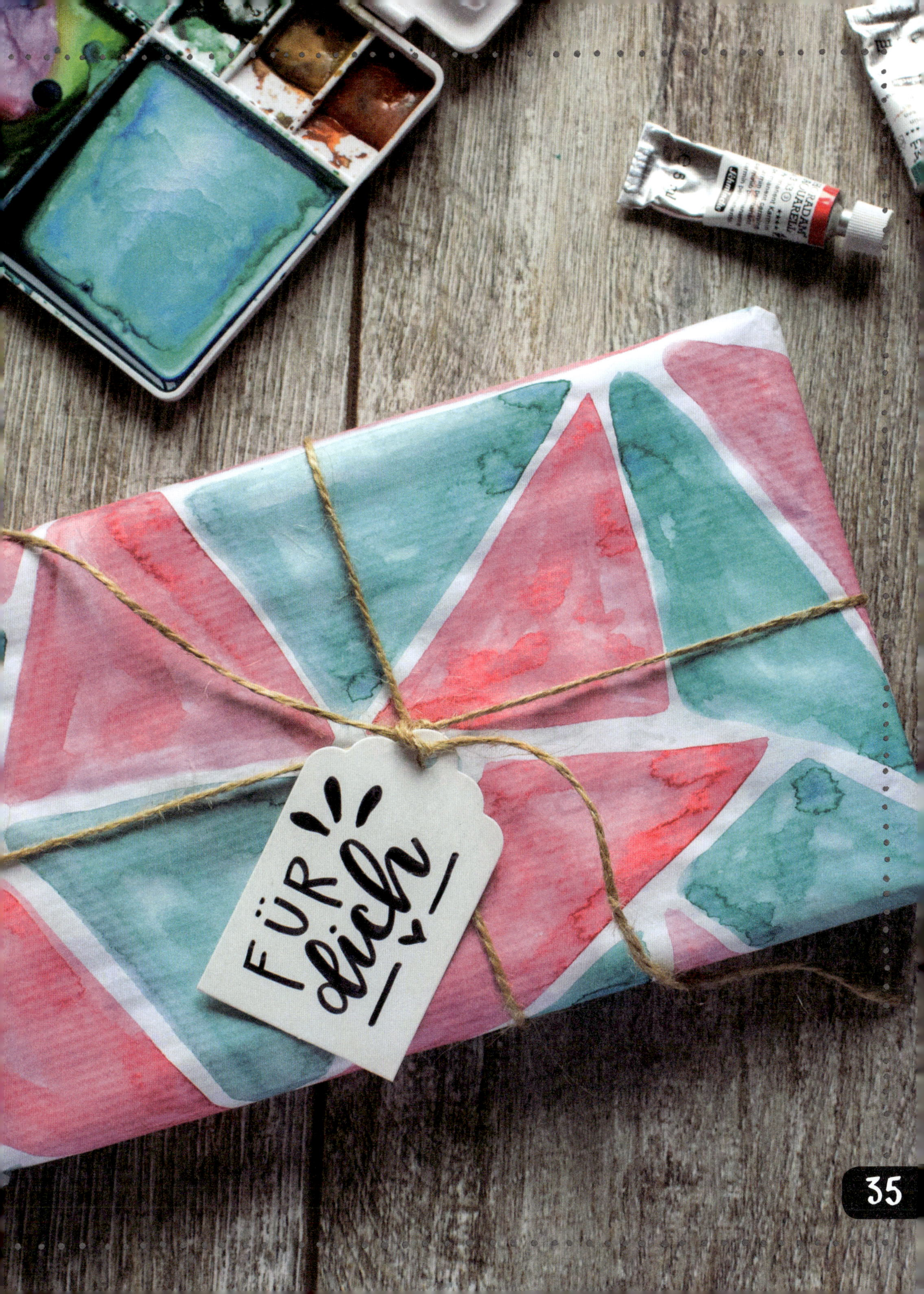
FÜR dich

Pimp It Up!

WATERCOLOUR AND PEN – A DYNAMIC DUO!

The great thing about watercolour is that you can combine it with other art techniques and materials, such as pens or inks. Drawing and painting complement each other perfectly and together form a powerful pairing. The contrast between the delicate, flowing colours of the watercolour paint and the hard lines of the pen ensures some lively compositions.

The most frequently asked question at this point is which do you use first - watercolour or pen? The answer is, it depends on your taste. I like to apply liquid colours first and then work on the details with a fine liner. But if you prefer, you can work the other way round.

TIP: If you prefer to work with pens or fineliner first, then they should be waterproof. Otherwise, the lines will blur when you apply wet paint.

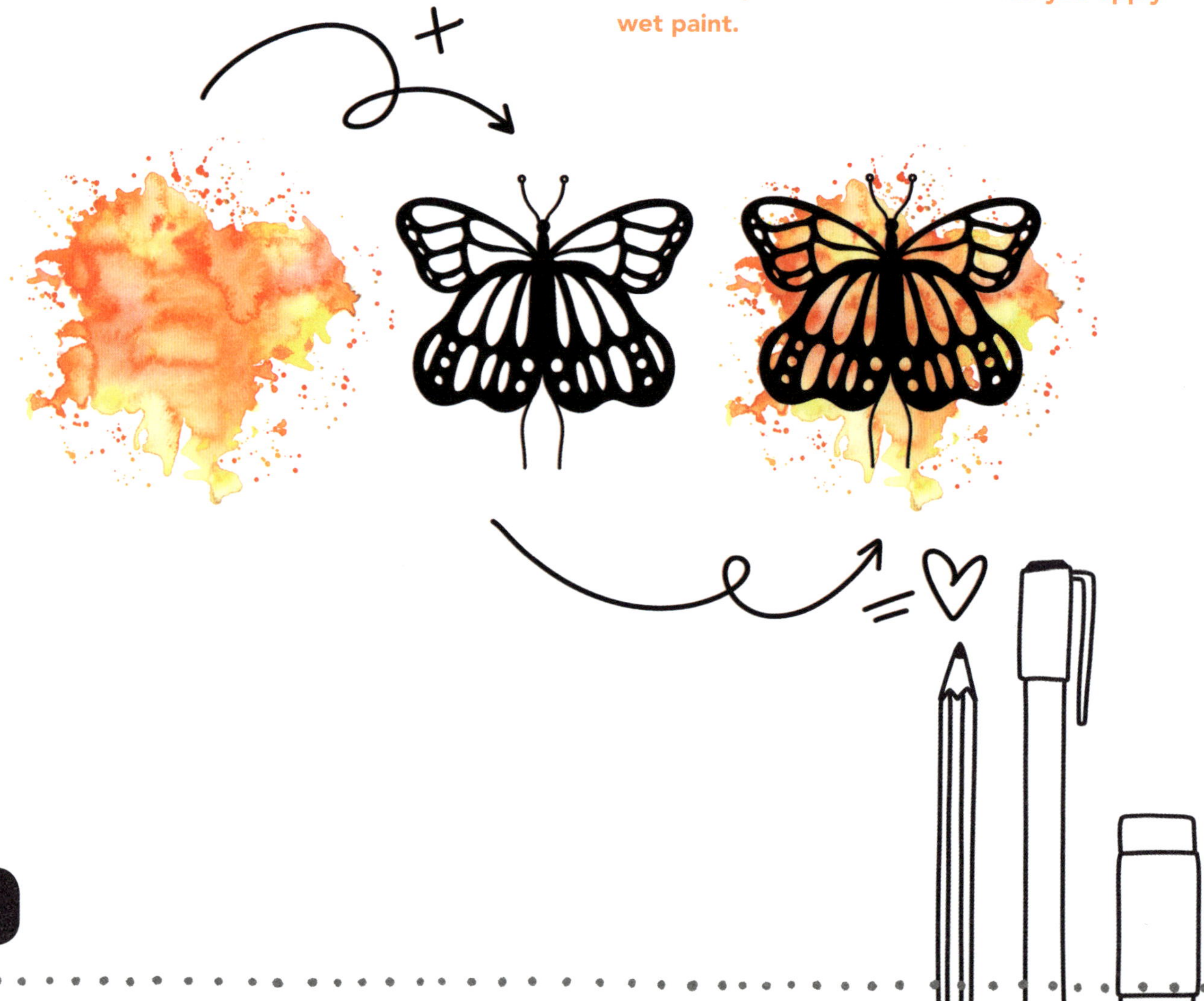

HOME IS …

In this project, we start out with watercolour and then continue with a black 0.5mm fineliner pen.

1. Create a watercolour background with four different colours that merge in the middle. Let the paint dry out thoroughly.

2. Use a hard pencil to sketch a house on your watercolour paper. I recommend that you make a few preliminary drawings in a sketch pad to practise your design. This helps you avoid having to rub out the pencil lines on your watercolour paper.

3. Now draw over the house with your fine liner pen. After a short wait, you can carefully erase any pencil lines that are visible. Some fineliner pen marks may be smudged by a rubber so be very careful at the beginning.

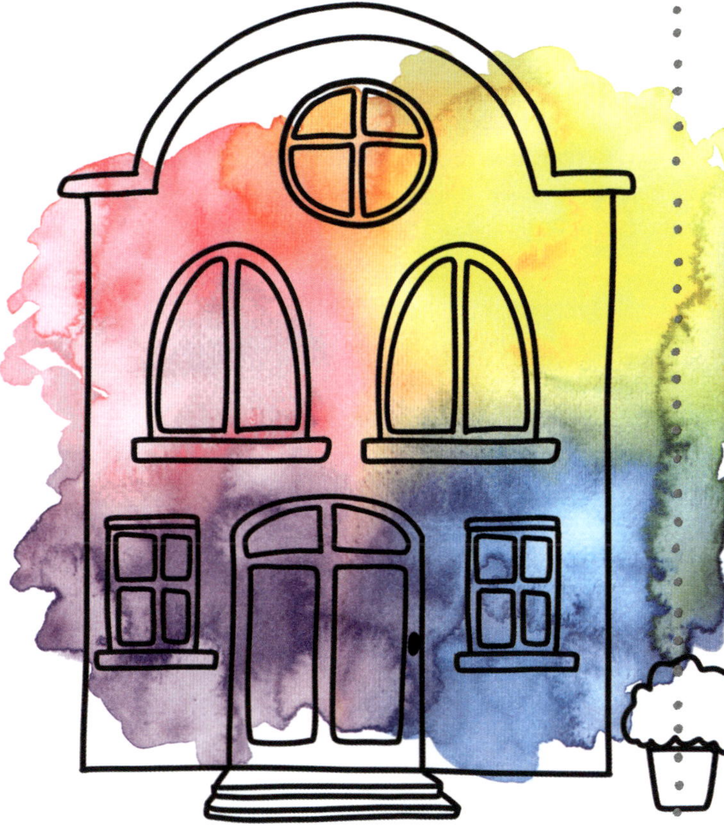

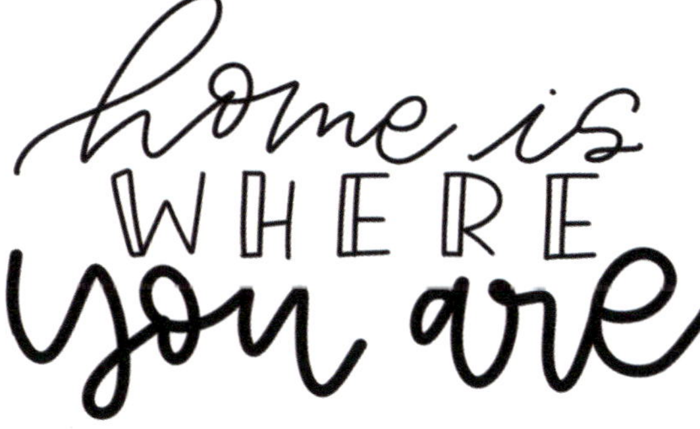

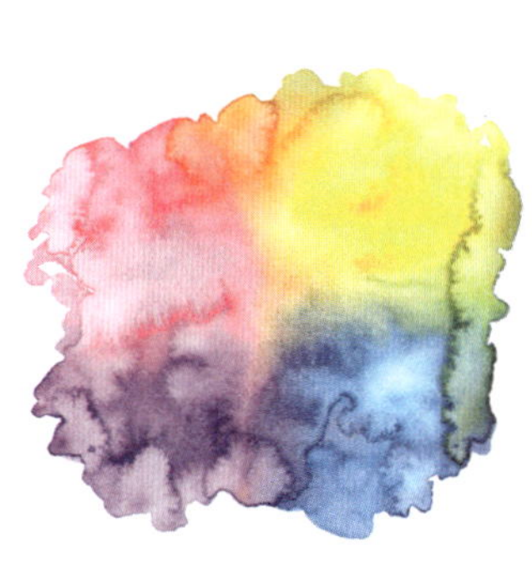

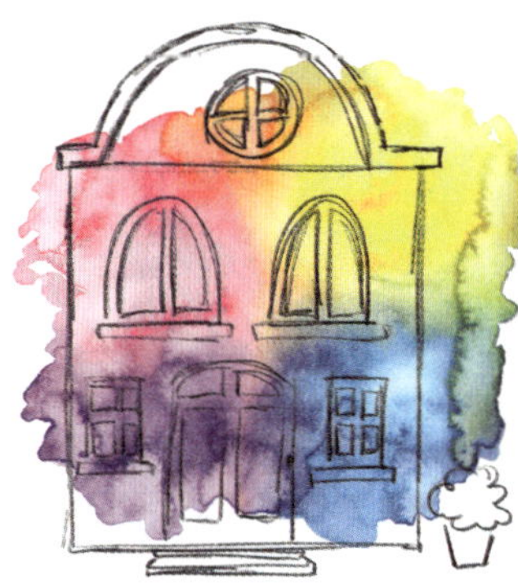

Flower Girl

With this circle of flowers, watercolour and fineliner pen have merged to create a wonderful picture. This time, however, we have start with the fineliner first and then added colour accents with watercolour. For this project, the fineliner should be waterproof and the width of the tip is only 0.2mm.

1. Use a pair of compasses or draw around a saucer or plate to create a circle on your paper. Then plot out the position of your flowers. I chose to include two roses and two large four-petalled flowers, filling in the gaps with several small flowers and leaves and ferns.

2. Because my drawing with the fineliner pen will be sketchy in style, I didn't draw in any further details with the pencil but started directly with the black pen. But you are welcome to sketch out the whole design with pencil and then draw over the lines with the fineliner.

3. When you've finished the pen drawing, erase your pencil lines before moving onto watercolour. Using a large round brush, first paint rough areas of pink and purple over the flowers. Then use shades of blue to go over the leaves and spaces in between. Complete the picture with brush lettering.

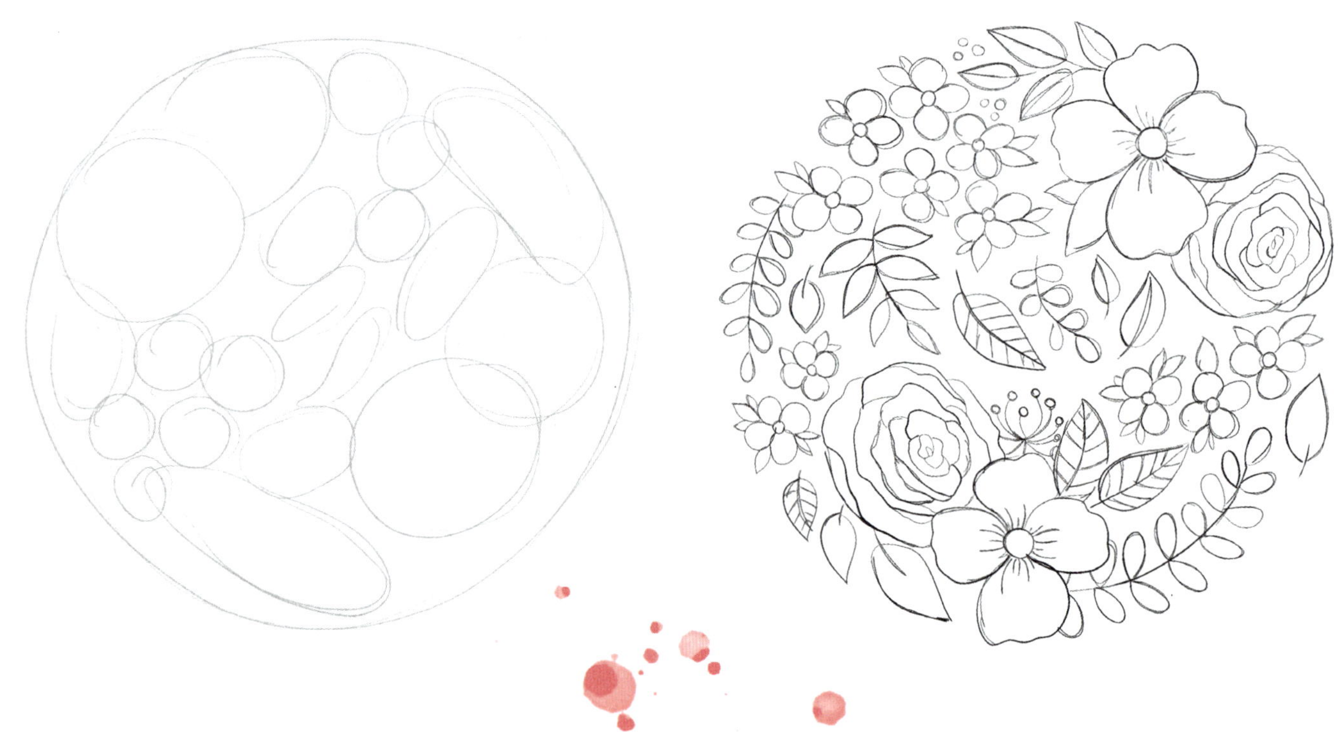

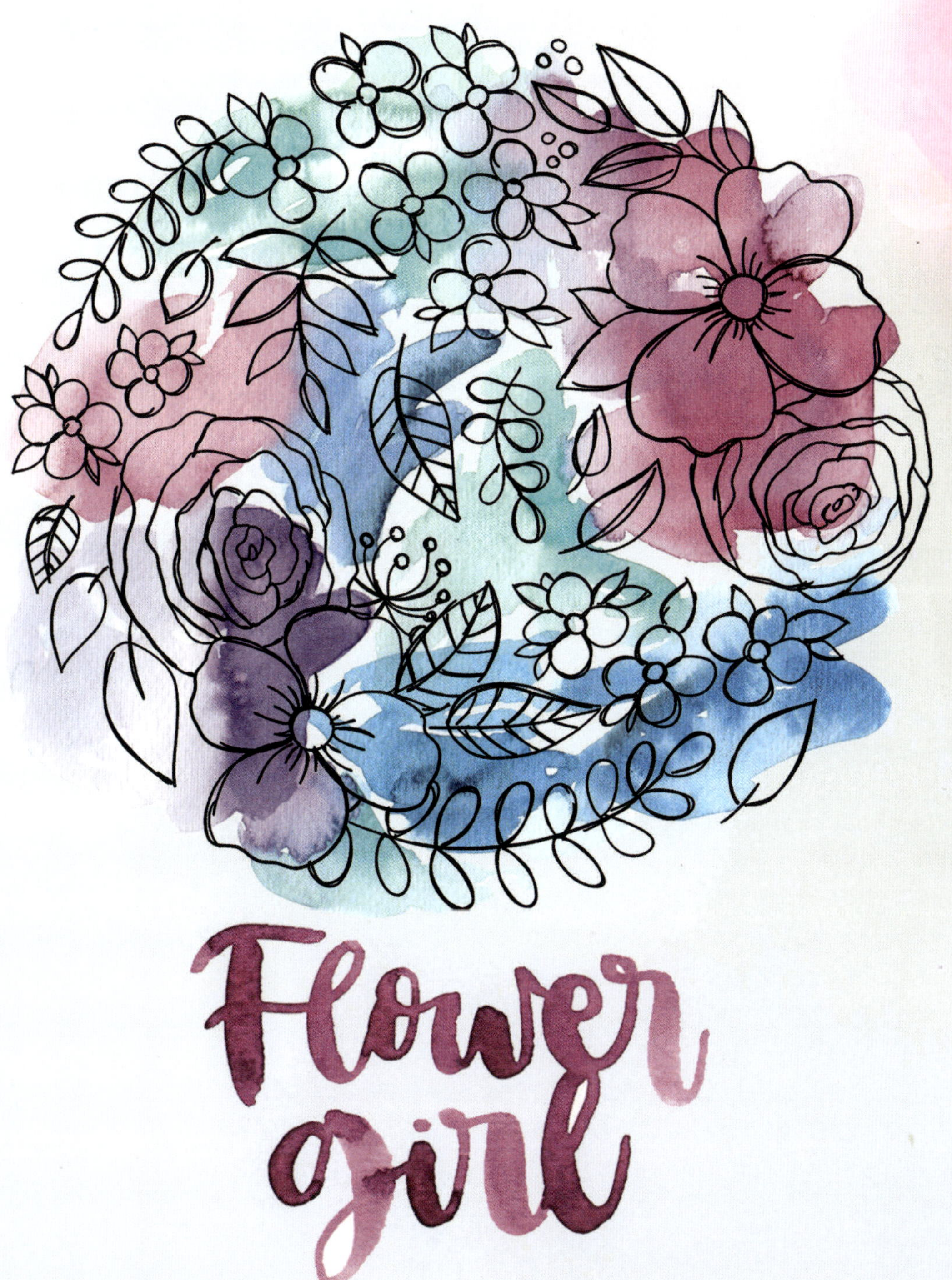

Flower
girl

Watercolour Night Skies

INTO THE NIGHT SKY

Starry skies are definitely one of the more complex watercolour backgrounds you can paint. They can stand alone as finished works, but they also work well with other illustrations or effects. They are not easy to paint because they combine two watercolour techniques – wet-on-wet and glazing.

SOME THEORY BEFORE THE COLOUR RUSH

Since we are going to work with three to five different shades, a little reminder of colour theory might be a good idea. The primary colours are red, yellow and blue. If you mix together red and yellow, you get orange; red and blue, you get violet; yellow and blue, you get green – these are called secondary colours. Tertiary colours are created when you mix a primary and a secondary colour. This creates, for example, red-orange, blue-violet or yellow-green.

Complementary colours are colours that lie opposite each other in the colour wheel, such as violet and yellow, green and red, orange and blue. They harmonize well with each other, but if you mix them with each other, they result in shades of grey to brown.

When painting coloured backgrounds, be careful about which colours you mix or the colour result may not be as bright as you want – especially with the wet-on-wet technique. So, enough of the theory, now we can start our first night sky picture!

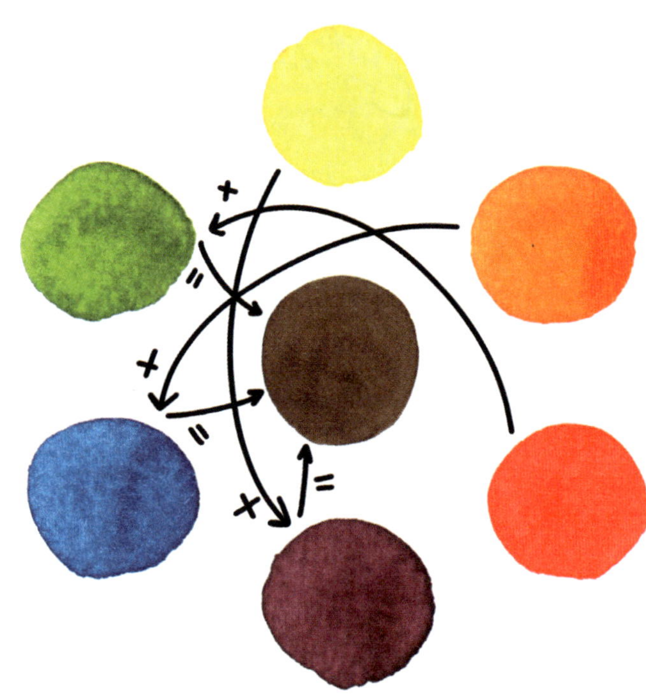

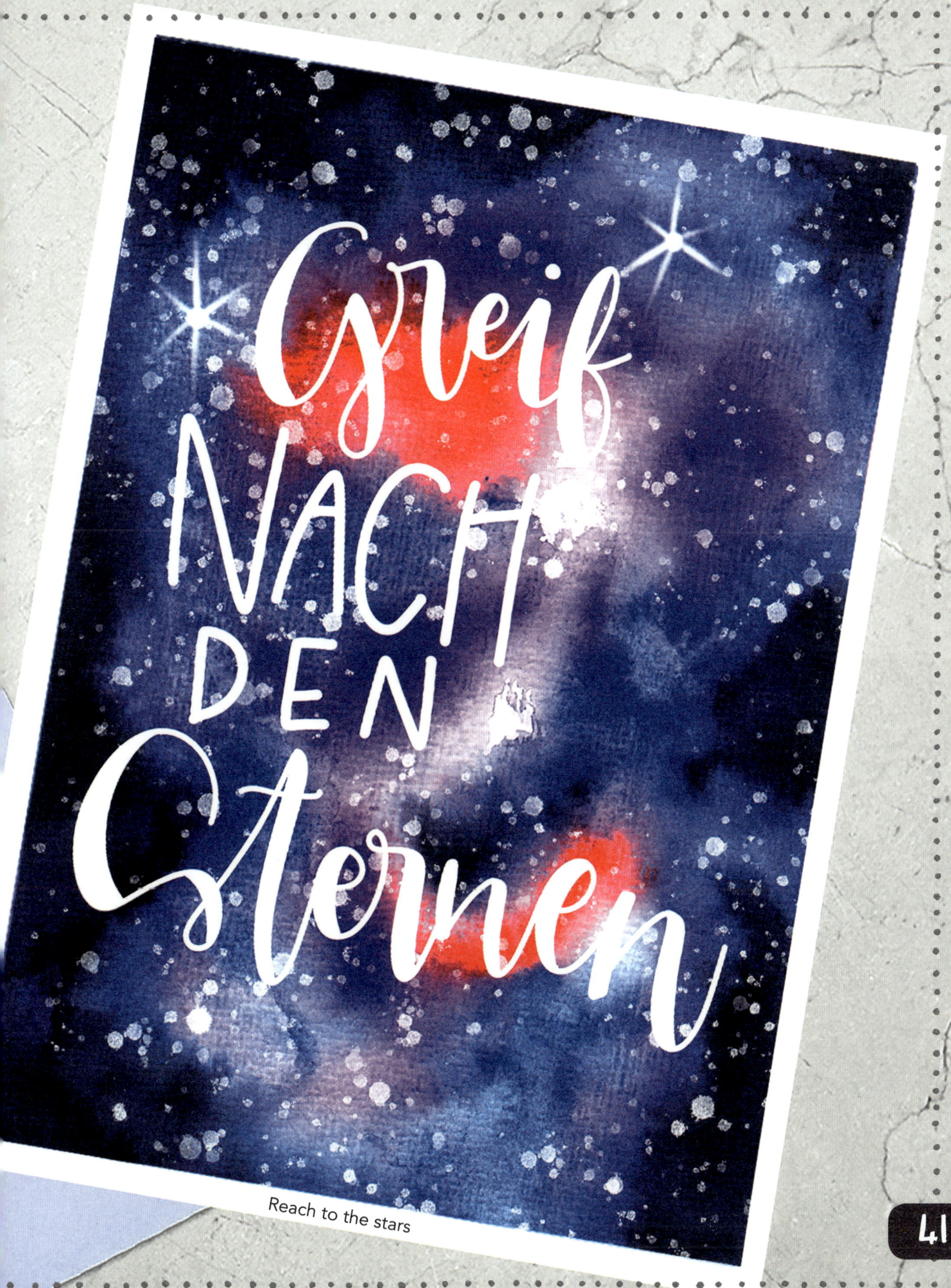

Reach to the stars

A WATERCOLOUR GALAXY

For this cool project I will show you a very special watercolour background using the wet-on-wet technique. The result looks very challenging but getting there is probably easier than you think.

MATERIAL

- Watercolour paints in pink, purple, and light and dark blue

- Watercolour paper

- Round brushes, sizes 4 and 10

- Jar or glass of water

- Paper towels

- Acrylic or gouache paint in white

1 Starting with a size 10 round brush, apply clear water to the watercolour paper.

2 Apply a thin dilution of pink, purple and light blue paint to the still damp colour, leaving some areas unpainted for white space.

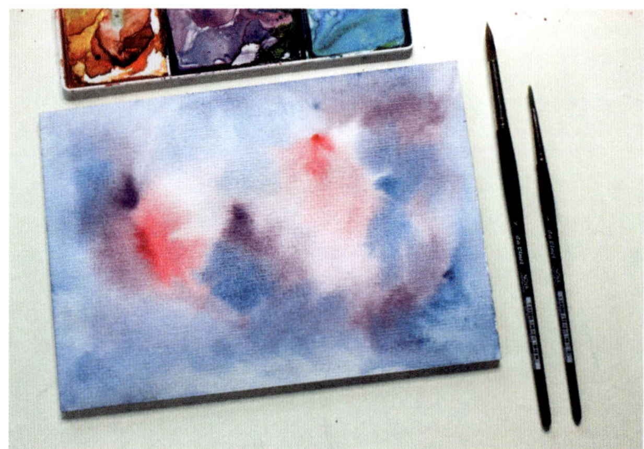

3 Now add some splodges of darker pink and purple paint.

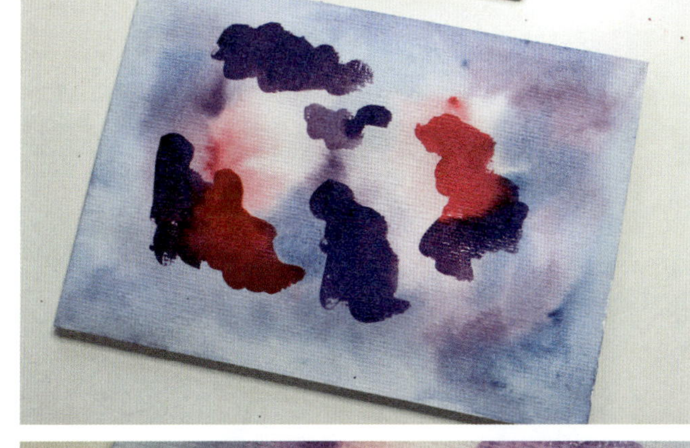

4 Use a clean, wet size 4 brush to soften the edges of the darker paint layers while still slightly damp.

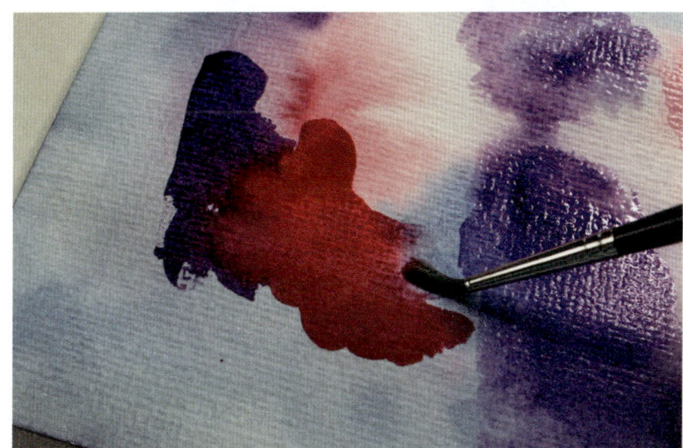

5 You can use paper towels to dab the very wet spots on your picture. Again, let everything dry well.

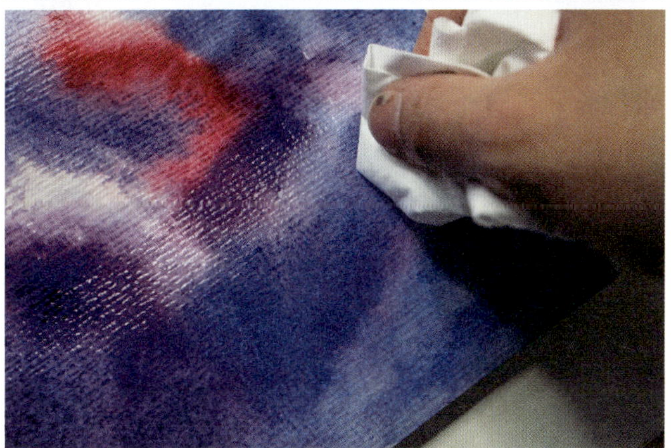

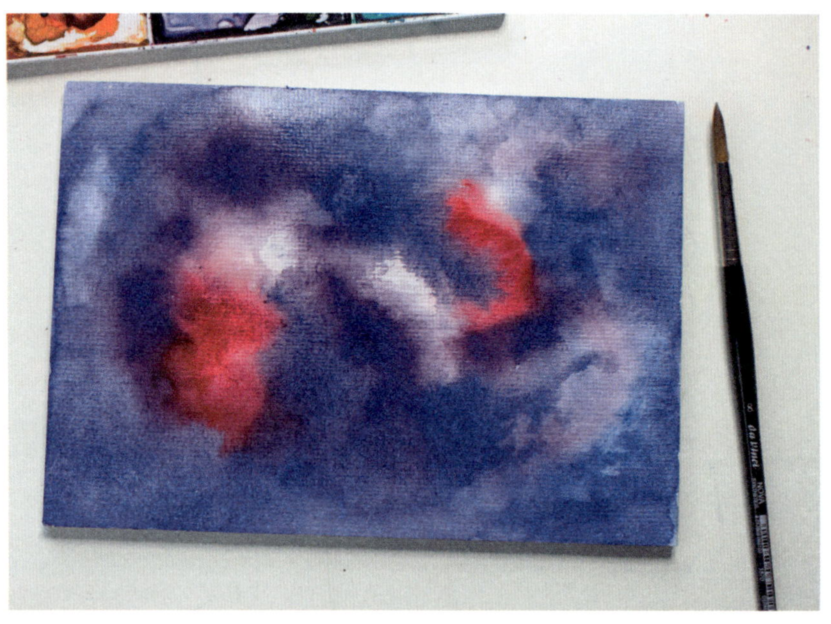

6 Now continue to add patches of dark blue. Soften the edges with a clean, wet brush as before.

7 Apply a very dark blue to the outer edges of the picture. You will have created a colourful galaxy with both very bright and very dark areas – the contrast is crucial here.

8 Mix up some white gouache or acrylic paint and use the toothbrush method (see page 27) to add some splashes for stars. Then paint on your lettering (see page 41).

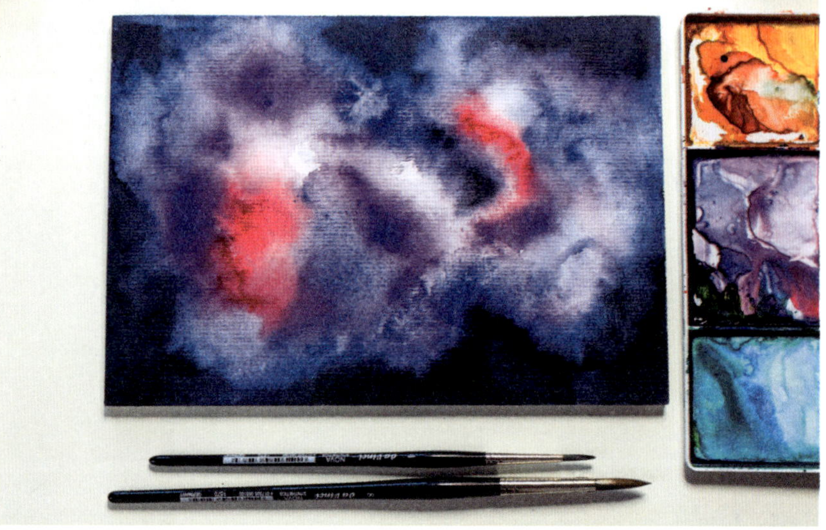

THE MOON IN THE SKY

Do you remember drinking straw technique for blowing paint from page 27? We are now going to use that to create a lunar picture.

MATERIAL

- Watercolour paints in turquoise, dark blue, grey and black
- Watercolour paper
- Pencil and saucer or pair of compasses
- Masking fluid
- Round brush, sizes 4 and 10
- Jar or glass of water
- Drinking straw
- Acrylic or gouache paint in white

1. Draw a circle in the middle of your watercolour paper then fill it completely with masking fluid. Leave to dry for about two hours.

2. Mix up some light turquoise paint and apply plenty of it around the circle. Then immediately start blowing the paint with a straw in an outward direction, radiating out from the circle. You will have to turn the sheet round as you blow.

Apply a darker shade of turquoise to the still damp paint around the edge of the circle. Leave to dry.

 A dark blue gives this image the necessary depth. Apply the paint, then soften the hard edges with a clean, damp brush as you did with the watercolour galaxy (see page 43). Then add splashes of dark blue with the brush or toothbrush method (see page 27). Let everything dry.

4 Spray some white gouache or acrylic paint onto the dark surfaces with a brush or toothbrush. Once this has dried, carefully rub off the masking liquid from the central circle. Apply clear water to the white paper and then add spots of grey and black paint. As you are using the wet-on-wet technique the grey and black will run across the circle, making it look like a moon.

5 If you like, decorate the illustration with lettering.

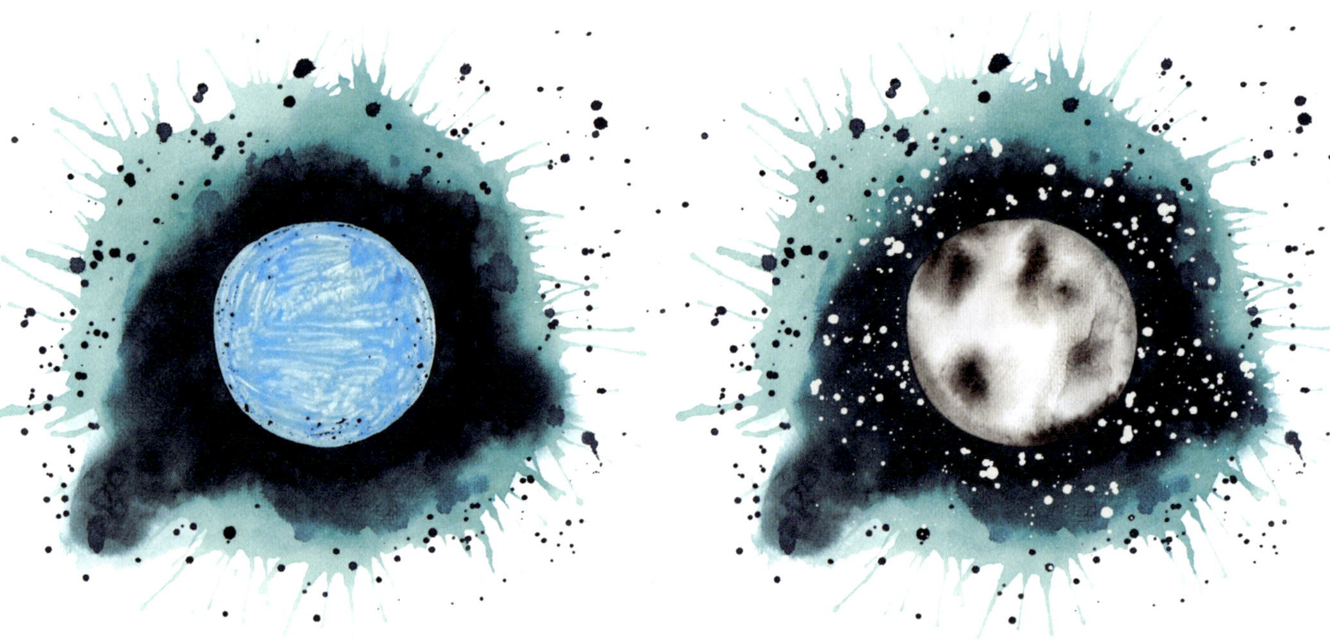

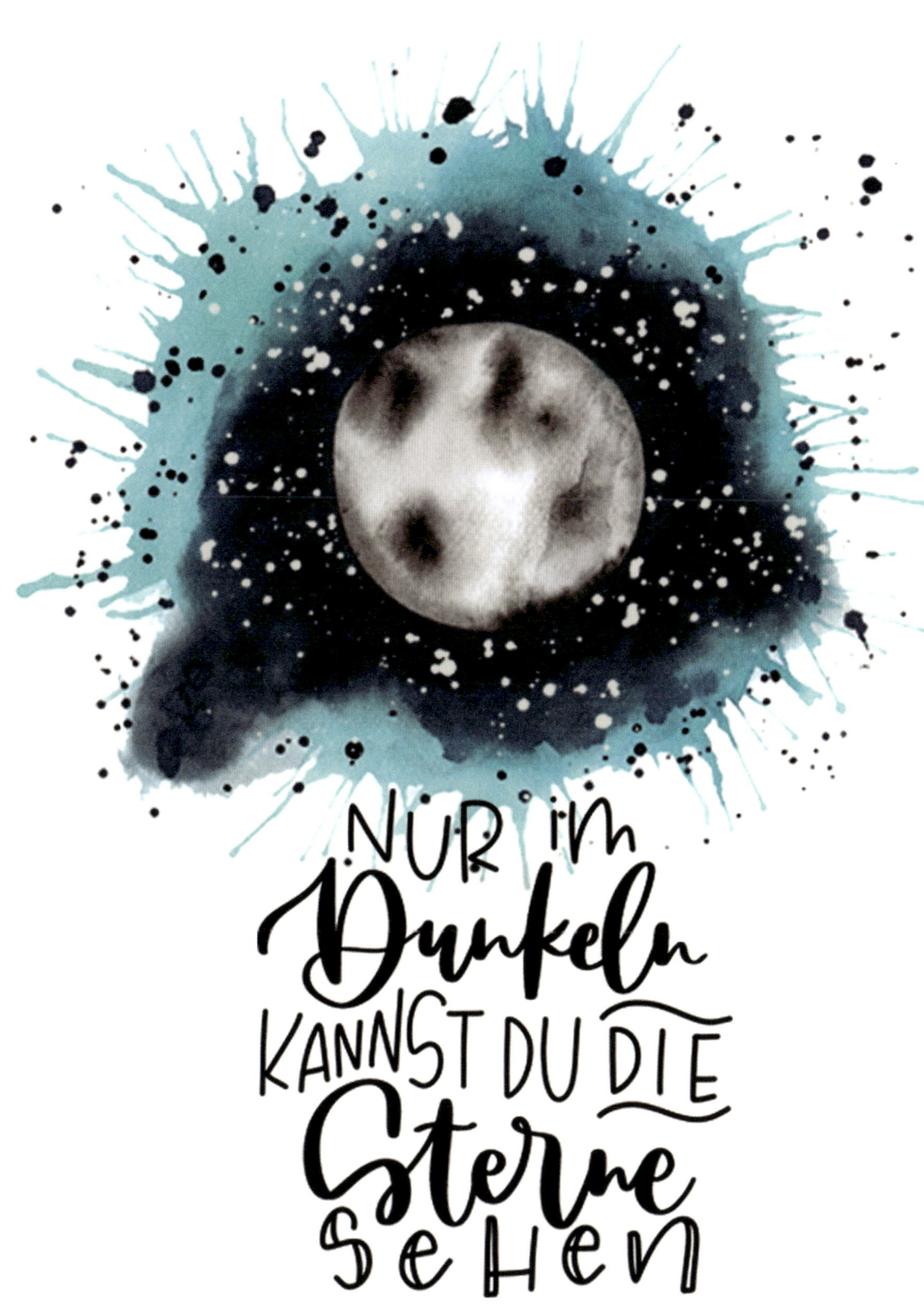

You can only see the stars in the dark

Even Backgrounds

MYSTICAL EVENING FOREST

In the previous projects, I showed you how to create watercolour backgrounds that are rather irregular. However, if you want a very even background, you should do this differently. The following project will help you explore the technique.

MATERIAL

- Ecoline watercolour paints in black and blue

- Large flat brush

- Round brush, size 4

- Watercolour paper

- Jar or glass of water

- Acrylic or gouache paint in white

1 First mix together one part black and two parts dark blue paint. Using a large flat brush, apply the paint downwards from the top of the paper in horizontal strokes. Dip the brush in clear water and pull the paint further down the page. There should be a uniform colour gradient from dark to light. Let everything dry well.

2 Using black paint, paint a line across the base for the ground, then add two fir trees on the right.

3 Here's how to paint a fir tree. Draw a vertical line for a trunk, then draw slightly curved lines coming away from the trunk from top to bottom. The lines should become longer towards the bottom of the tree so it appears conical.

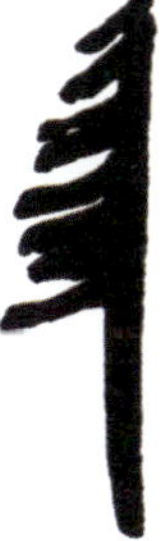

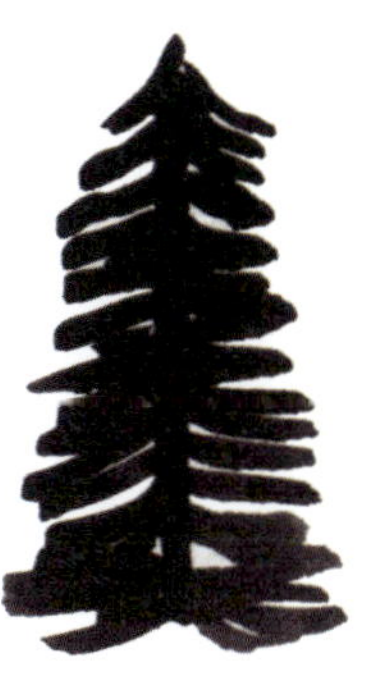

4. Add more fir trees in different sizes. Finally, spray some white gouache or acrylic paint onto the upper dark area with a brush or toothbrush to create a mystical evening forest with a starry sky and fir-tree silhouettes.

5. Add some lettering to give your evening forest a special extra dimension.

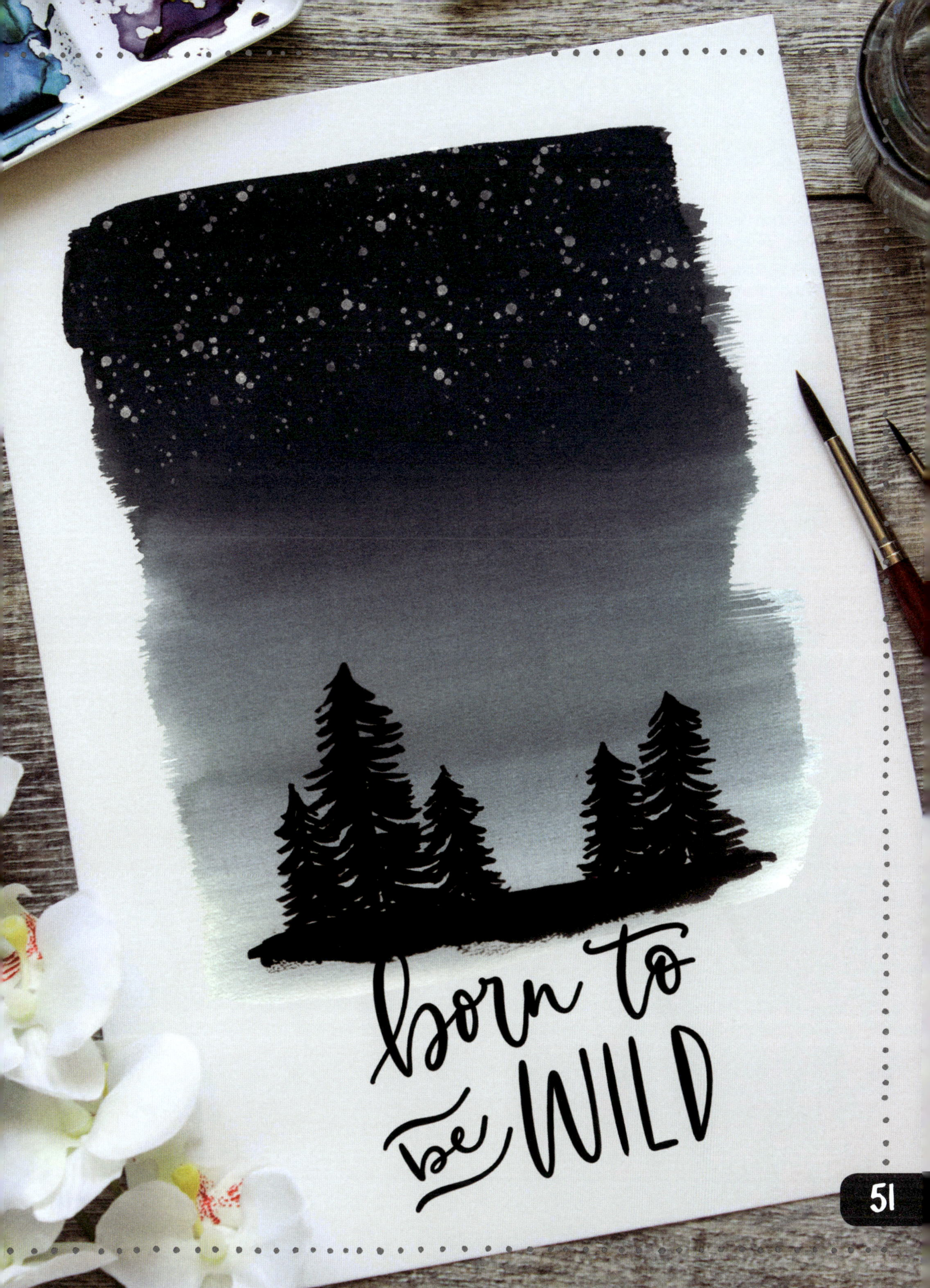

born to
be WILD

Loose & Floral

I am a big fan of what you might call 'fast and loose' watercolour. By this I mean a quick and easy style where you paint shapes loosely and quickly with your brush. The aim is not to to produce completely realistic images and not to go into too much detail. The great thing about this technique is that you have to do only a little preliminary drawing with a pencil and – then after a little practice – you can quickly create impressive works of art.

On the following pages you will see how we have combined some beautiful flowers and leaves in simple projects to make lovely image. But first, let's look the basics of painting flowers and leaves.

LEAVES AND BLOSSOMS

Leaves are some of the easiest things that you can paint with a brush without doing a preliminary drawing.

Below, I've shown you two varients of a simple leaf – sample #1 and sample #2.

SAMPLE #1

With the tip of your brush, paint a short stalk about 1.5cm long on your paper. Put the end of your brush on the end of the stalk, then pull the brush up the paper to form the leaf, lifing it off at the top to form the tip.

SAMPLE #2

Paint a short stalk, then place the brush on the left side of an imaginary line coming out of the stalk and paint an arc that leads back to the stalk. You should have a rough crescent shape. Do the same on the right of the imaginary line, leaving a white space in the middle. This is how you create a leaf with a central vein.

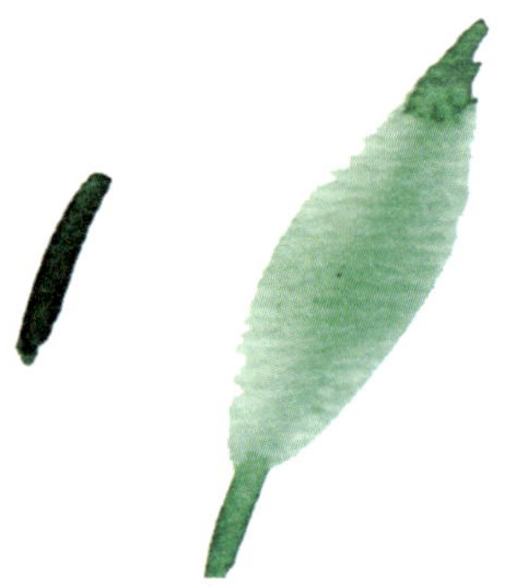

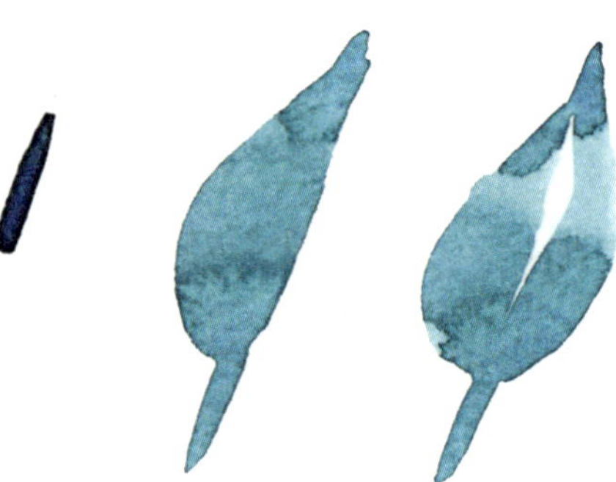

Palm leaves look complex, but they actually consist of only one stem and many small leaves. Paint a thin, curved line, then paint small thin leaves along this line, similar to sample #1. With a palm leaf, the leaves become smaller towards the top. Complete the right side then repeat on the left side.

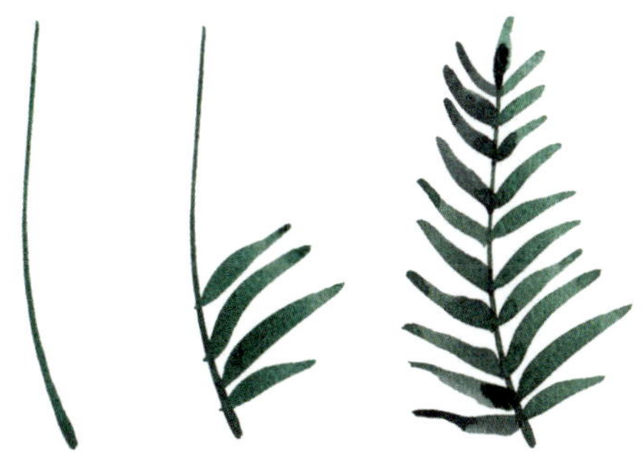

OTHER VARIANTS

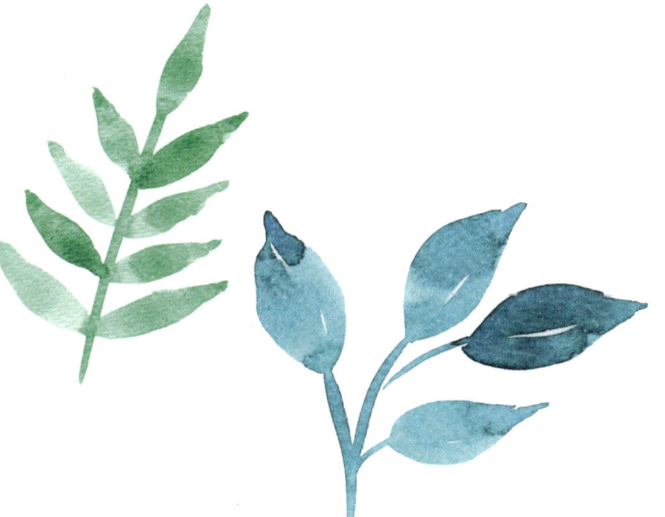

A FIVE-PETALLED BLOSSOM

Painting flowers not only brings joy to the heart, but it is also wonderfully relaxing, which makes practising even nicer. Let's start with a simple five-petalled blossom. Decide on a centre point, then paint a loop outwards from this and fill it with paint. It's good to leave a few white areas. Repeat the process to form four more petals.

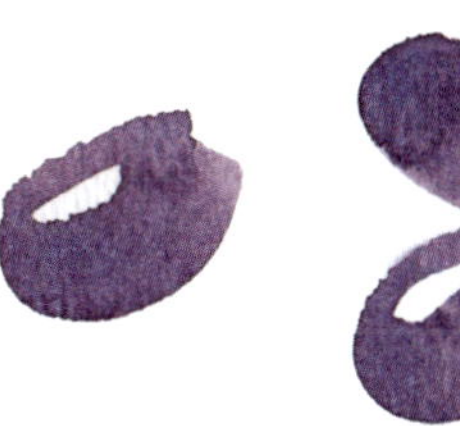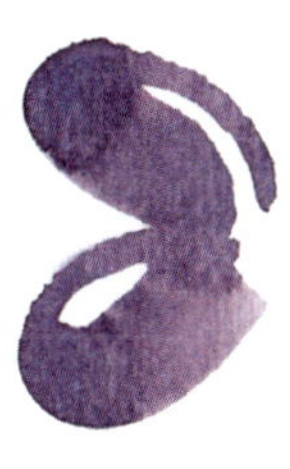

ROSES

For a rose, place your brush tip on an imaginary centre and pull the brush outward in a spiral shape and in wavy lines. The further you come out, the longer you make the shapes.

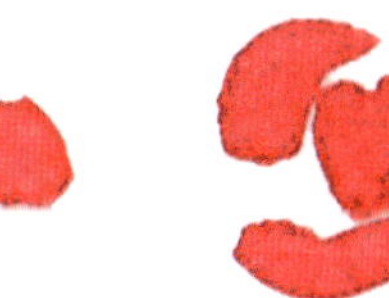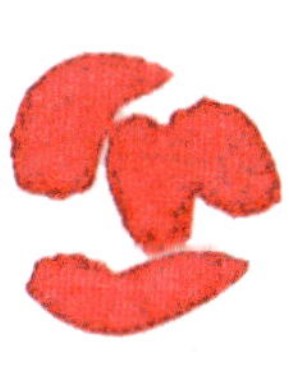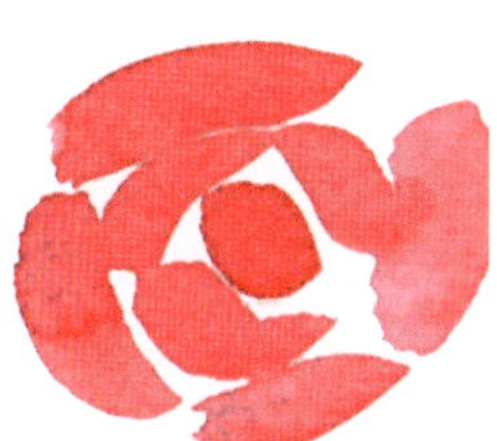

LAVENDER

To paint lavender, start with a grey line as the stalk. Using a violet-blue, dab the brush along the stalk, making the dots smaller towards the top end of the stem. Dab another row along the opposite side

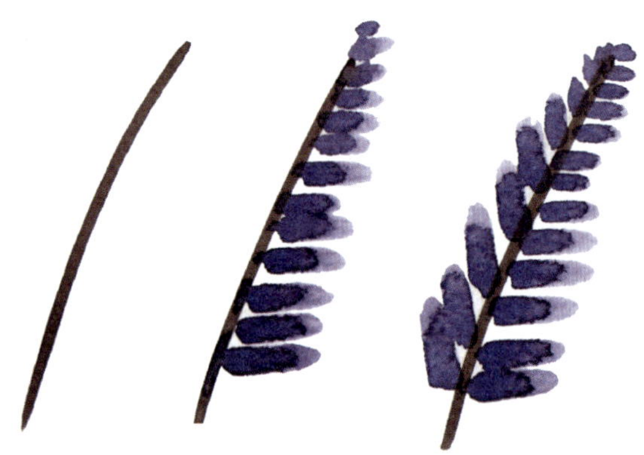

SUNFLOWER

Start a sunflower by painting a brown disc. Using yellow paint, put the tip of your brush on the outer edge of the disc and pull it out to form petals like the sun's rays. This brush movement is similar to that in sample #1 on page 52. Repeat so that the petals go around the circle once.

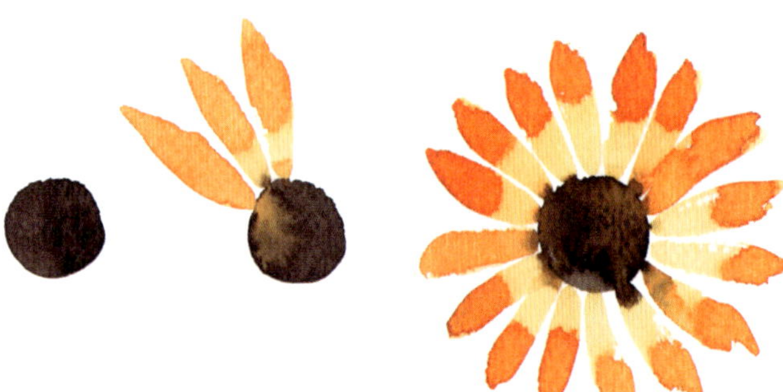

HYDRANGEA

For a hydrangea, it's best to start with a pencil circle. Fill the circle with many small flowers, similar to the five-petalled flower but with only four petals. Allow the small flowers to touch in several places and use paint in pink and purple shades. Finally, paint a few large leaves around the flowerhead.

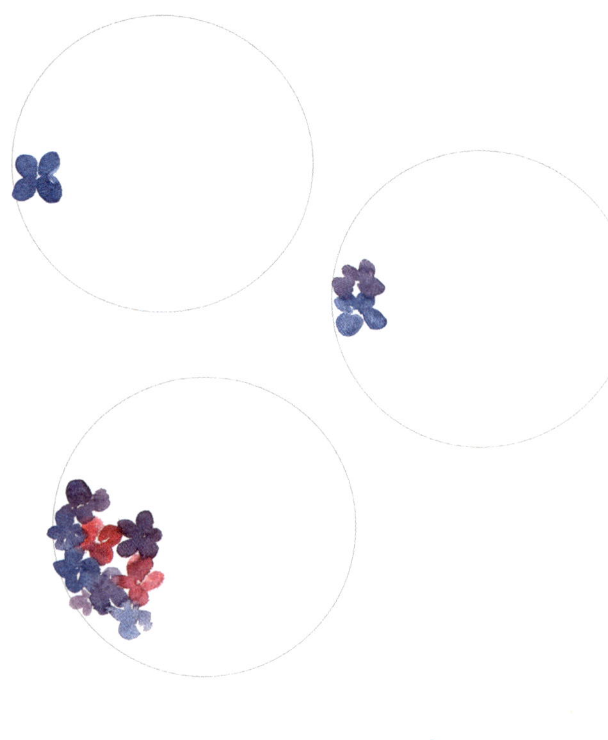

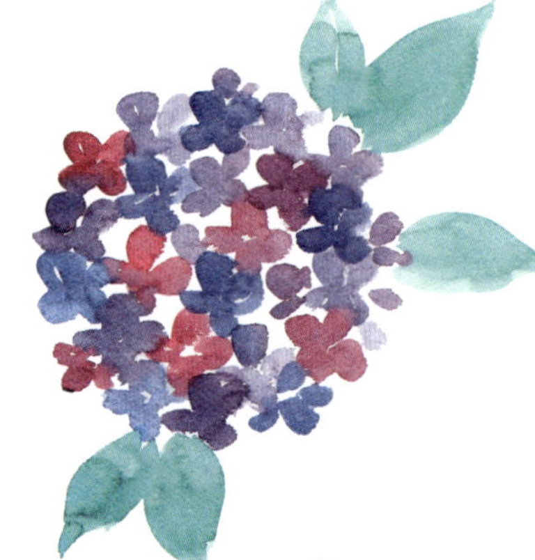

A Bunch of Flowers

For our first full floral project, I've chosen to paint a lovely bouquet that you could give away for almost any occasion. We've used size 4 and 6 round brushes for this painting.

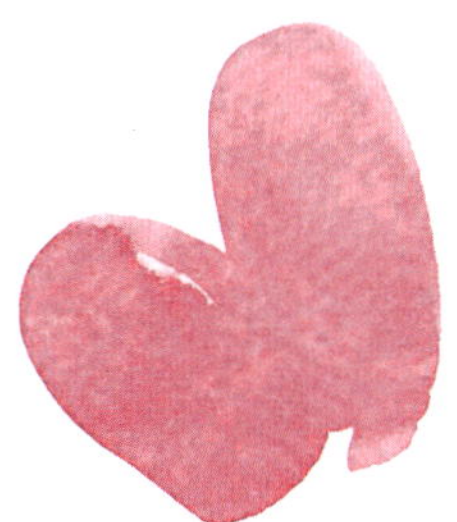

1 Use a size 6 round brush to paint a five-petal blossom in side view by first painting a small loop and then a larger one.

2 Place another small loop next to the large one, then draw oval spots of colour next to the outer loops. These petals look as if they are more in the background.

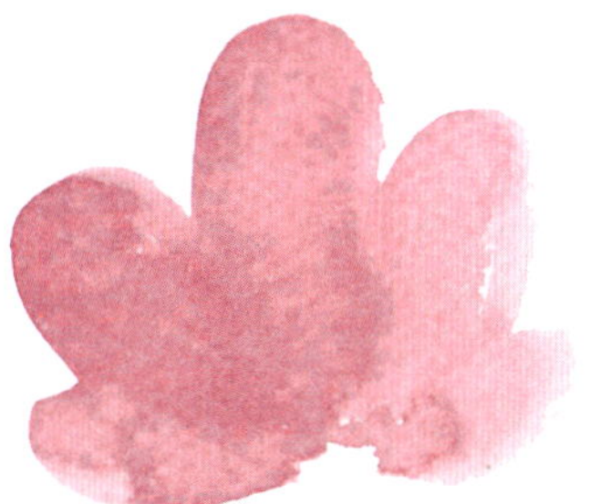

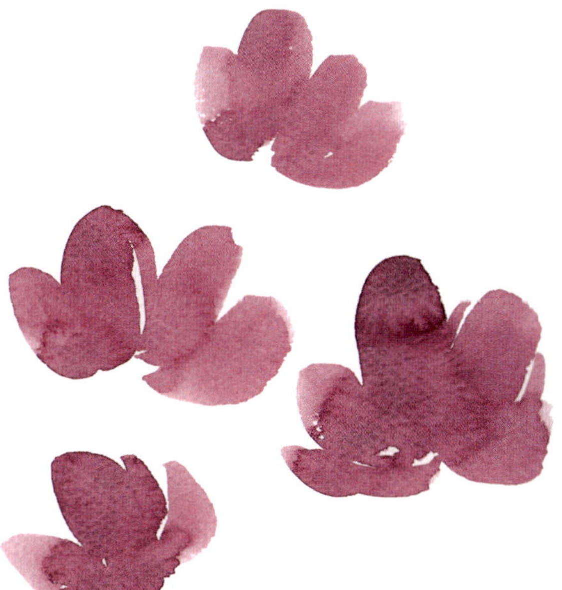

3 Put four more of these flowers on the paper. There can be three or four petals – the irregularity reflects what is found in nature.

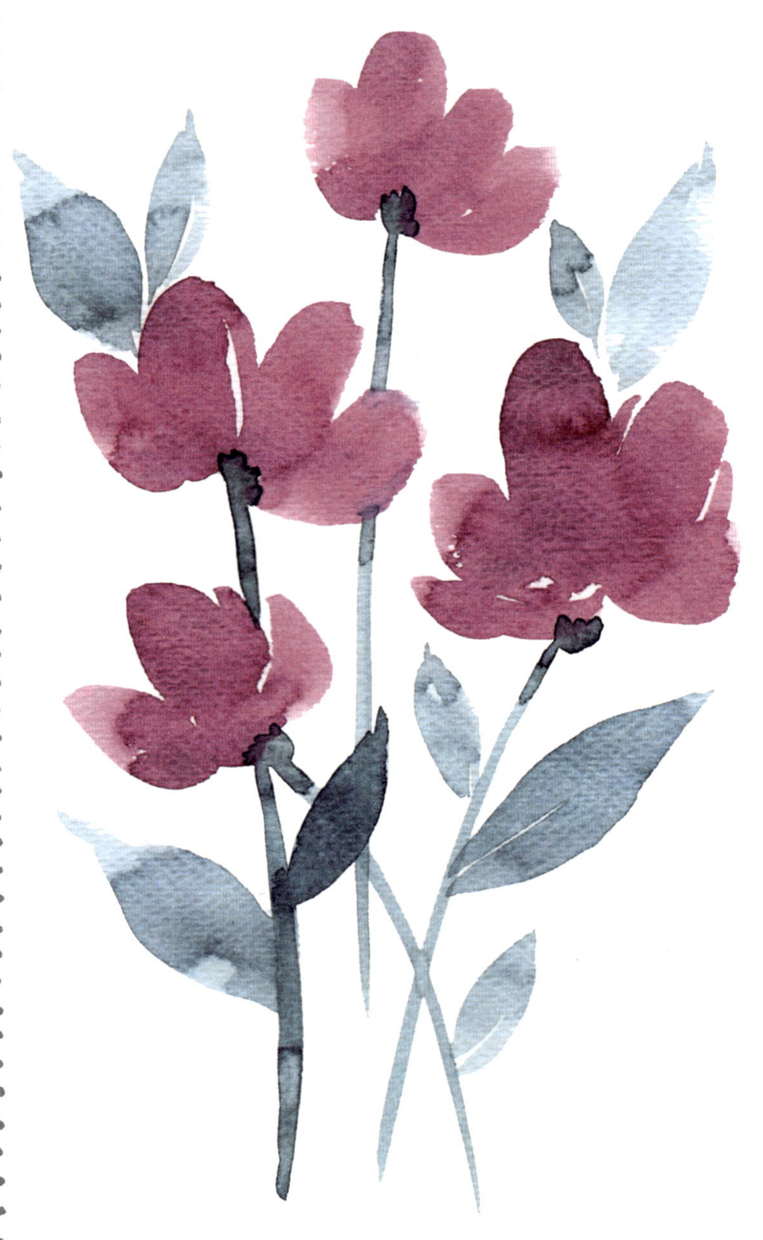

4 Paint stalks coming out of the flowers, then add leaves. I chose the style of leaf shown in sample #2 and painted it in different sizes.

5 The second kind of flower in this bouquet consists only of an group of dots connected by stalks and a stem, painted with a size 4 round brush.

6 Add a lettering message (see page 58) and you can give away a colourful work of art that will last longer than a bunch of real flowers!

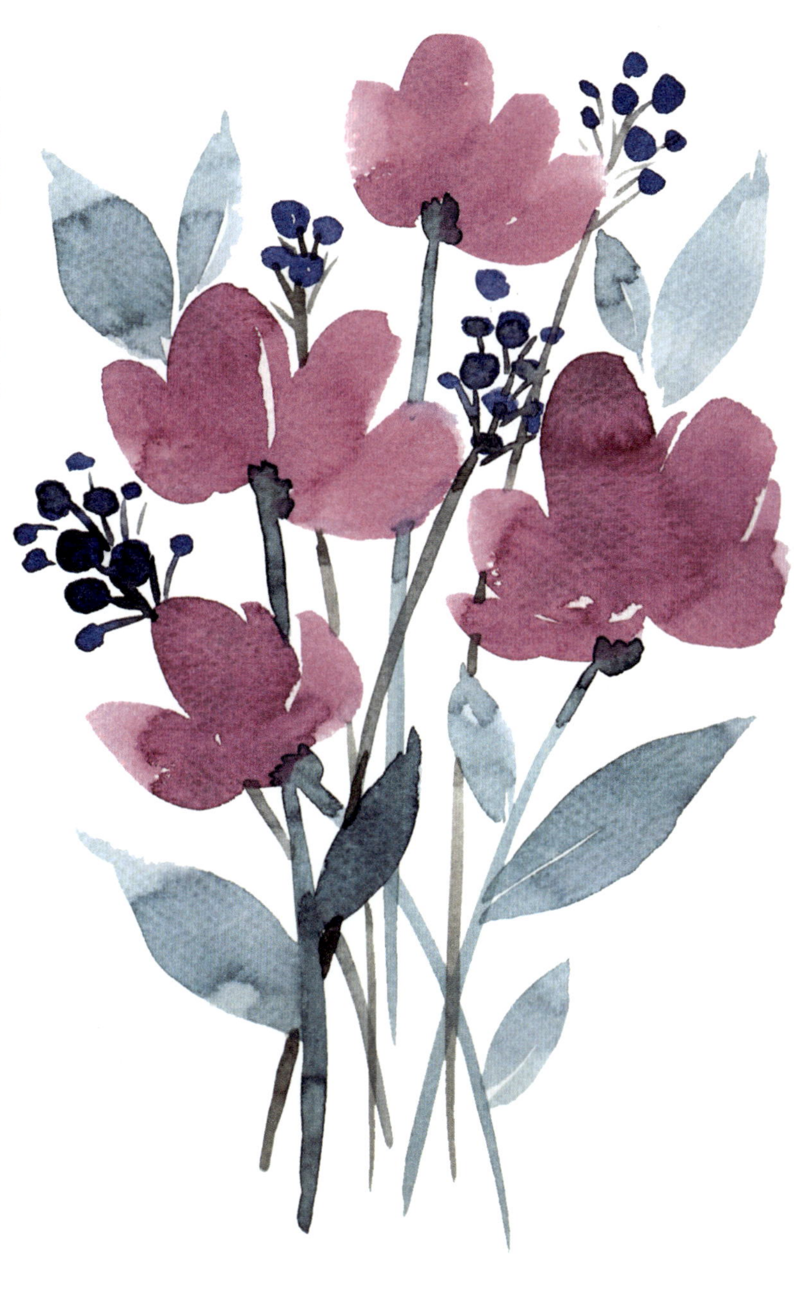

Du bist mir wichtig.
You are important for me

Autumnal Flower Wreath

With different blooms and leaves, a wide variety of floral wreaths can be created. Different combinations of colour can create very different moods – as with this autumnal flower wreath. Sizes 2 and 6 brushes have been used for this project.

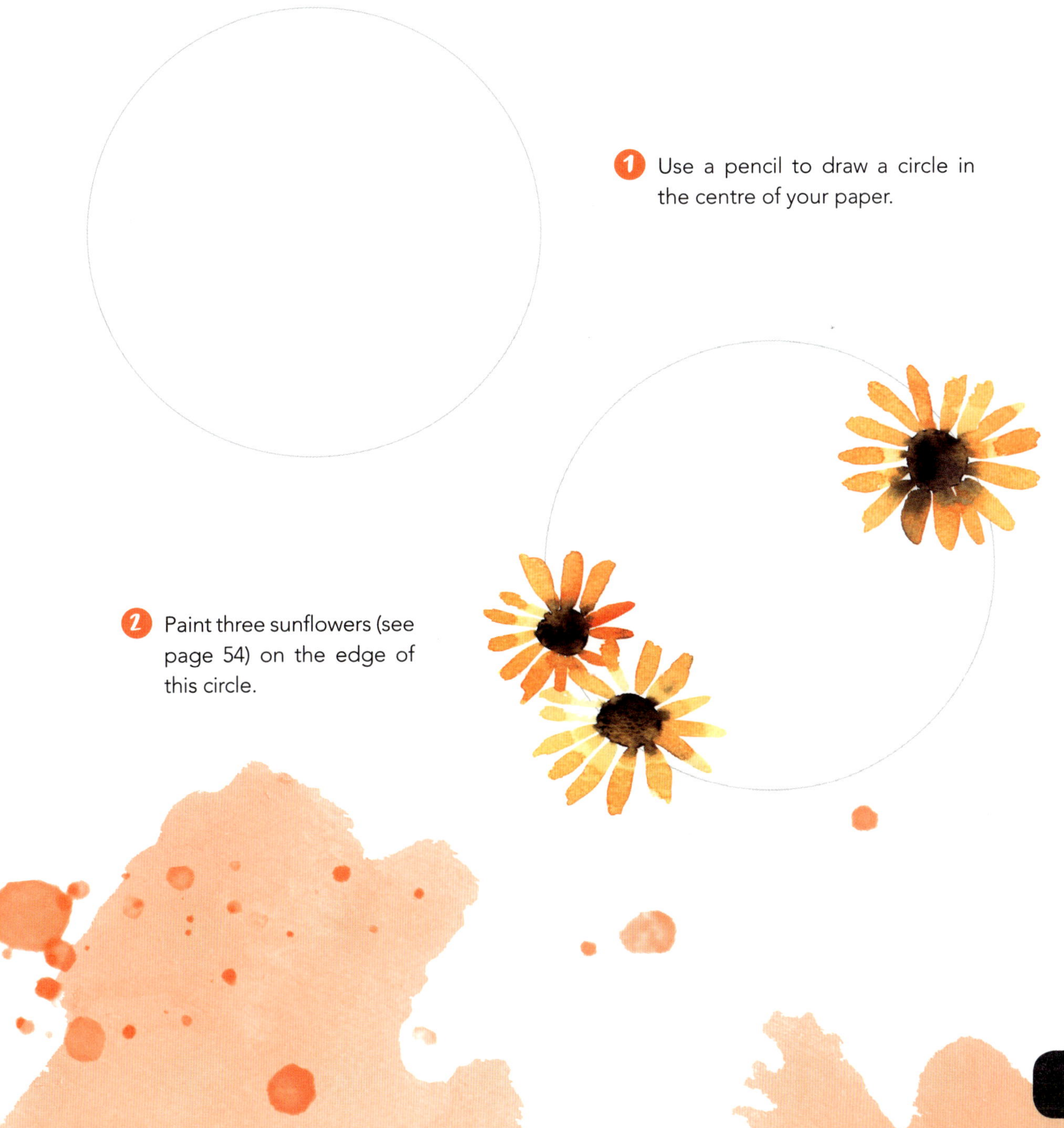

1 Use a pencil to draw a circle in the centre of your paper.

2 Paint three sunflowers (see page 54) on the edge of this circle.

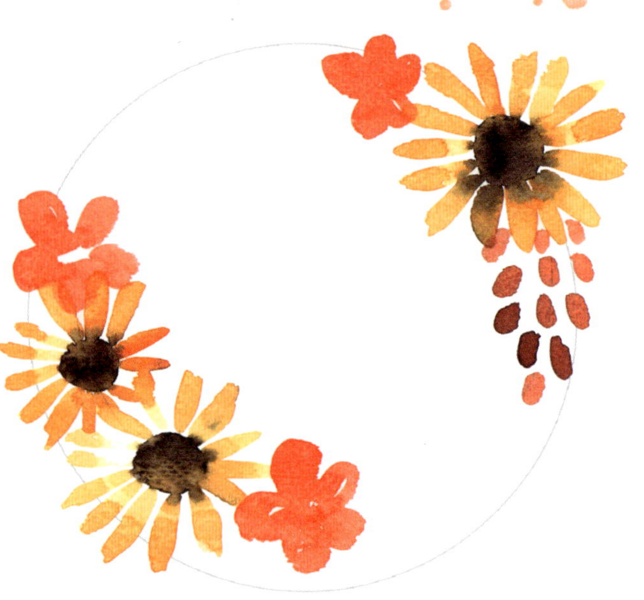

3 Paint three red five-petalled blossoms. Add twelve small red ovals in a rough triangle shape below the right sunflower.

4 Paint in some green leaves, then add some stalks between the small red ovals.

5 Paint in some twining brown lines between the groups of flowers, following the line of the drawn circle.

6 The space in the middle of a floral wreath is the perfect space for lettering.

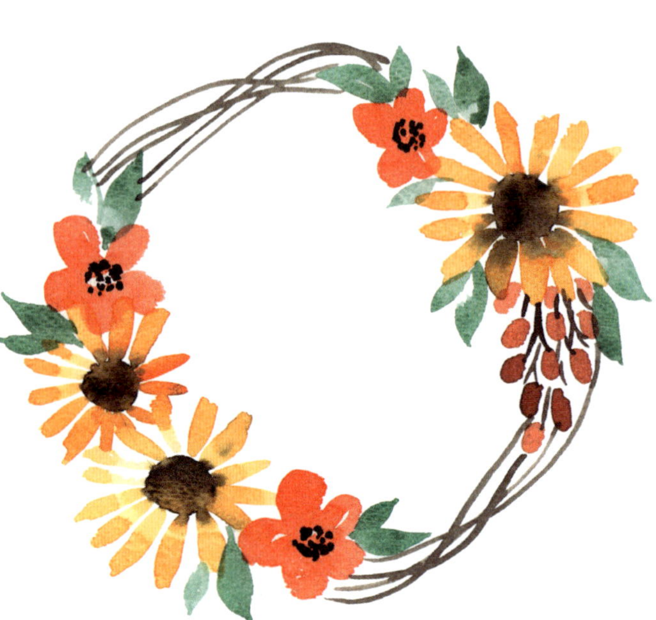

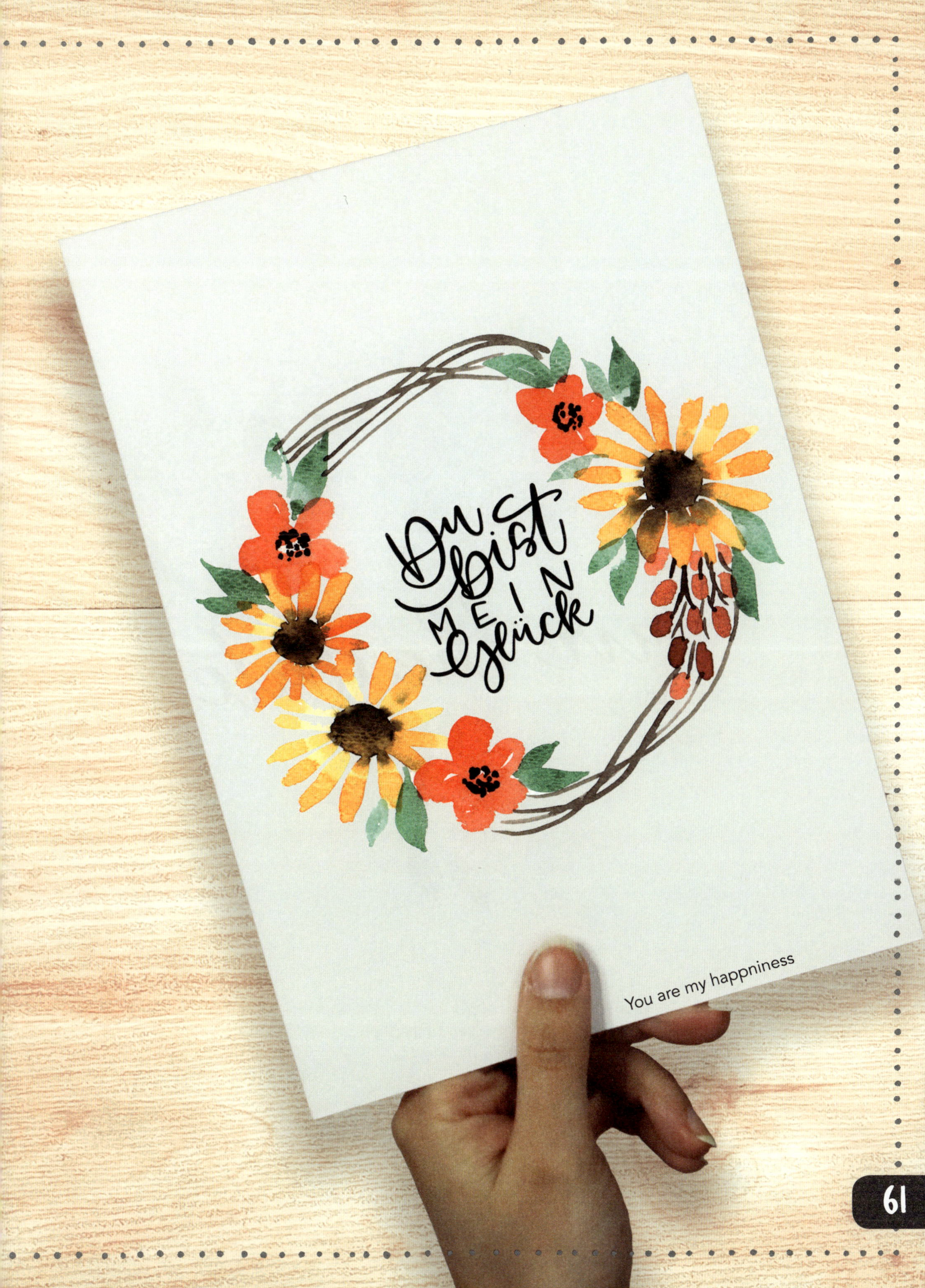

Du bist mein Glück
You are my happniness

Save the date

'Save the Date' with Roses

1. Draw two parallel pencil lines, about 15cm long and 5cm apart.

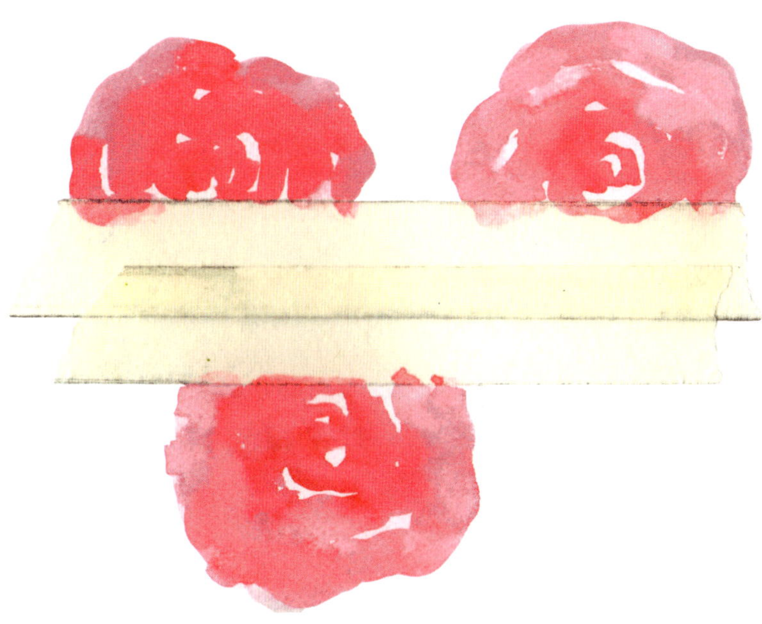

2. Cover the area between the lines with removable masking tape. Paint three partial roses outside and just overlapping the parallel lines.

3 Create four buds by painting a large and small loops directly to the right and left of the roses. Let the paint dry briefly. Add stalks to the buds and a few green leaves at the base of each.

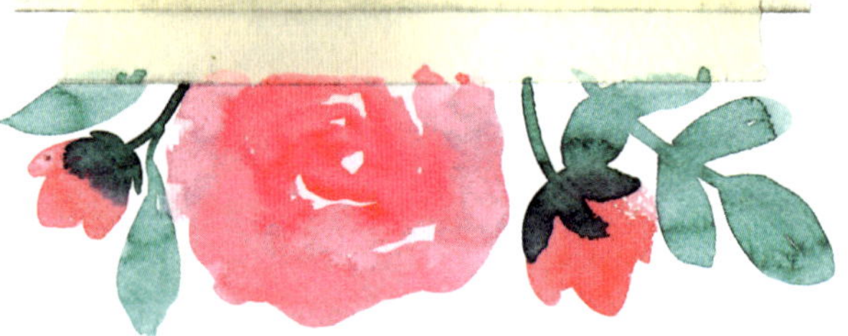

4 Add some pale coloured leaves.

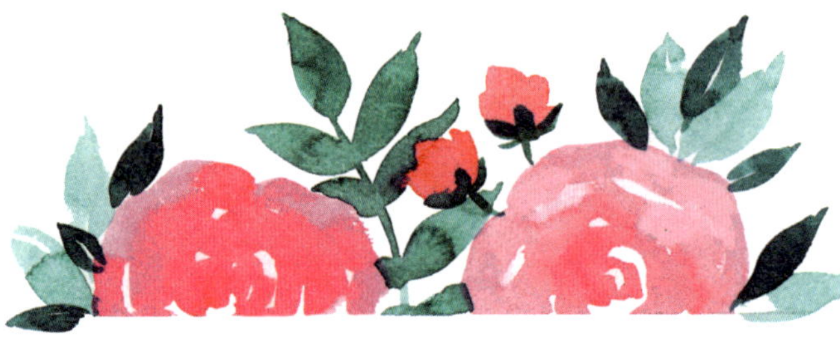

5 When the first leaves have dried, use a stronger shade to paint darker leaves over the lighter ones. This gives the picture more depth and makes it more interesting. Remove the masking tape and add your lettering.

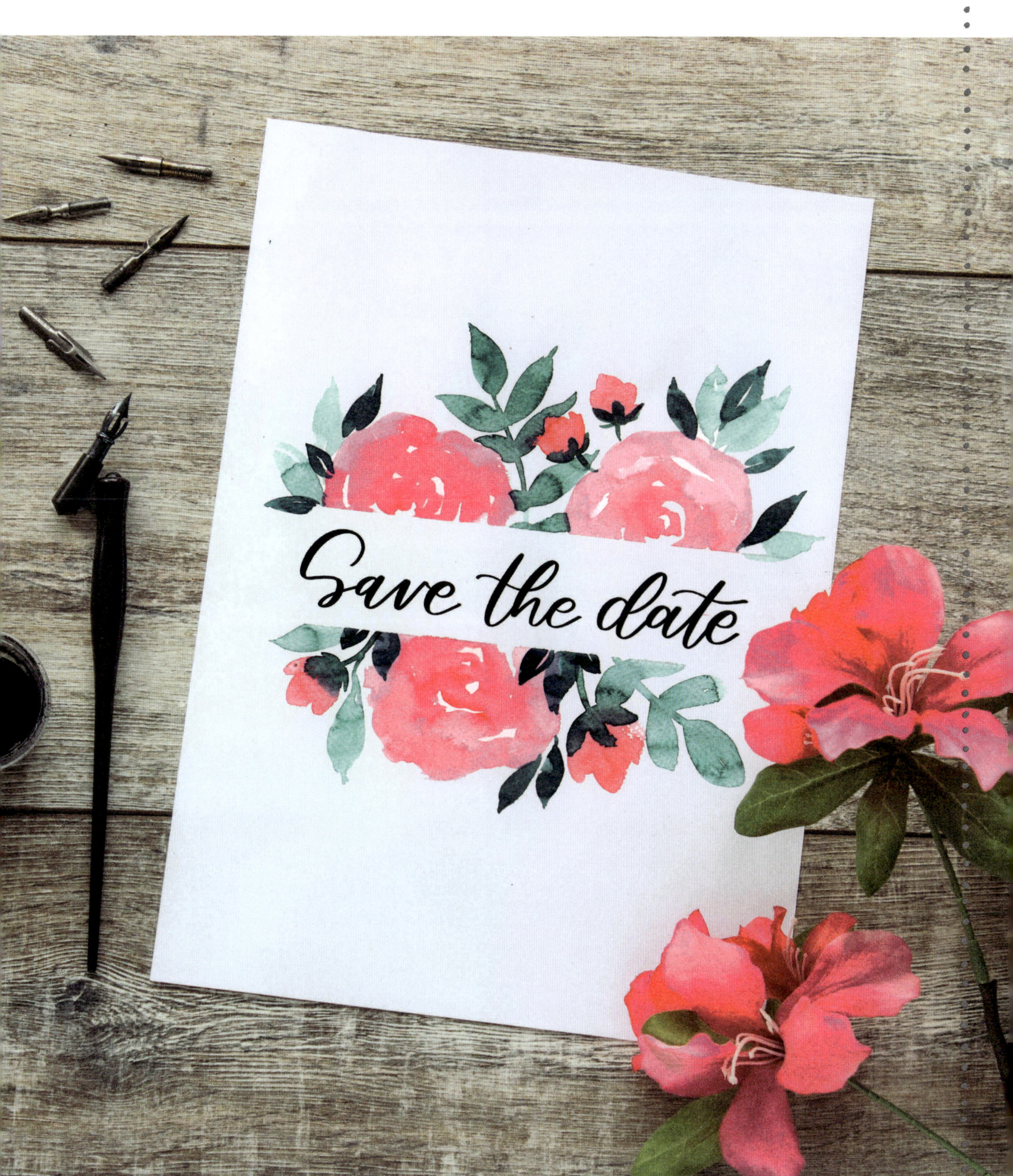
Save the date

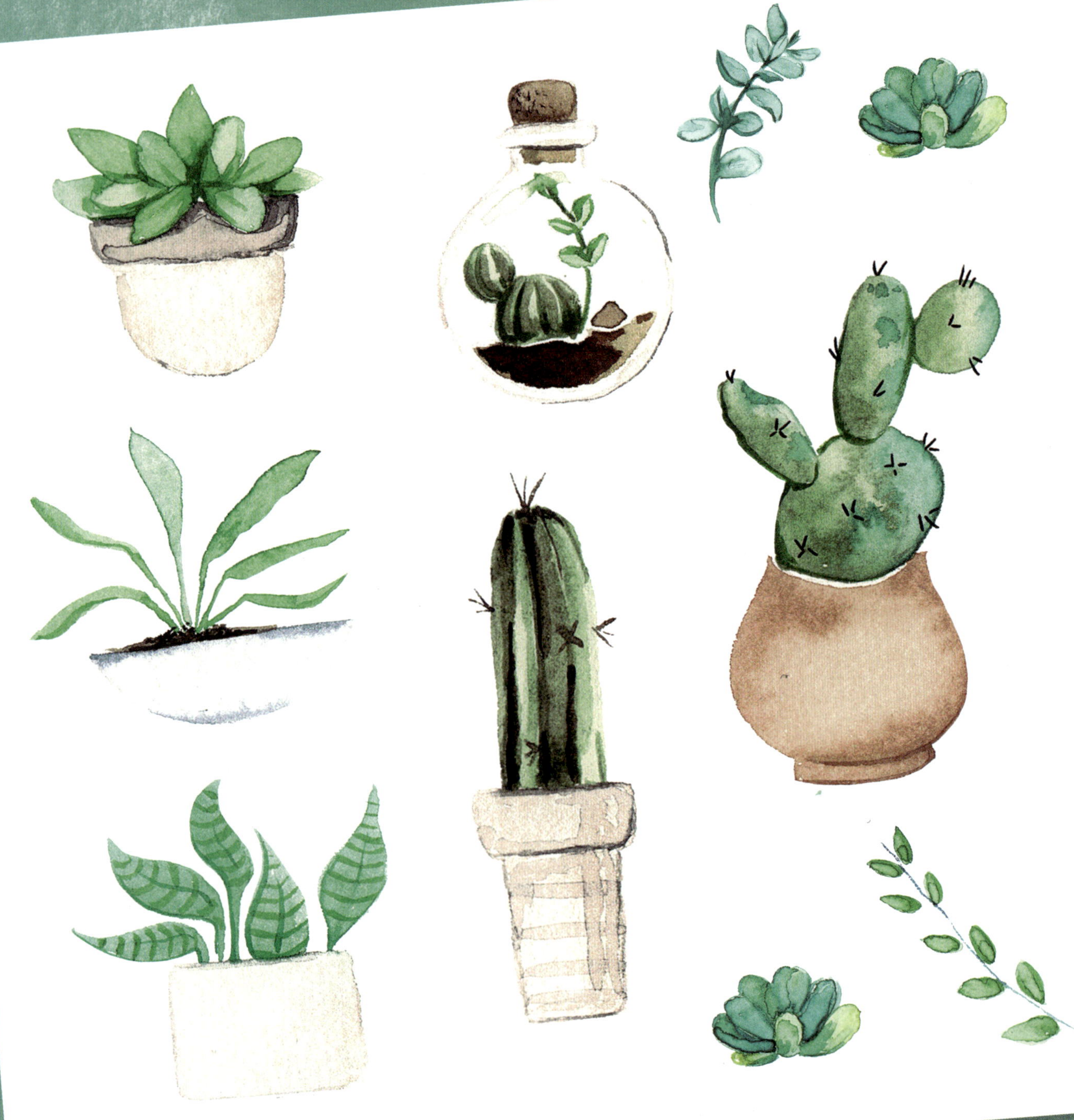

Leaves, Succulents & Cacti

If you love those sometimes-spiky, little green survivors like I do, then this is the place for you! I'll show you the brush and watercolour techniques you'll need to bring twigs, cacti and succulents to life on your paper. Combine your plant-inspired pictures with a suitable lettering and your creations can become real little works of art to hang or give away.

All you need is a small box of watercolour paint with 12 colours – that's plenty for getting started. Take a little time to experiment and you can mix almost any colour yourself. For each project, I will show you the creation process step by step, from sketch to painting to lettering. Then you can go on to put all manner of twigs, leaves, cacti and succulents, in pots or in hanging baskets, onto paper.

You can send a message of love to a person close to your heart, create a funny cactus family or paint an inspiring wreath for yourself, the choice is up to you. At the end of the chapter, you will find a library of plant images to give you plenty of ideas and inspiration.

Get painting and have some fun!

Tanja

You & me

For me, the best thing in life is being with a loved one. For a while, I have been think about what pictures I can create for our home. I wanted something not too cheesy and which would suit both of us – individual and with a personal touch. So here is something with a little bit of green, a little bit of nature and a lot of love for our home.

PRELIMINARY SKETCH

1. Using an HB pencil, draw a ribbon-like banner slightly below the middle of your watercolour paper. Make sure that it's not too small, because you will be adding text to it later.

2. Now sketch in two or three leafy branches behind the banner. It should look as if the banner is bunching the branches together.

3. Then draw in a border of branches around the paper. Vary the shapes of the branches and leaves and keep the areas to the left and right of the banner free of drawing.

TIP: Make sure that you draw your sketch lightly so that you don't have to erase much later.

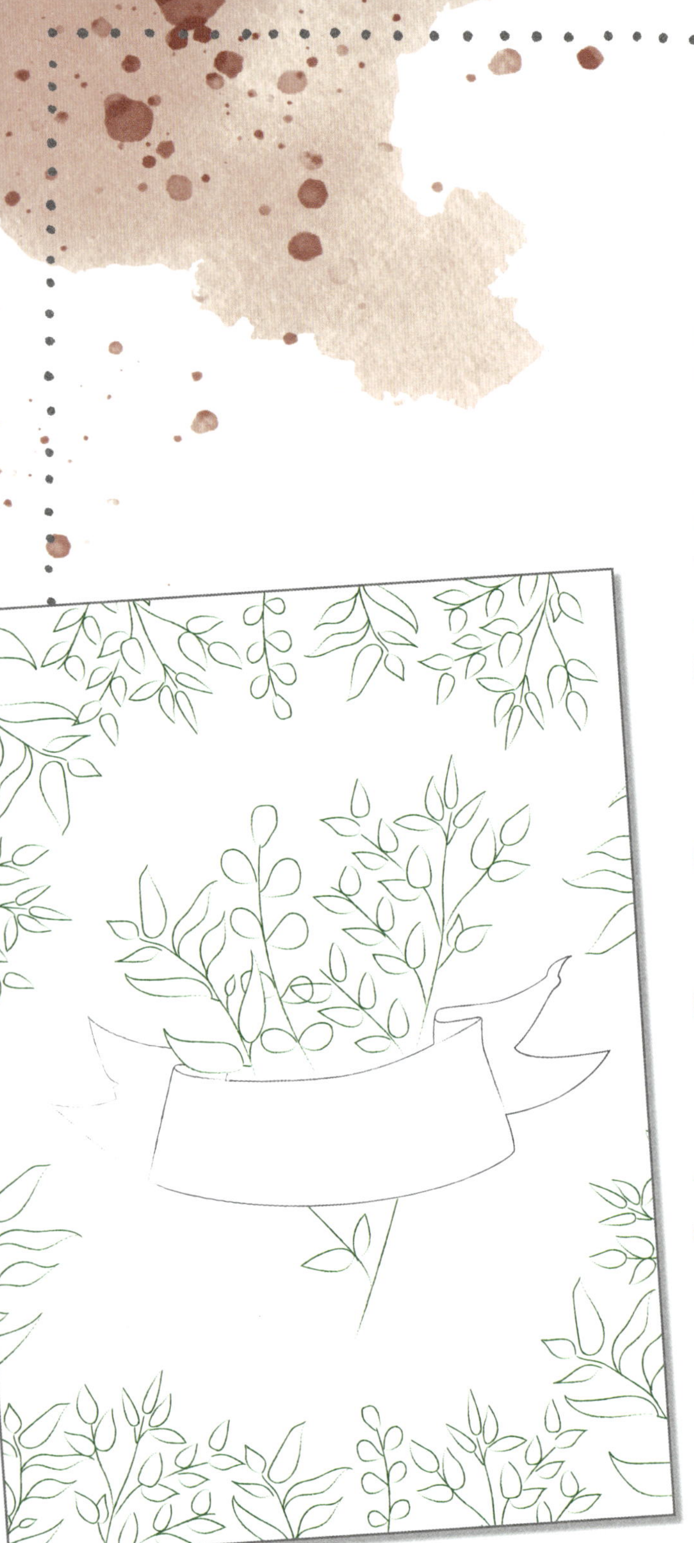

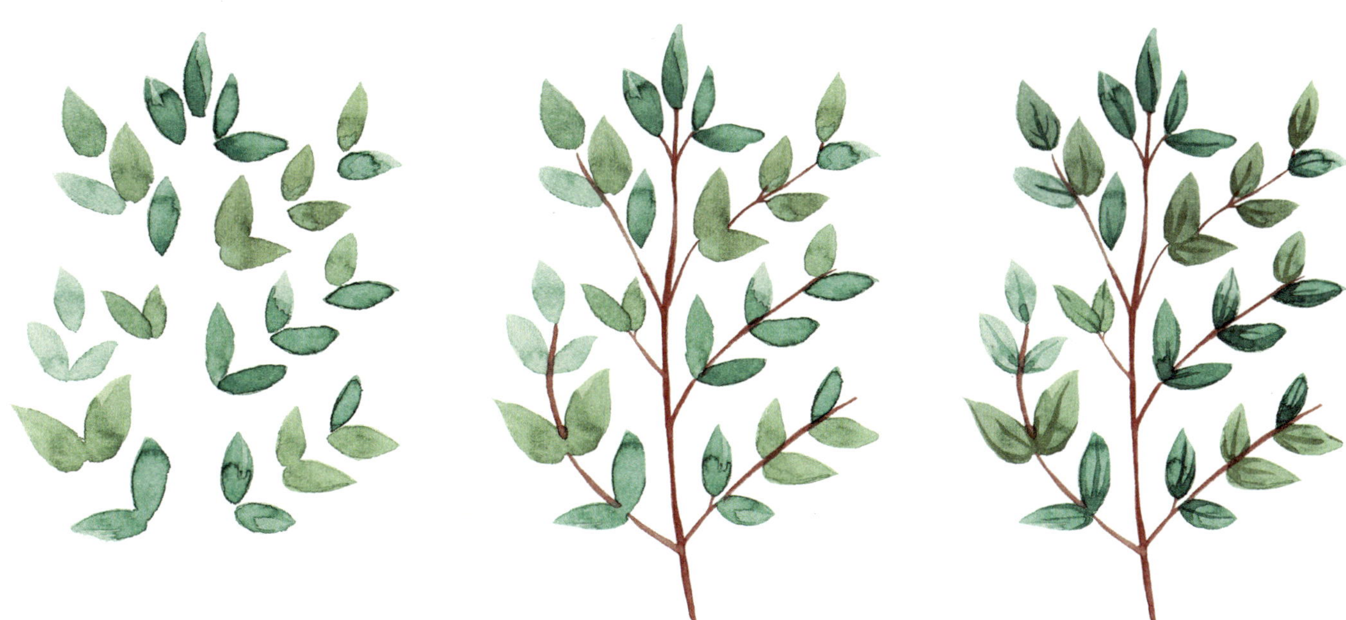

THE PAINTING

4 Mix up two to three different shades of green for your branches. In my design, I decided on three different types of branch. Start by painting just one type so that there will a uniformity to your overall design.

5 Now start to paint individual leaves with a very watery shade of green. Immediately add a dab of a darker shade to the underside of each leaf. This mixes both colours and creates a shadow. While you are waiting for the leaves to dry, you can begin paint the other types of branch in the other shades of green.

6 Mix up a shade of brown and paint the stems and twigs that connect your leaves.

7 Let your painting dry well before you work more details into leaves and branches with a thin brush. Make sure you use more paint and work with very little water on your brush.

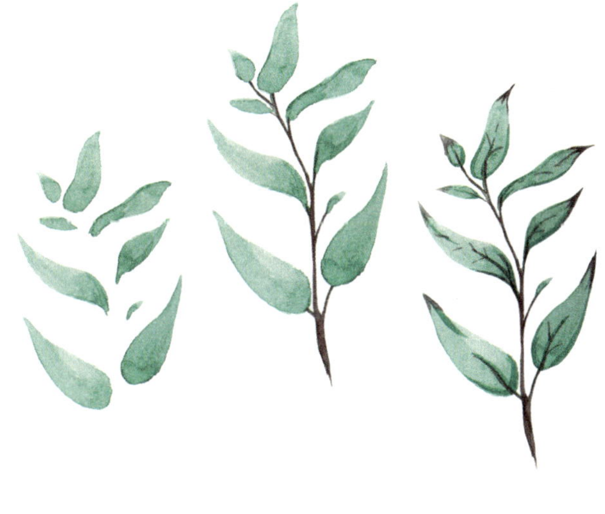

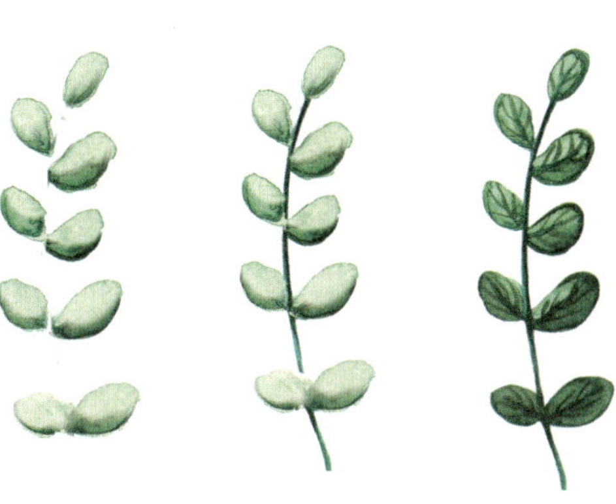

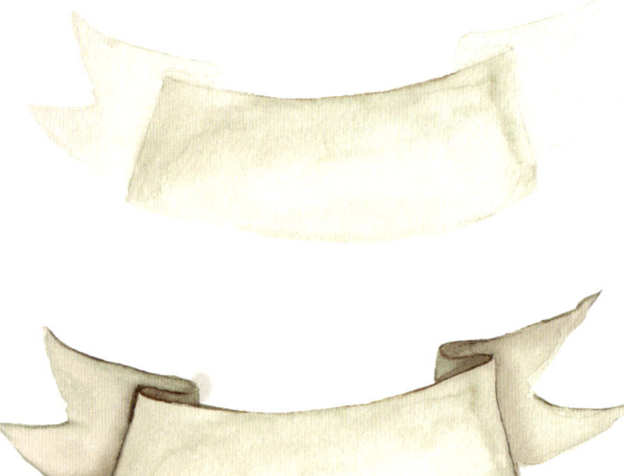

8 When all the leaves are done and you are satisfied with the result, it's time to paint the banner. Mix up a light shade of brown for this. Again, start with a very light, watery colour and let the whole thing dry a little.

9 Paint in darker areas and shadows layer by layer. Then let the banner dry completely.

10 For the perfect finishing touch, you can paint the edges with an even darker tone. This gives the shape additional strength.

ADDING LETTERING

11 After the banner is completely dry, lightly draw in your lettering with a pencil.

12 When you are satisfied with the result, use a brush or brush pen to go over the letters. When everything is dry, carefully erase the pencil lines.

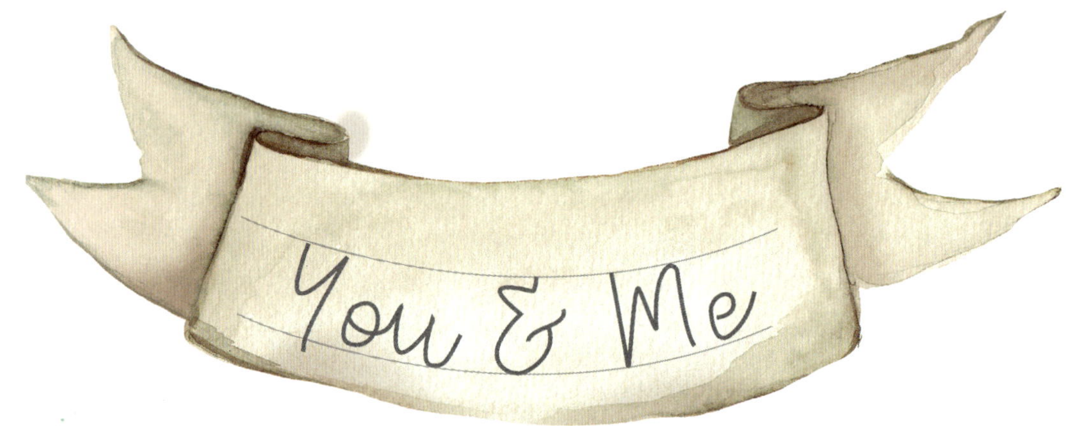

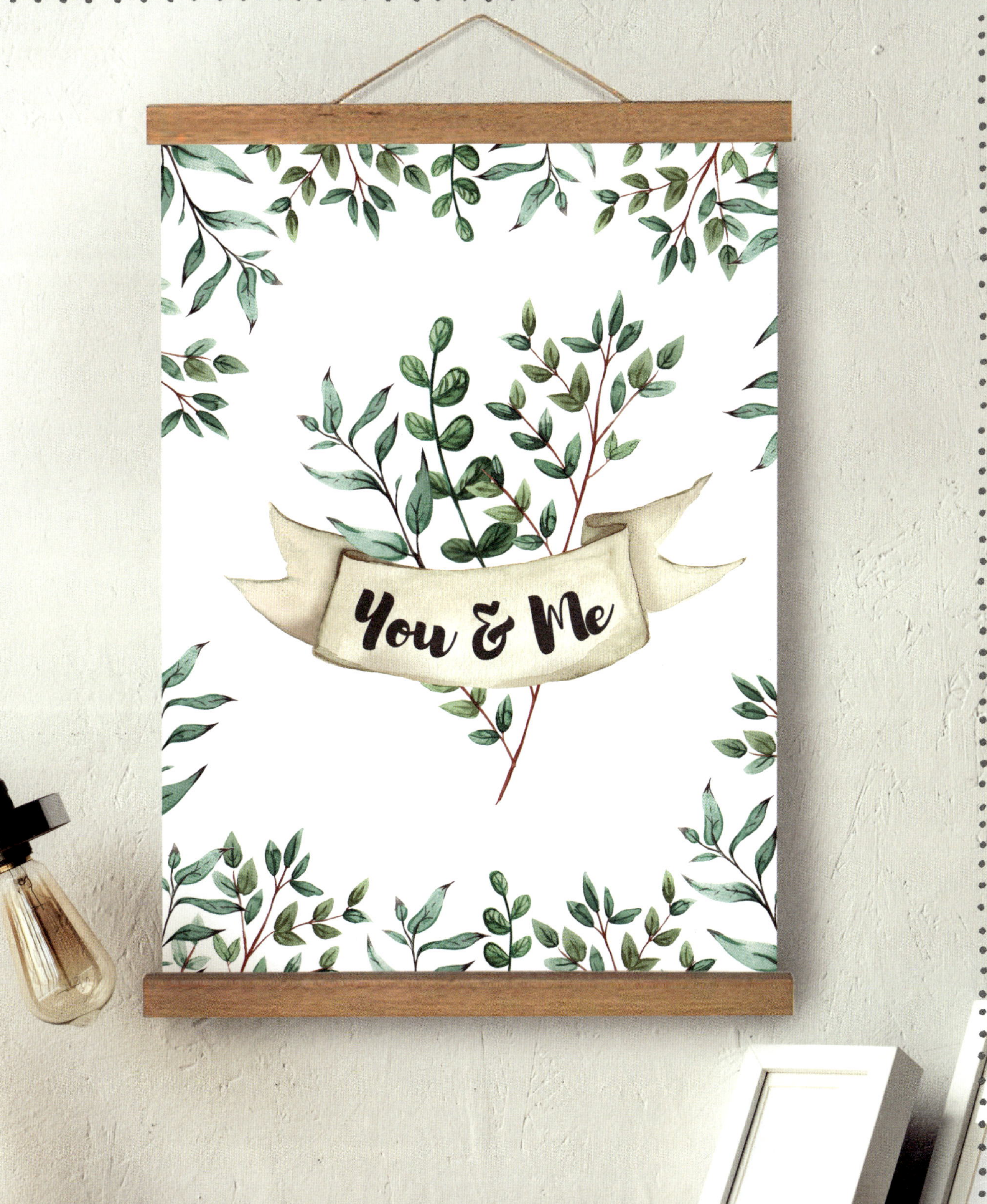
You & Me

Leaf Wreath – Be Happy

Wreaths of leaves and flowers are all over the internet – who hasn't seen photos of them on Pinterest, Instagram and the like? But have you ever tried to paint such a wreath of leaves? You might be surprised, but with a little bit of planning, it's actually quite easy.

PRELIMINARY SKETCH

1 Use a pair of compasses to draw a circle in the centre of your paper. Alternatively, use a cereal bowl or a small plate and draw around this.

2 Start by drawing in the larger leaves with a pencil. Make sure they are loosely but evenly distributed around the circle.

3 To make your wreath design more interesting, fill the gaps with small twigs, leaves or berries.

THE PAINTING

4 When your sketch is done, mix up two to three different shades of green for your leaves.

5 I start with the light tones and, as I am right handed, I begin painting at the bottom left. This way I avoid blurring the damp paint with my hand as I work.

6 Two brush strokes are all that's needed to paint most leaves. Put the brush tip on the tip of the leaf and bring the brush down. Increase the pressure on your brush and the stroke will become wider and wider. At the base of the leaf, reduce the pressure again and the shape narrows. Repeat on the other side of the leaf. The shapes may overlap or you can leave a little white space between. Vary the way you paint the leaves to give the image more interest.

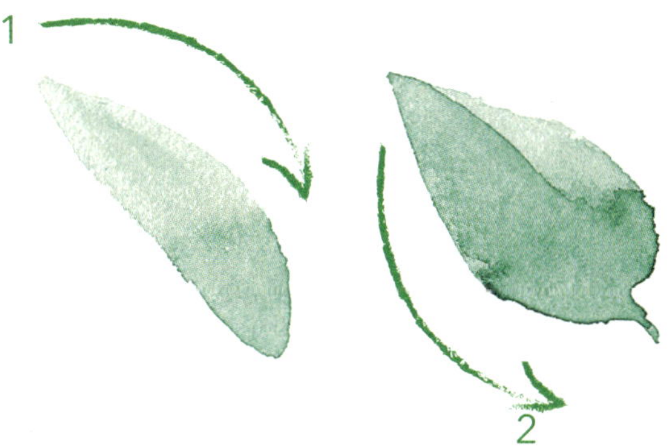

7 Complete the wreath by painting in the small twigs, berries or single leaves. overlaporyoucan leave a little white space between. Vary the way you paint the leaves to give the image more interest.

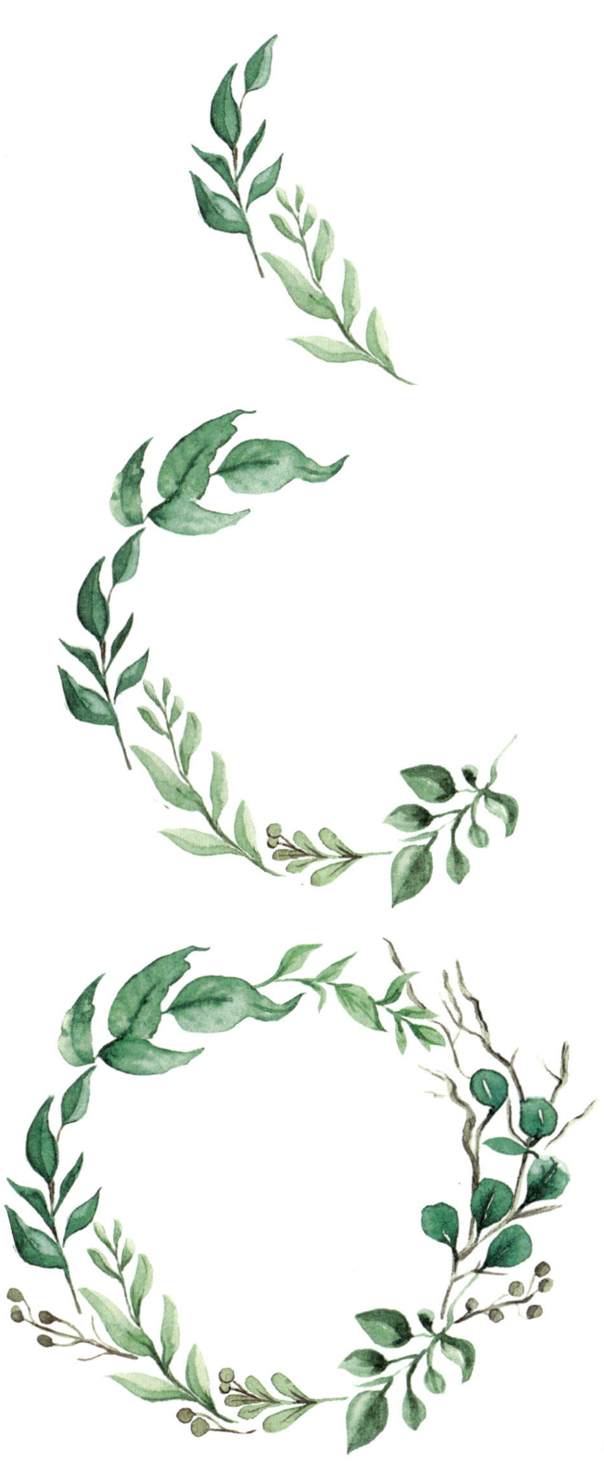

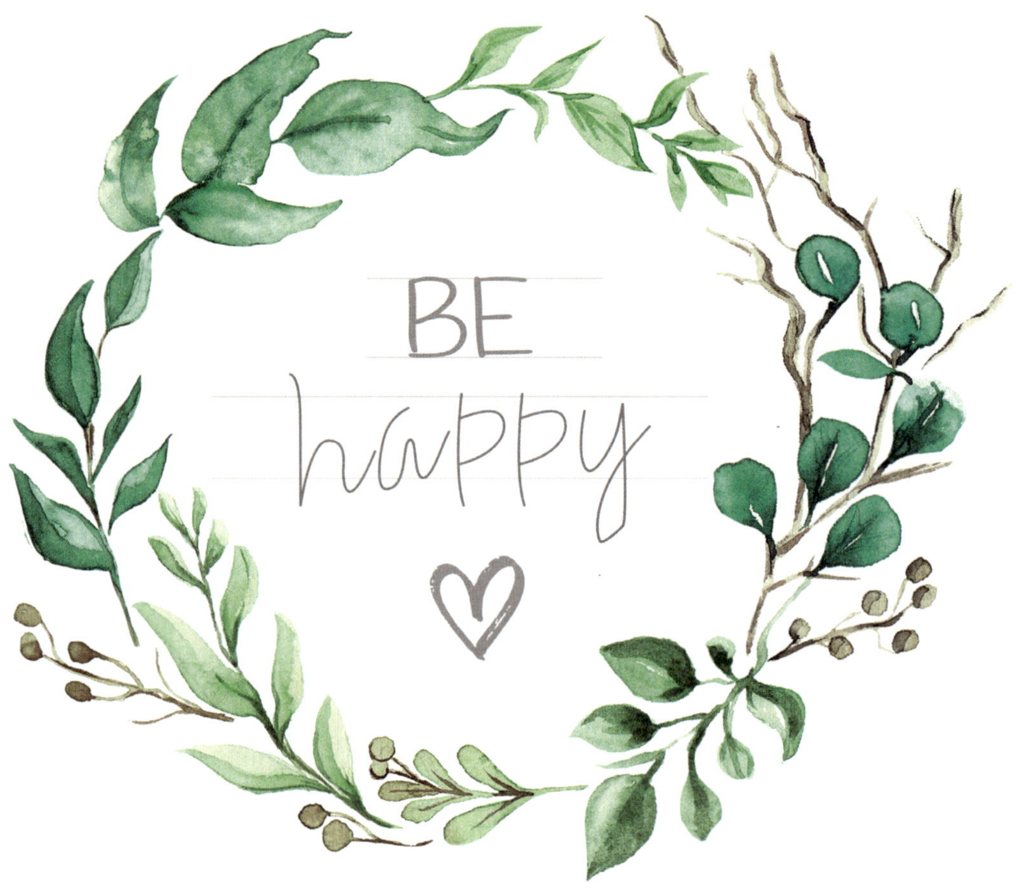

ADDING LETTERING

8 Sketch in your words in the middle of the wreath in pencil. To make sure that the lines of text are parallel, use a ruler to mark in faint guidelines.

9 When you are happy with the lettering, paint it in letter by letter. If liked, you can add a little heart shape below the words.

When everything is dry, very carefully erase your pencil lines.

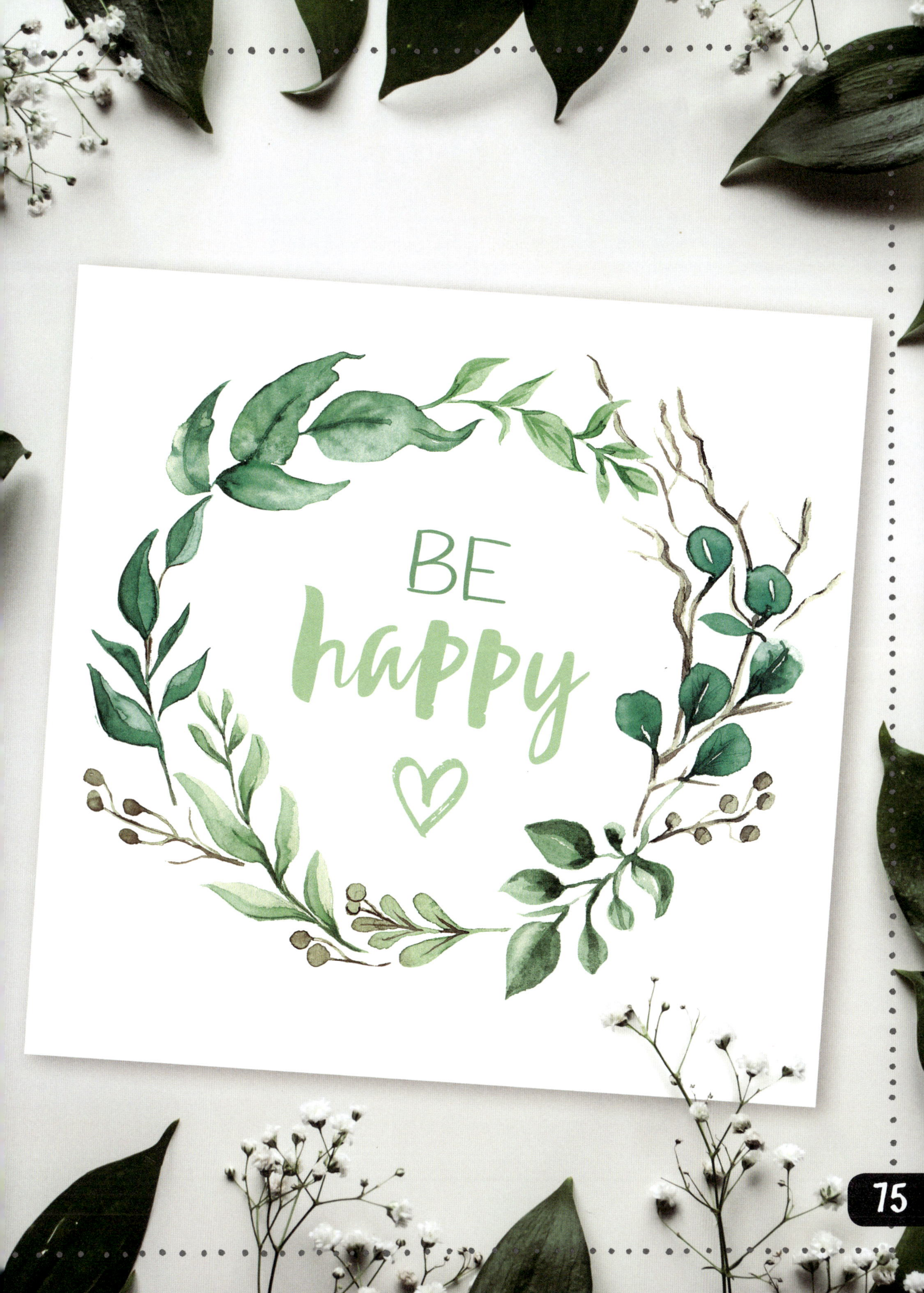
BE
happy

Eucalyptus Twigs

Eucalyptus trees have beautifully coloured and interesting leaves. Branches of eucalyptus are often found in florists' arrangements and they smell so wonderfully fresh. Here you can paint a version that never fades.

PRELIMINARY SKETCH

1 The sketch is very simple and quick - draw in a long stem and add some round leaves. Again, make sure that the sketch is very lightly drawn.

WATERCOLOUR

2 Mix up a bluish shade of green on your palette. Use a wet brush to moisten all the places where the leaves will be.

3 Start with a light shade and gradually dab the colour onto the moistened leaves. These will be the bright areas later.

4 Do not let the surfaces dry, but dab stronger colours into the areas you want to be darker. In this way, the colours mix with exciting gradients.

5 Leave everything until completely dry before painting in the stems of your eucalyptus twigs with a thin brush.

6 When your illustration is completely dry, you can gently erase the pencil lines and reveal your everlasting eucalyptus twigs.

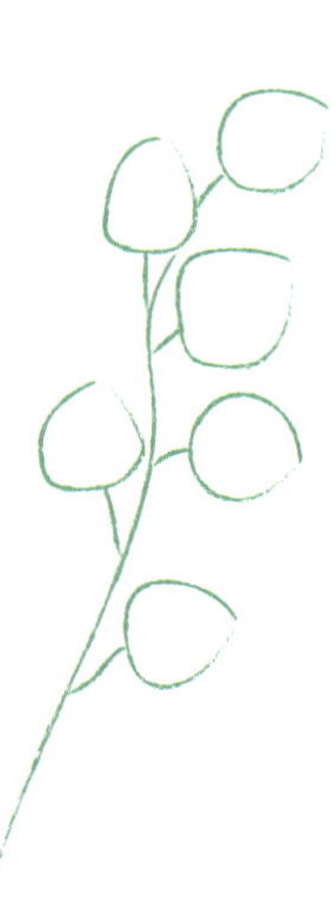

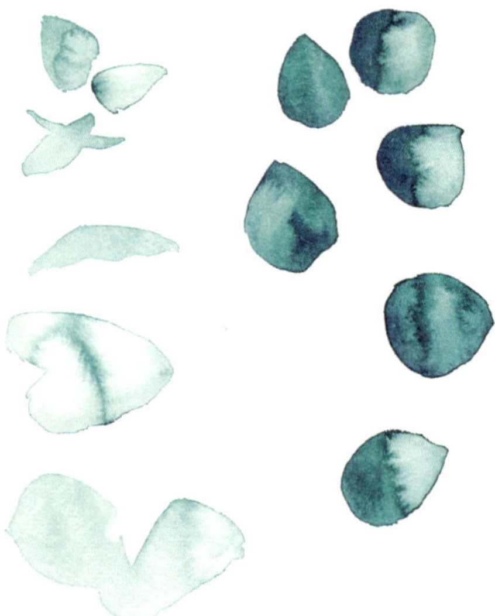

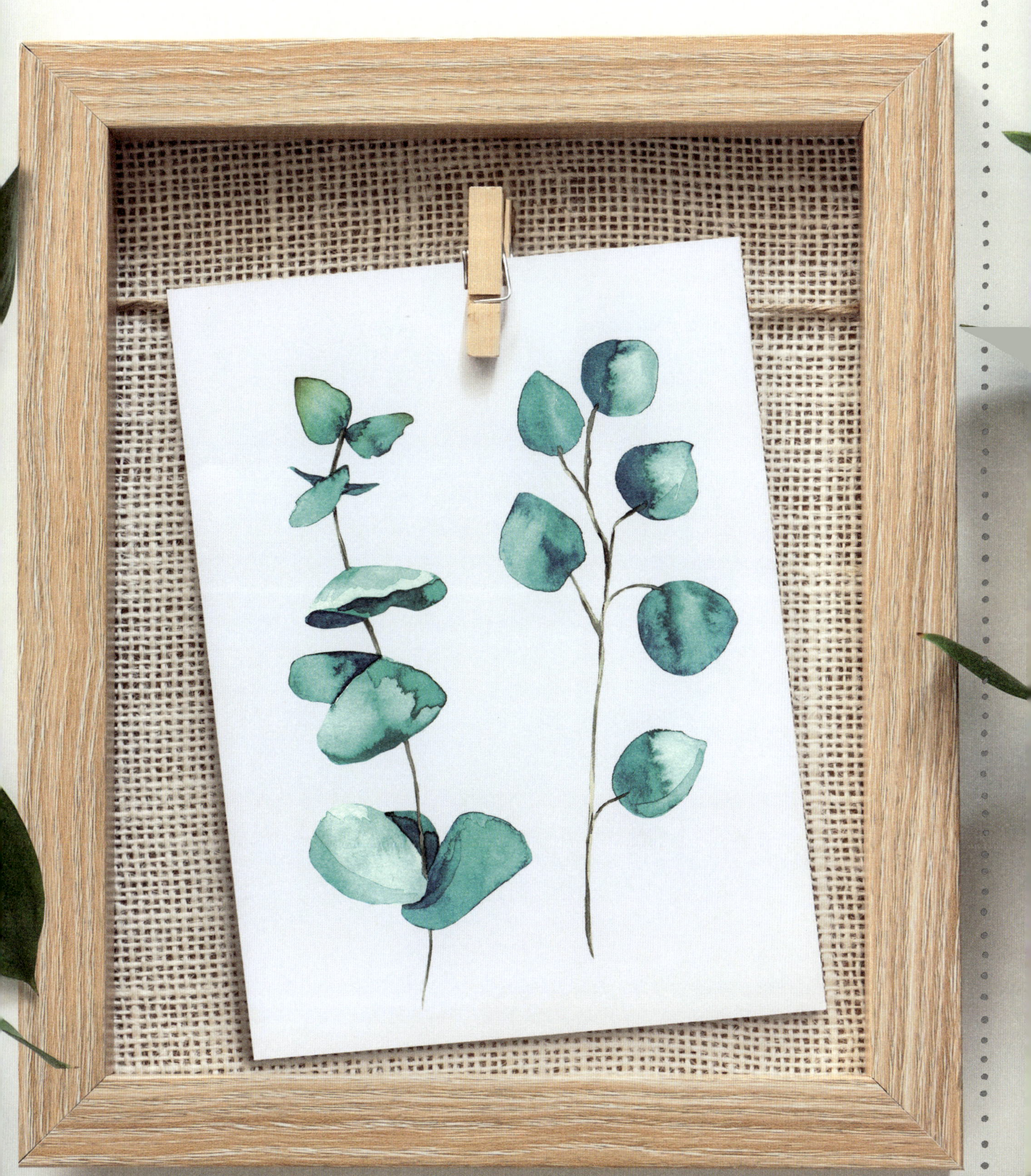

Love Always Survives

Love is wonderful and, of course, we hope that it never fades. There are always ups and downs, but with a little care love can survive forever, like a succulent plant in a desert. That's why this sempervivum (which means 'ever living') makes the perfect symbol for long-lasting love.

PRELIMINARY SKETCH

1 Fold an A4 sheet of watercolour paper in half, to form a card. Draw three concentric circles on the front of the card. Start with the largest and draw the two smaller ones inside, spaced evenly apart.

2 Lightly sketch in the leaves with an HB pencil. These plants naturally have a circular form so use the circles as a guide to the placement of the leaves. The leaves get bigger from the inside outwards.

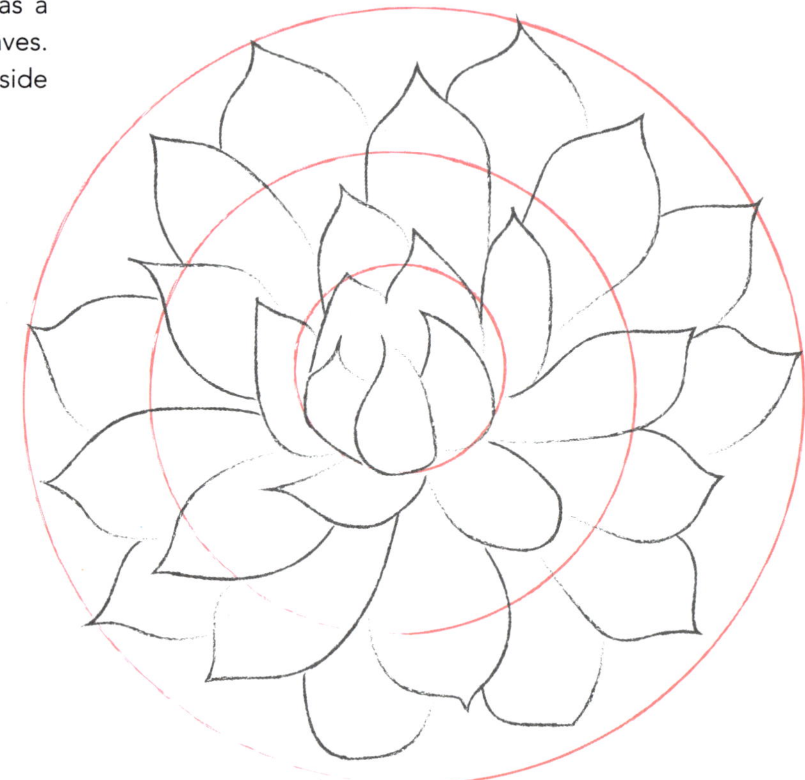

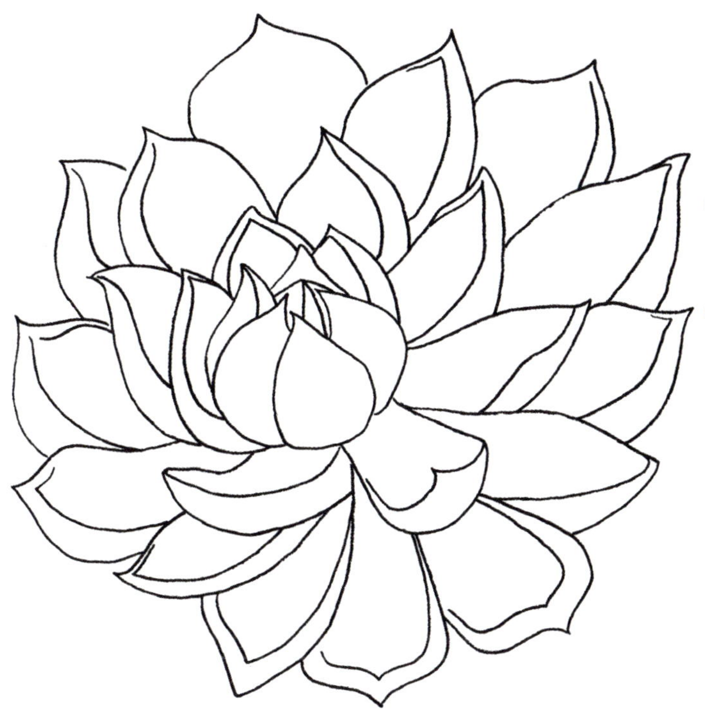

USING A FINE LINER

3. With a waterproof fineliner pen, now go over your sketch.

4. After the fineliner is dry, you can gently erase the sketch. But be careful not to damage the surface of the paper.

THE PAINTING

5. Mix up a shade of turquoise and of pink. Start with the turquoise, well diluted, as this forms the basis for your leaves.

6. Paint in individual leaves one by one. Make sure that you aren't painting leaves that touch each other so the colours do not run into each other.

7. Using a stronger shade of turquoise, paint the darker areas of the leaves, towards their base, while still moist so the colours run. This gives the leaves a more three-dimensional look. To add a bit of colour, I dabbed a few touches of pink into the moist colour at the tips.

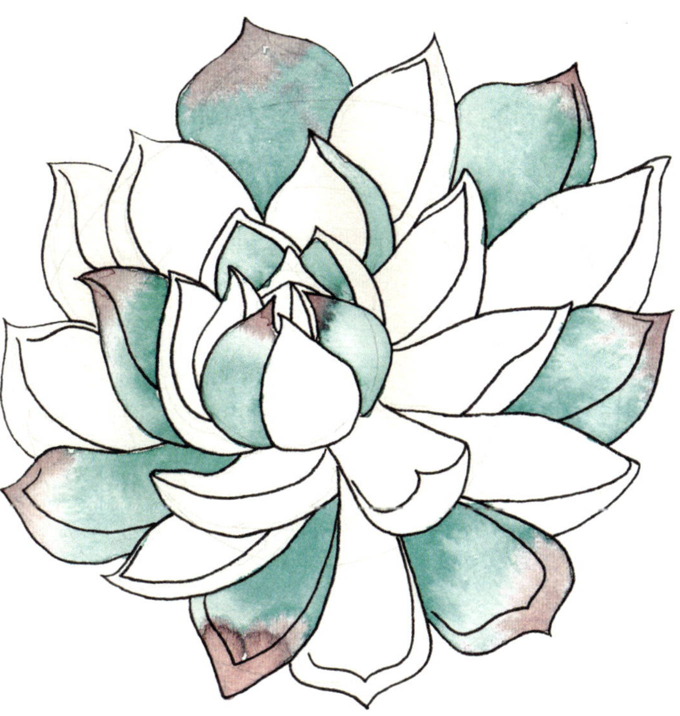

8 When your first leaves have dried properly, you can paint in the others until your entire succulent is complete. Strengthen the pink areas at the tip of each leaf.

9 Finally, dip your brush in damp paint and spray a few splashes here and there over the picture (see page 27) to add a bit of extra interest.

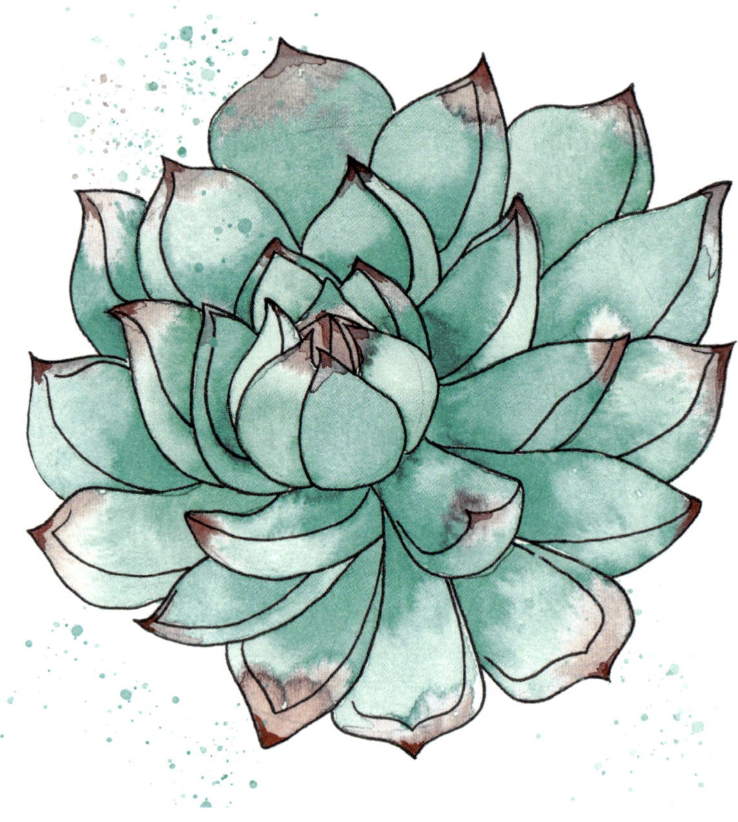

ADDING LETTERING

10 Using a pencil and ruler, add some guidelines for your lettering. Sketch out your lettering in pencil.

11 When you are happy with the sketched letters, go over them with a fine liner pen.

Your message of love for that special person in your heart is ready!

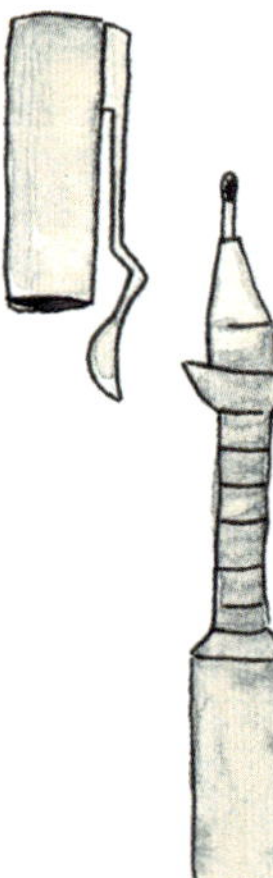

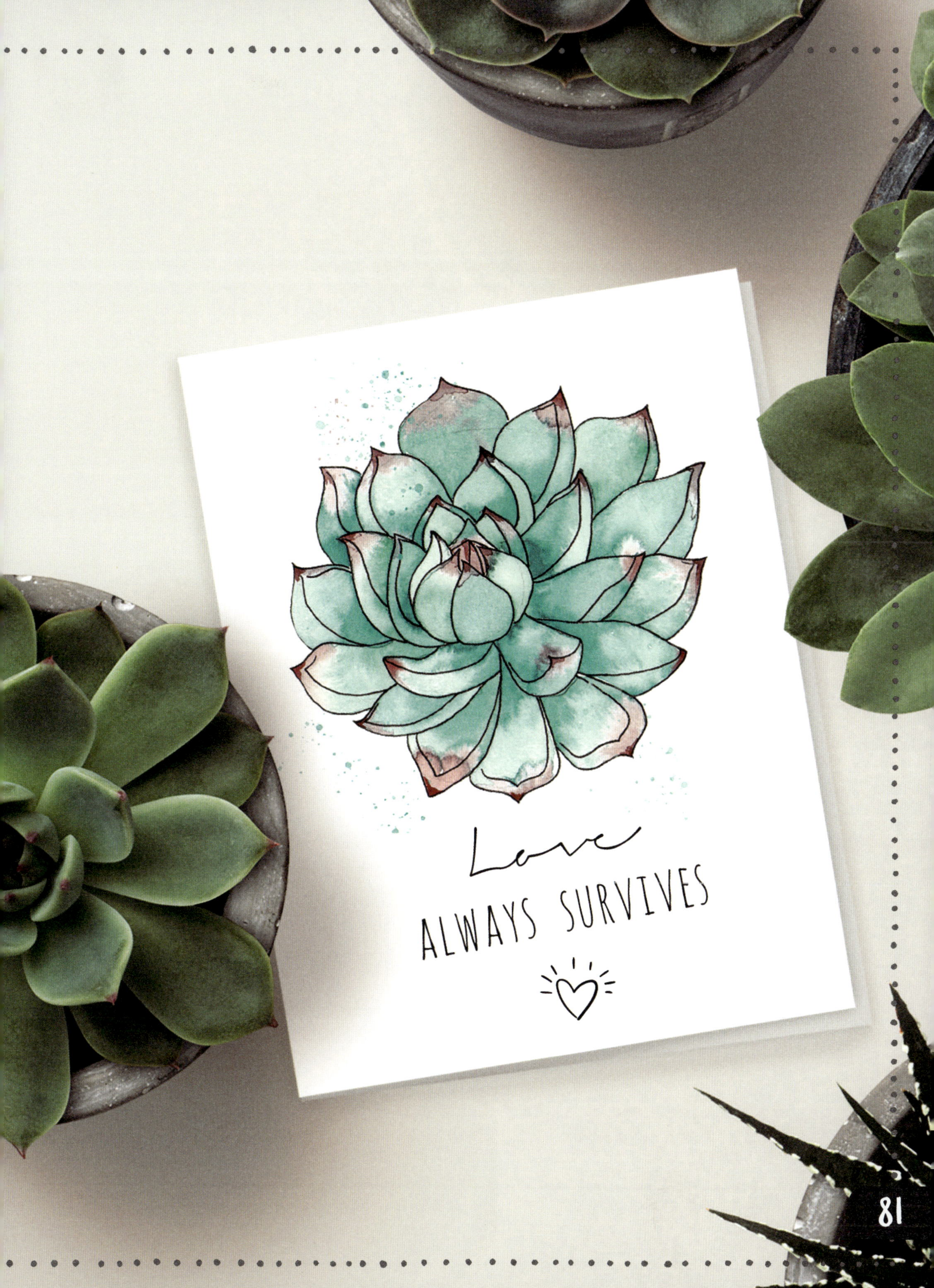

Love
ALWAYS SURVIVES

Love Grows Here

PRELIMINARY SKETCH

1 Draw out your design with an HB pencil, making sure that you place it on your paper so there is plenty of room for the lettering you'll be adding later.

2 Start by drawing the hanging baskets. You can use a ruler to help with this.

3 Draw in a few plants and leafy tendrils in the baskets.

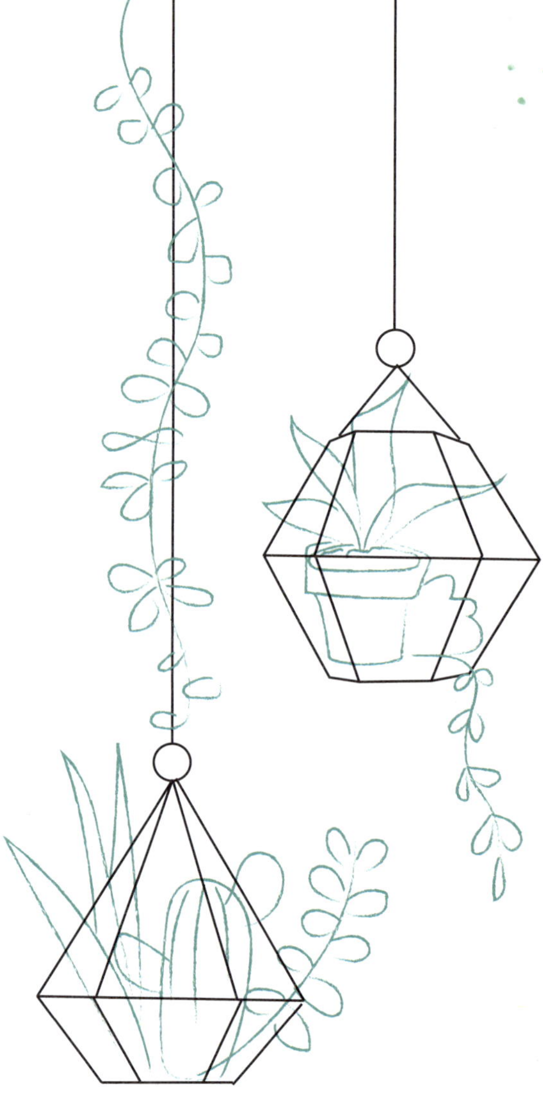

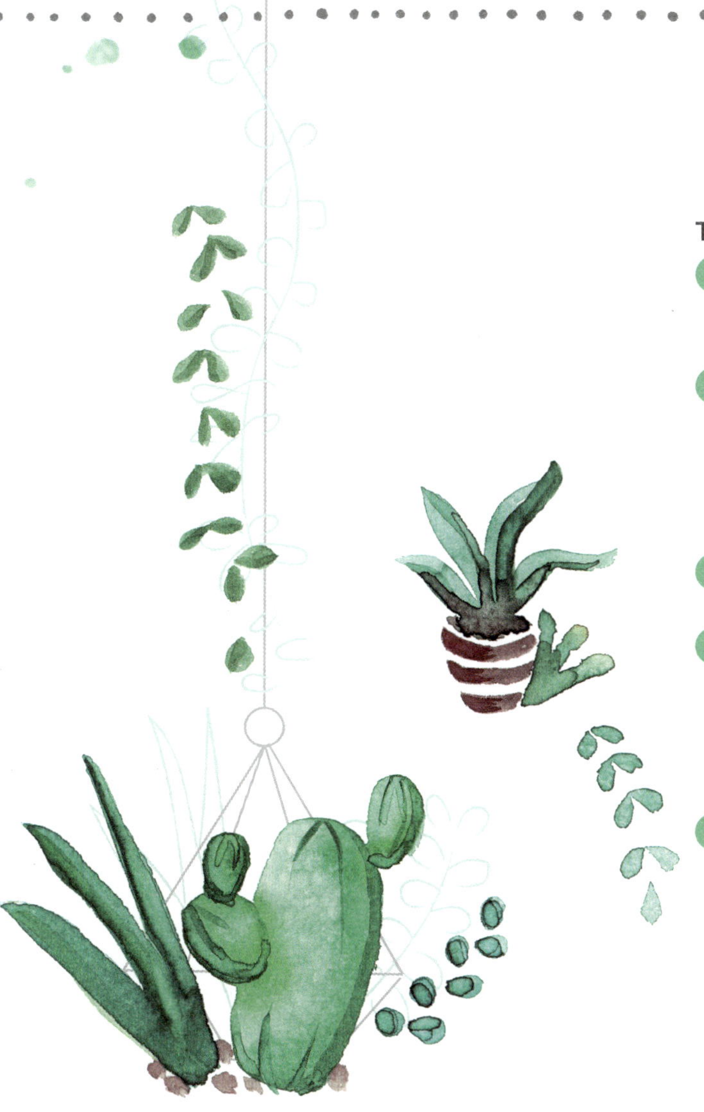

THE PAINTING

4 Mix up the colours you want in your palette.

5 When painting, start on the left side of the motif (or the right if you are left handed). Start with the lighter colours and work towards the darker ones.

6 First paint in the leaves, cacti and succulents.

7 Let these dry. Complete your illustration with further details such as cactus spines, plant stems and the pot, including the soil.

8 When you are finished, let everything dry very well. If you are in a hurry, you can speed things up by gently blowing the paper with a hair dryer.

USING A FINE LINER

9 Using a fineliner and a ruler, draw in the the hanging baskets. You can also draw in the lines freehand, but it is easier to use a ruler.

10 Draw in the hanging cord. Draw over a few of the leaves so that it looks as if the tendrils wind around the hanging cord.

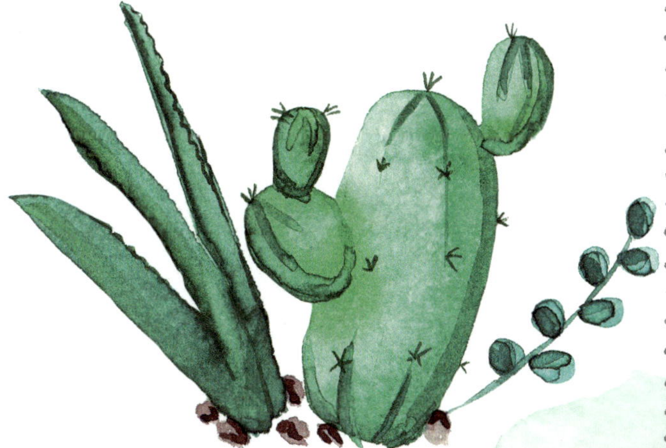

ADDING LETTERING

11 Sketch in the message with an HB pencil. If you allow the words the 'dance' on the page, the lettering will have a looser look.

12 Go over your lettering with a felt pen or fineliner and add a few dots here and there for extra decoration.

13 Finally, carefully erase all the pencil lines.

Display the picture on a clipboard for an inspiring piece of home decor!

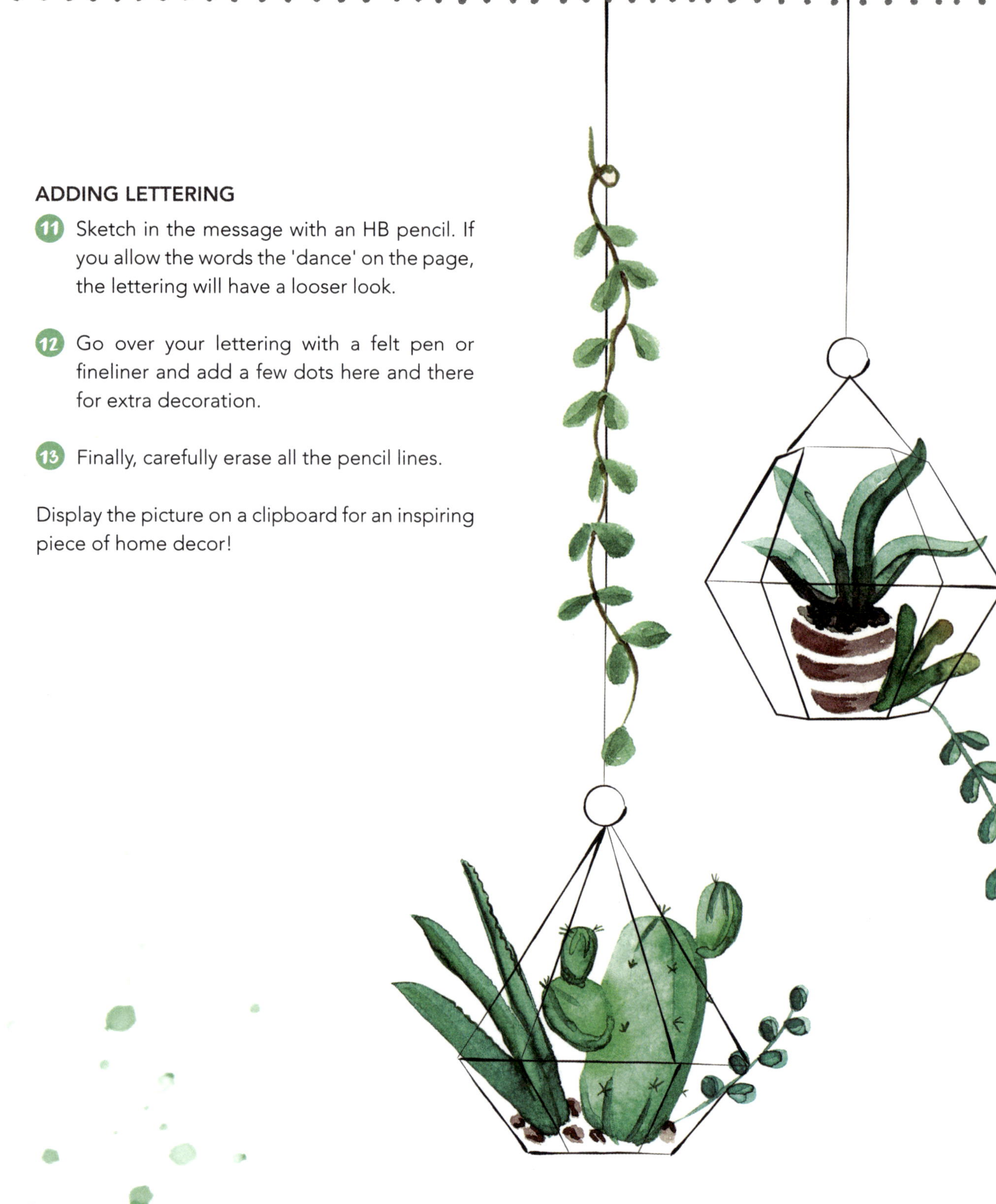

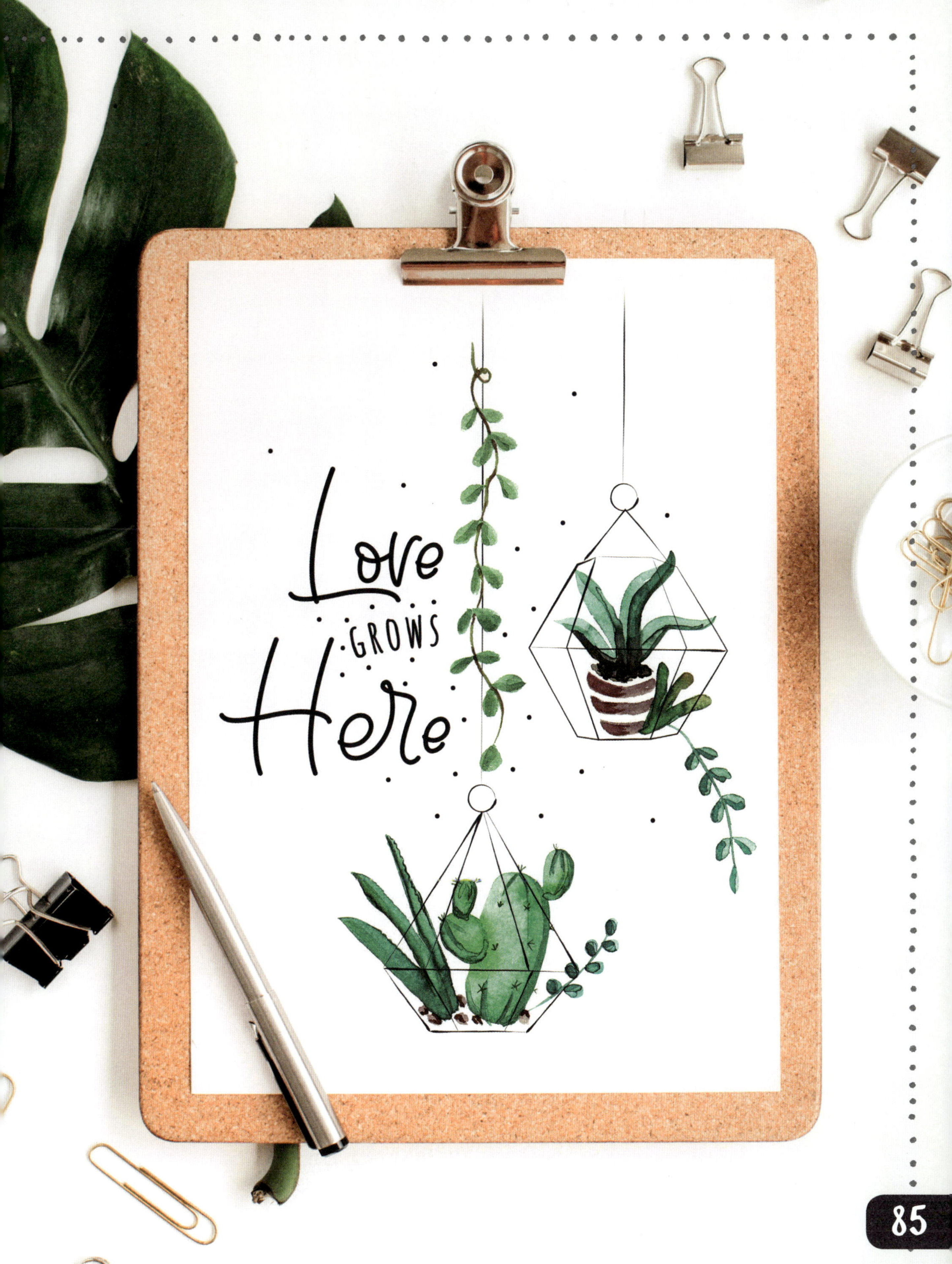

Love
GROWS
Here

Pretty Prickly

Small cacti are a bit like humans! A motley mix of different shapes and sizes with corners and edges. Everyone is different but together you make the perfect family.

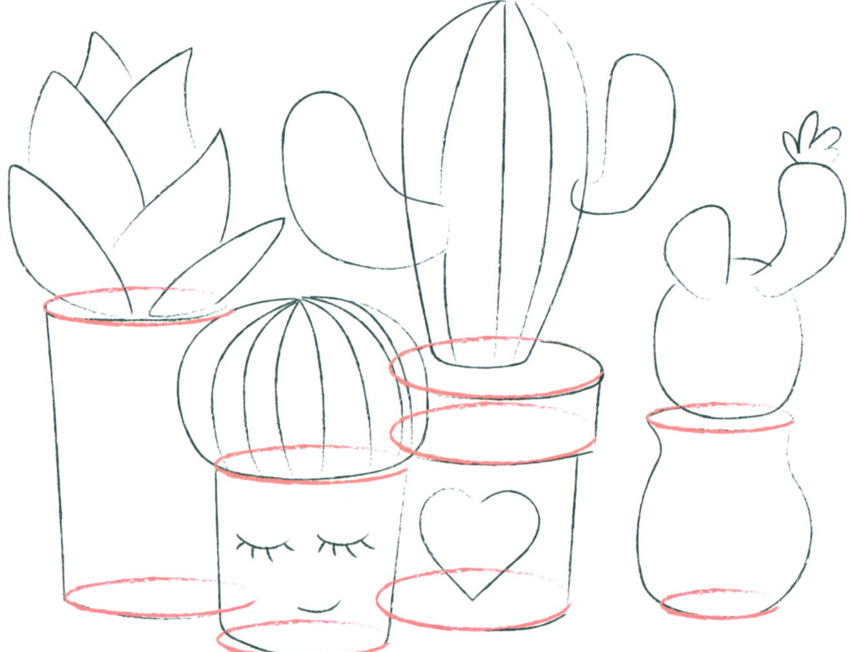

PRELIMINARY SKETCH

1. Do a pencil sketch of your little cactus family. You can also draw with a watercolour pencil so you don't have to erase anything later. But make sure you use a suitable colour.

2. Remember not to line up all the pots. Sketch them so some appear in front and some behind. This gives the picture more spatial depth.

TIP: You can draw flower pots by using a series of ellipses. Look at my sketch – the pink guidelines are used to show the different sized ellipses for each pot.

3 Mix up a shade of green and start painting the individual cacti with a very thin paint.

4 If your colour has dried slightly, you can add the darker areas layer by layer with a stronger green.

5 Let your cacti dry very well before starting on the pots.

With the pots, you should also work layer by layer, from light to dark.

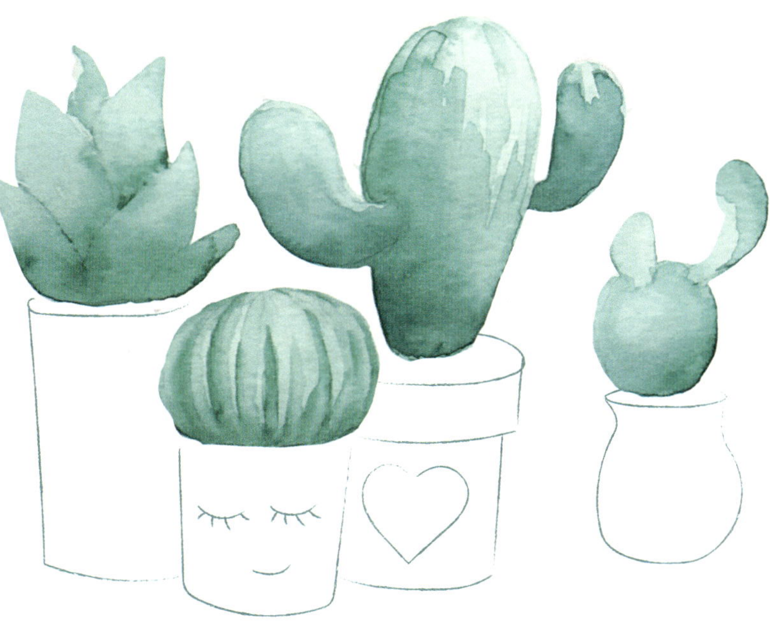

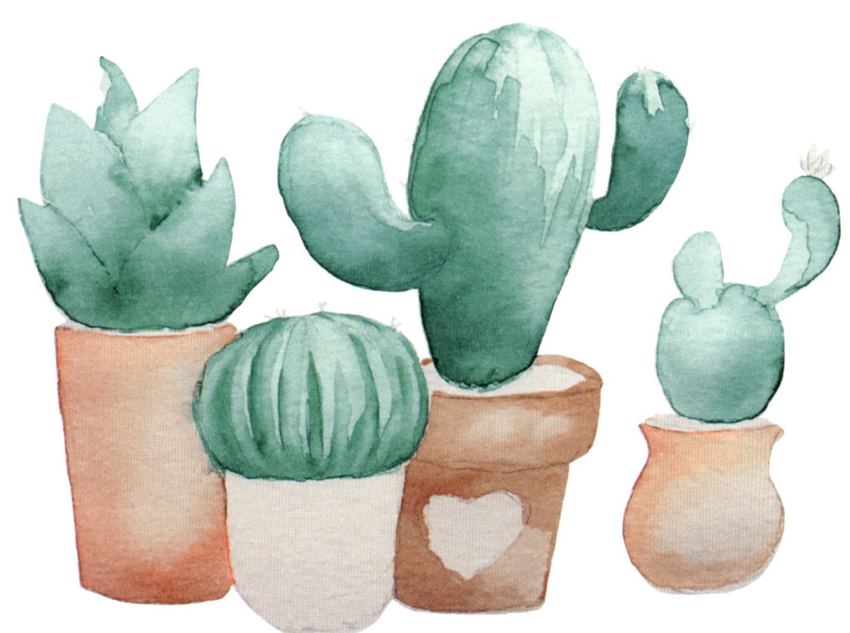

6 For the last step, take a thin brush and a strong colour and add details like prickles or maybe a pattern on the leaves of the cacti. If you like, give a pot a face. Make sure your work is completely dry, otherwise the colours will run together.

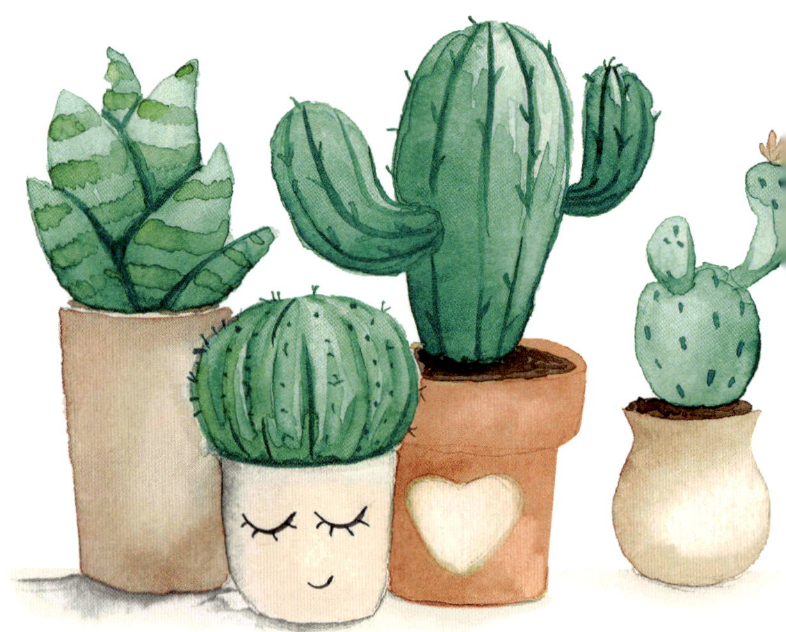

ADDING LETTERING

7 Using a pencil and ruler, sketch out a message under your cute cactus family. If you are happy with the positioning and style, carefully go over each letter with a fineliner pen.

8 Finally, gently erase any visible pencil lines – and your spiky family is done.

PRETTY PRICKLY!

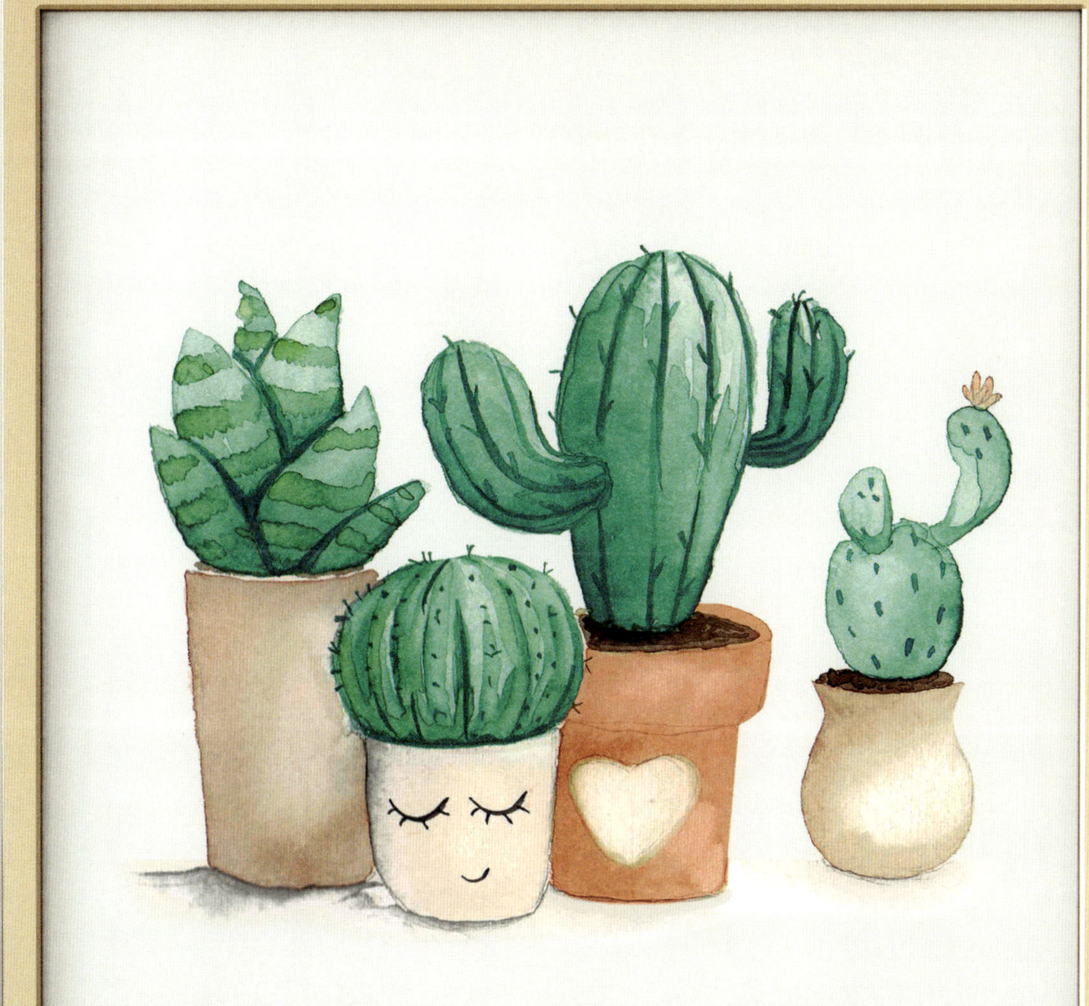

PRETTY PRICKLY!

You are smart

A circle of different plants and motifs – something that is multifaceted as you are. Something prickly, something green and something pink to together to make something perfect and beautiful – just like you!

PRELIMINARY SKETCH

1 Using a pair of compasses and a pencil, lightly draw a circle in the centre of your paper. Alternatively, you can draw round a small plate or bowl.

2 Lightly draw in your cacti and leaves with an HB pencil. Start with the larger cacti first, then fill the gaps with leaves and blossoms. Make sure that the elements are evenly spaced around the circle.

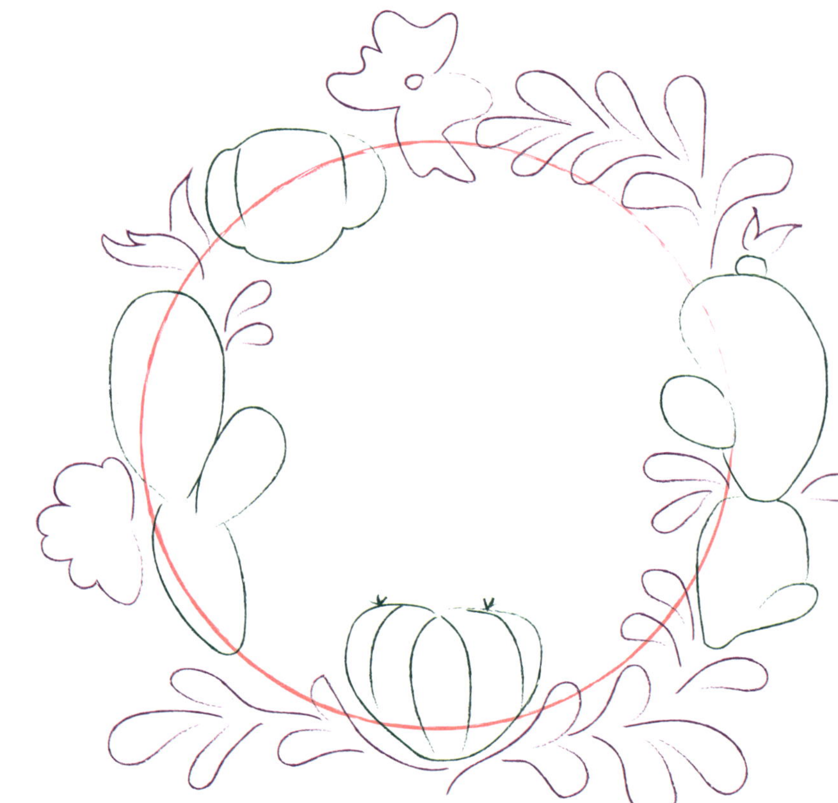

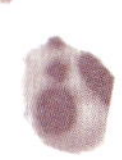

THE PAINTING

3 Mix up different shades of green and pink. Start by painting your cacti with a light shade of green. Feel free to choose different shades of green for the different types of cactus.

4 Paint shadows on your cacti with a darker shade to make them look more realistic.

5 When they're dry, use a fine brush to add a few details like shadows and spikes.

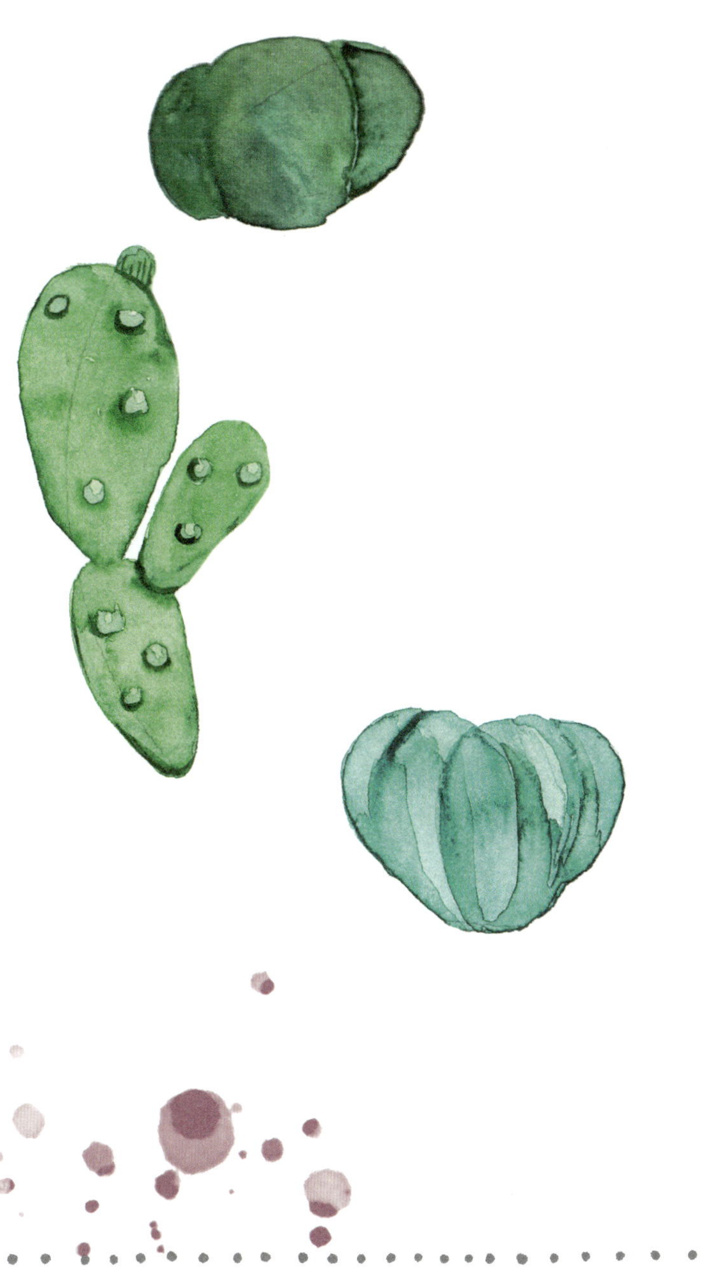

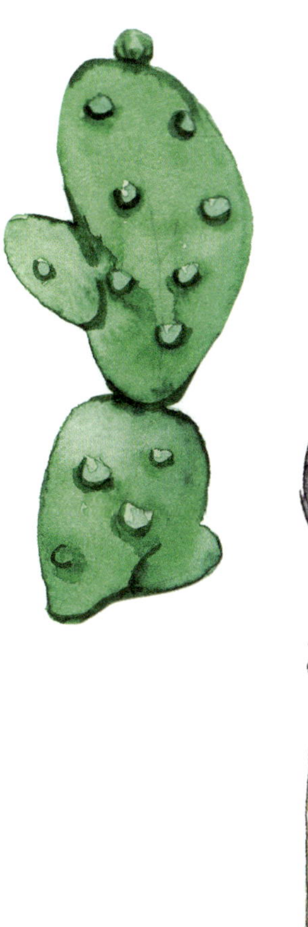

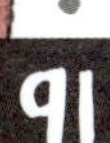

6 Fill the gaps between the cacti with leaves, tendrils and blossoms. Start with a light pink shade, then dab in a few shadows here and there with a stronger colour on the still-damp surfaces.

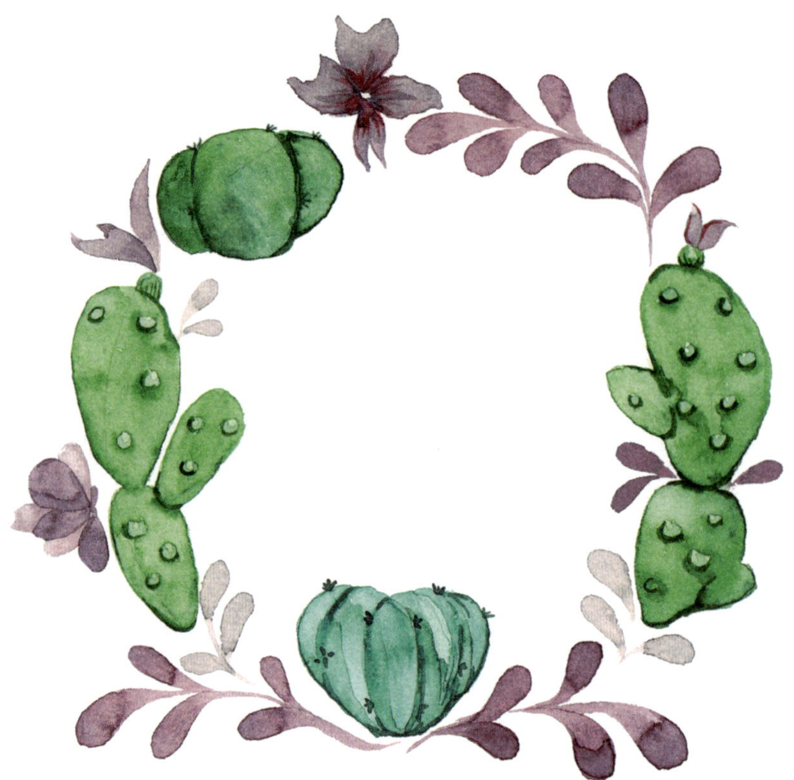

ADDING LETTERING

7 Make sure that your painting is completely dry. Add some faint pencil guidelines for your text to help you get your lettering straight.

8 If you are feeling brave, you can start right away with your brush. But if you prefer to err on the safe side, draw the words with a pencil before going over them with a brush or pen.

And your motivational cactus wreath is finished!

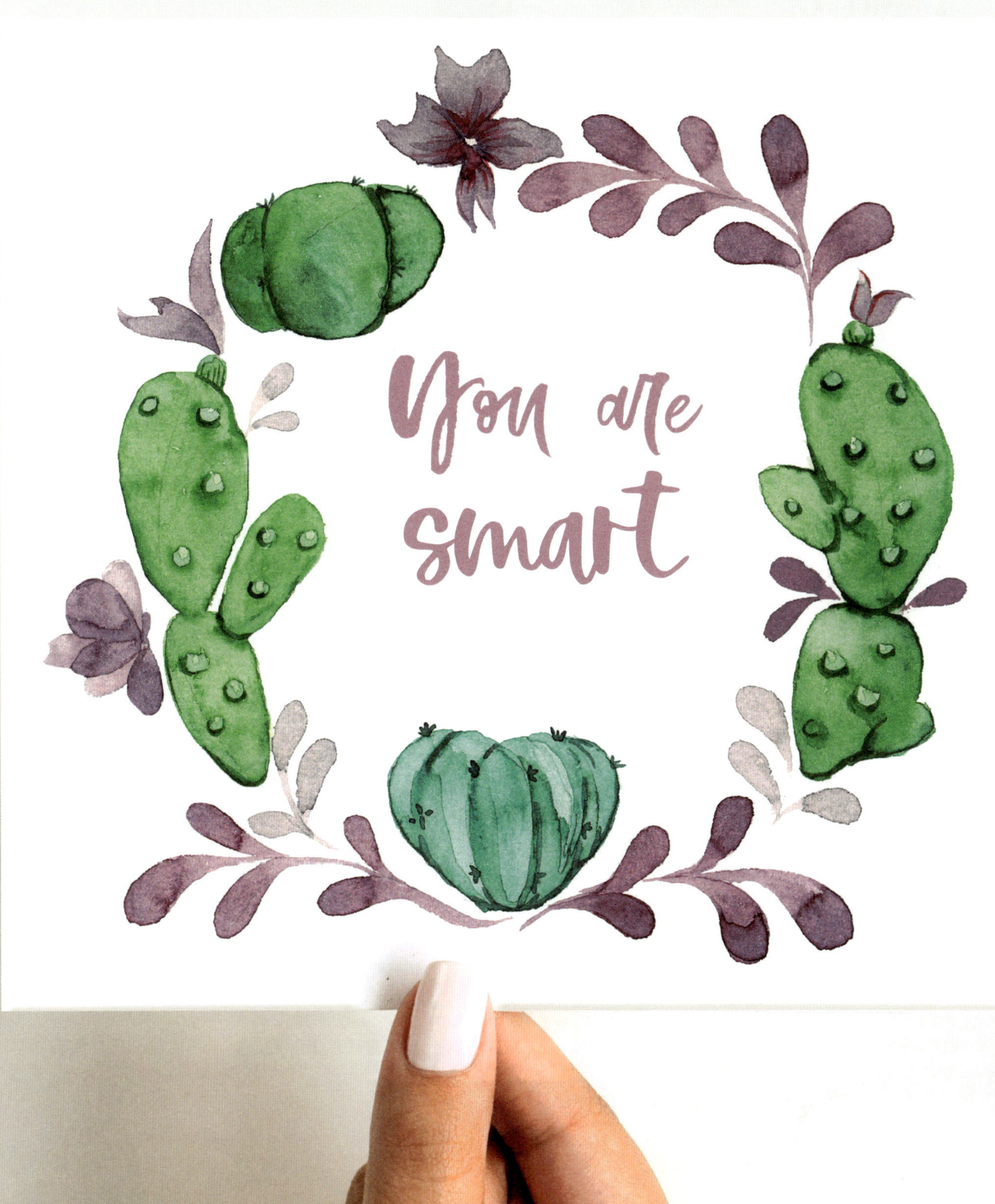

You are
smart

Don't Touch Me

As well as simply capturing the beauty of succulents, leaves and cacti, I love to add something to smile about. That is why I'm introducing Clara, the little cactus, to you.
With her blissful smile and pretty flower, she'll conjure up a big grin on your face while you're painting her, and she can warm your heart every day.

PREMLIMINARY SKETCH

1. Draw your little cactus lady in a mug with an HB pencil or a few watercolour crayons.

2. Make sure that top and bottom edges of the mug have no straight edges but are slightly curved.

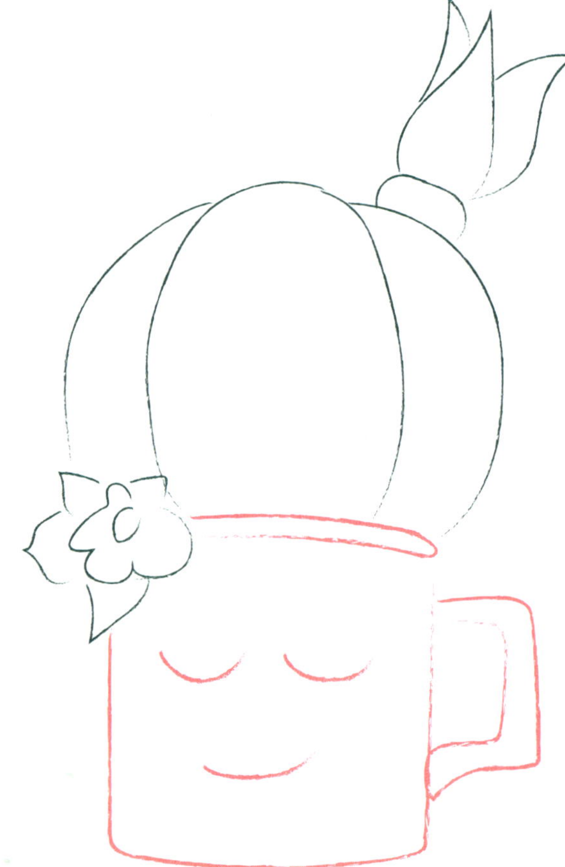

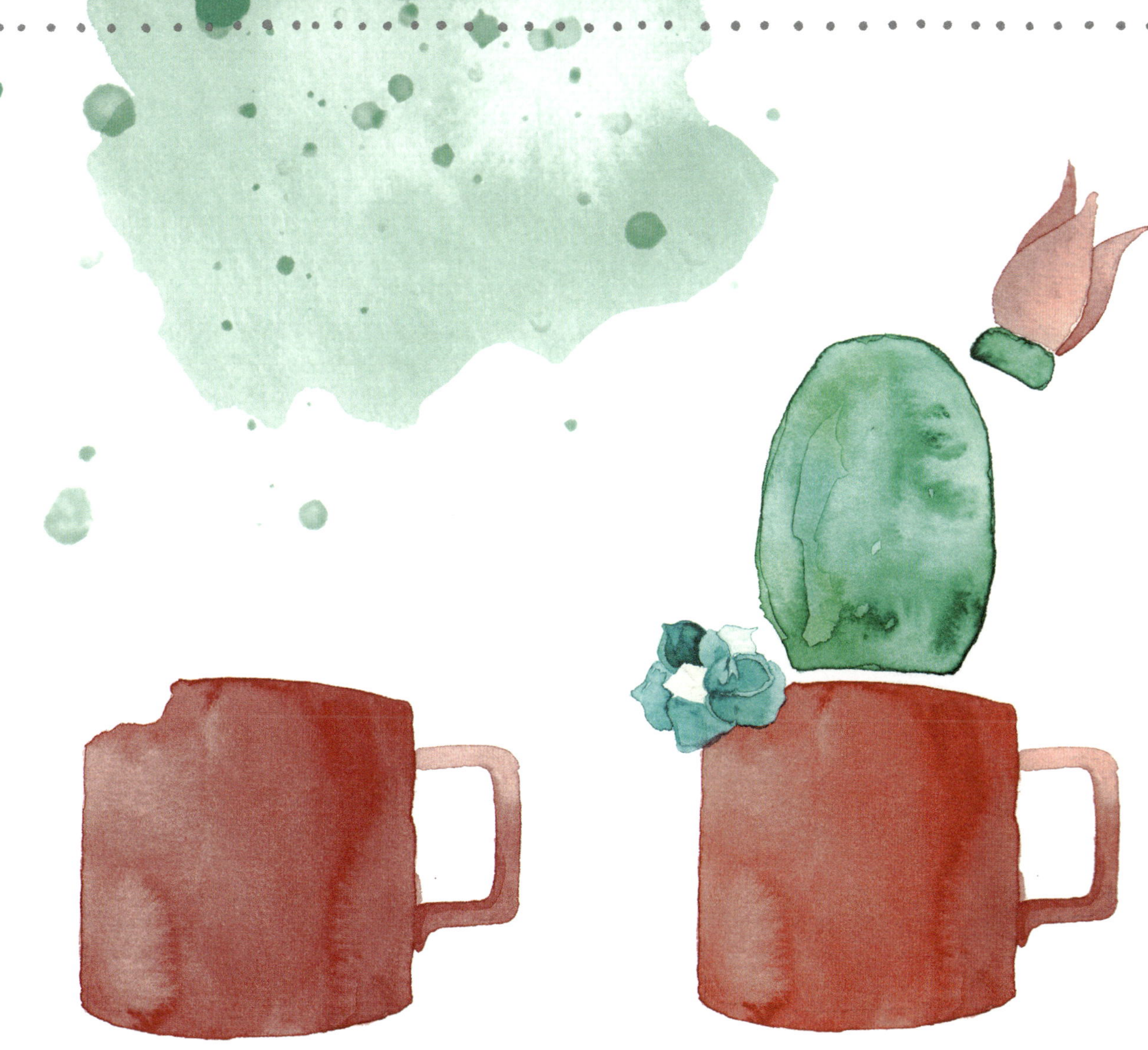

THE PAINTING

3 Choose three colours – one for the mug and the flower, and a green for the large cactus and a second green for the small succulent.

4 Dilute the colour you chose for the mug with water – in this case, red. This light colour serves as the base tone. Apply it carefully to all edges of the surface and fill the inner surface of the mug. Make sure that the surface is damp.

5 With a stronger colour, dab along the edges that are meant to be darker.

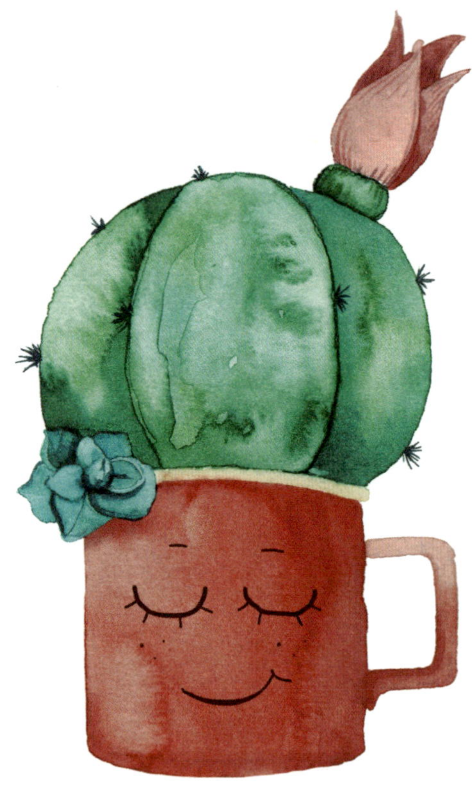

6. Do the same for the cacti. Start with the large area in the middle and let the colours run together. Do not start the next area until the first is completely dry. This gives you clear edges and transitions and prevents unwanted colour gradients.

7. Let the painting dry before using a fine brush to paint in the details such as cactus spikes and the smiley face.

LETTERING

8. Roughly sketch out your lettering.

9. Go over it carefully with a brush pen. If you like, try creating a gradient with two shades of colour.

10. Once everything has dried, carefully erase the pencil lines. For extra interest, you can use a brush and paint to add a few decorative splashes to your illustration (see page 27).

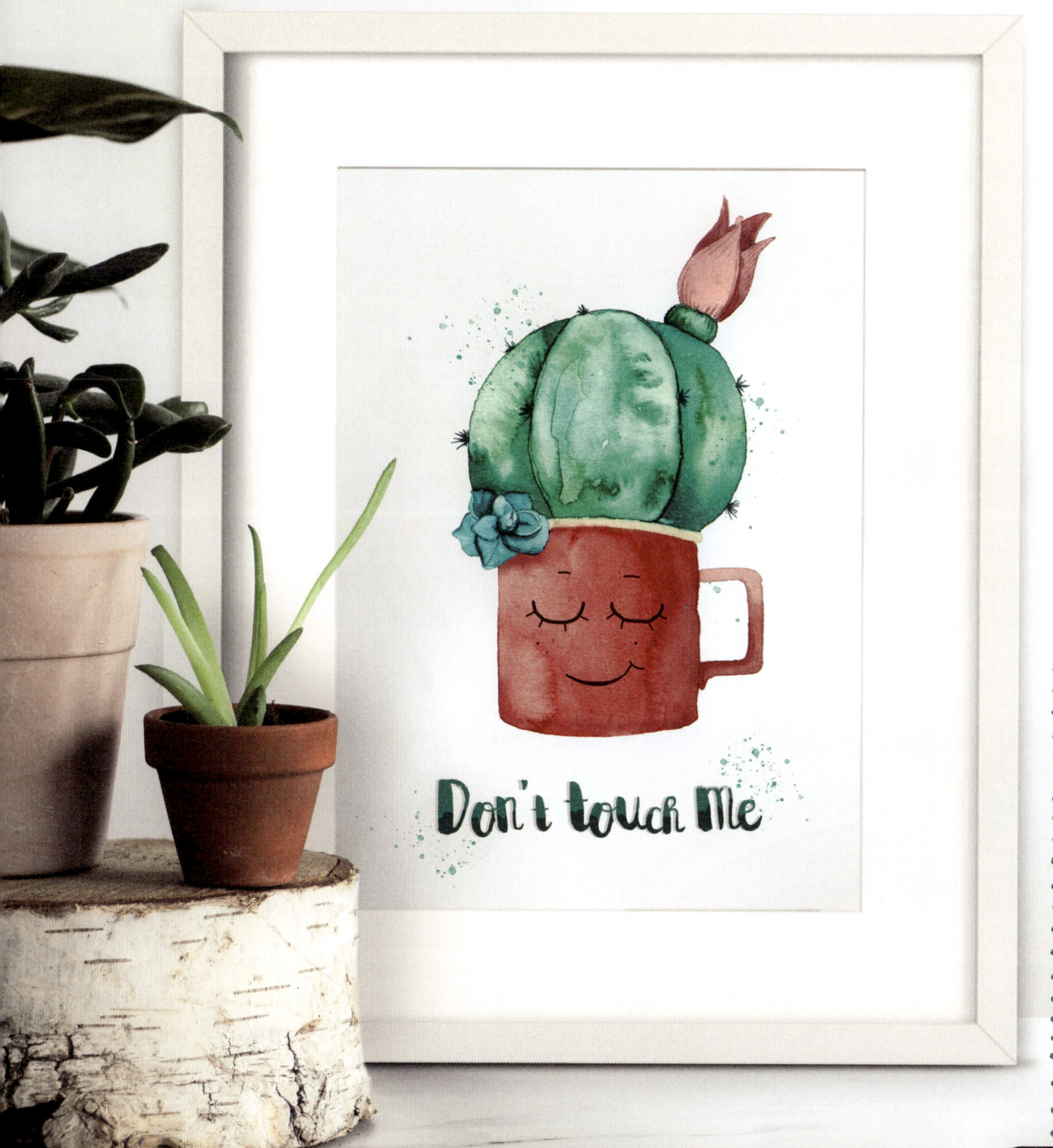

Don't touch Me

Leafy Library

Here are a few extra leaves, succulents and cacti – I hope you have fun trying them out.

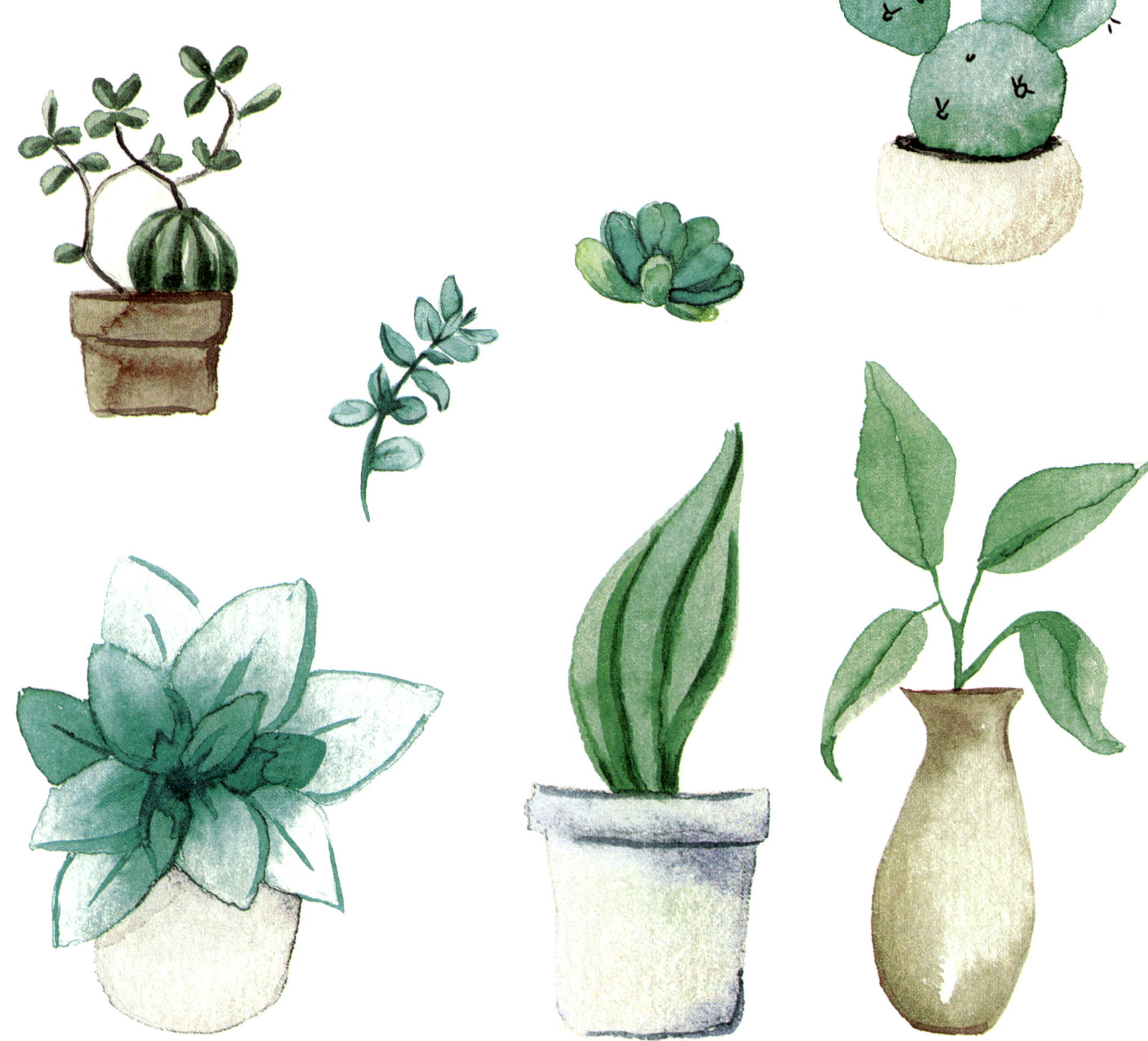

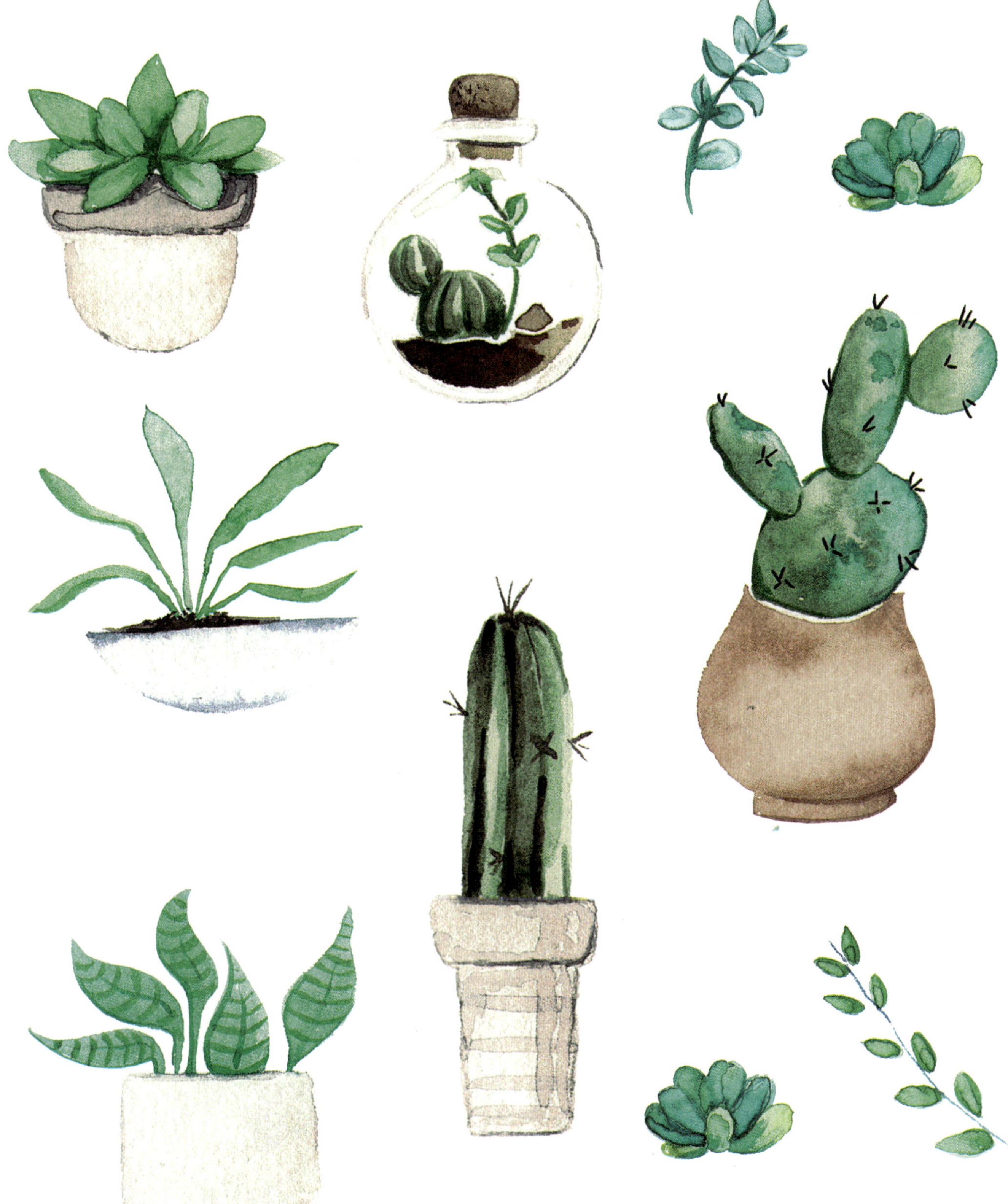

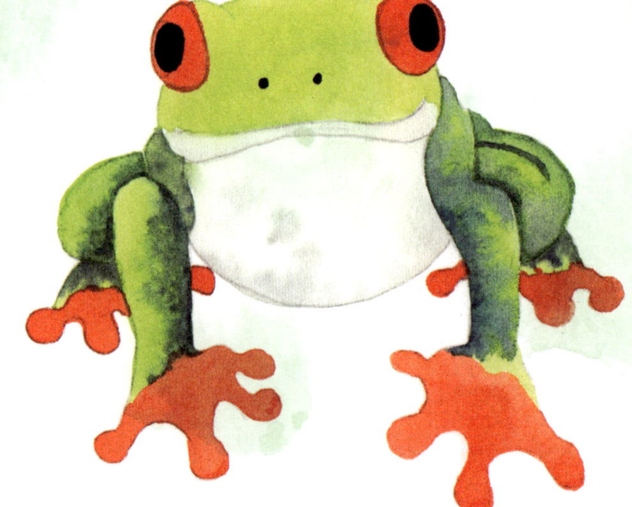

welcome
TO THE
jungle

Fantastic Beasts

In this chapter we are going to introduce you to the world of watercolour animals. It is colourful, diverse and incredibly rich in a wide variety of shapes and forms. Painting animals is not that difficult – you will see how easy it is to get started with creatures that have simple shapes and smooth surfaces, such as whales, penguins or elephants.

And then colour comes into play, with creatures such as flamingoes and king penguins that have bright and high-contrast colouring. Animals with fur and varied plumage, such as raccoons, badgers and budgies, are a bit more demanding. Here, too, we will show you how to achieve a convincing and lively picture step by step. We also have a lot of tips for you to ensure that you get a fantastic finished result.

Personally, we think that the combination of illustration and lettering is unbeatable. That's why we'll be showing you how to paint a cute alpaca that we hope will encourage you to complement your watercolour animals with hand-lettered sayings. You'll see how this can give your illustrations a very special meaning. We hope you enjoy the creative challenge!

Inay & Berry

Klaus the Whale

The whale is one of the easiest animals you can render in watercolour. It has a relatively simple shape and an even surface, so you can quickly achieve a great result. The nice thing is that there are many different types of whales that can be illustrated in a similar way – perfect for practising.
All you need for this illustration are watercolour paints, a jar or glass of water, a pencil, some watercolour paper and a medium-sized brush.

1 Start with a sketch. Draw it carefully on your watercolour paper and try to avoid rubbing out too much. If you are satisfied with your sketch, you can think about the colours in the next step. There are no limits to your imagination. Several shades of blue can look particularly beautiful for animals that live in the water.

TIP: When painting animals, it is often not easy to draw their shapes from memory. In this case, it's OK to draw from photos. Once you have sketched the basic shape of the animal, you can change a few things here and there. For example, with Klaus the whale, I made the fore fins a little longer.

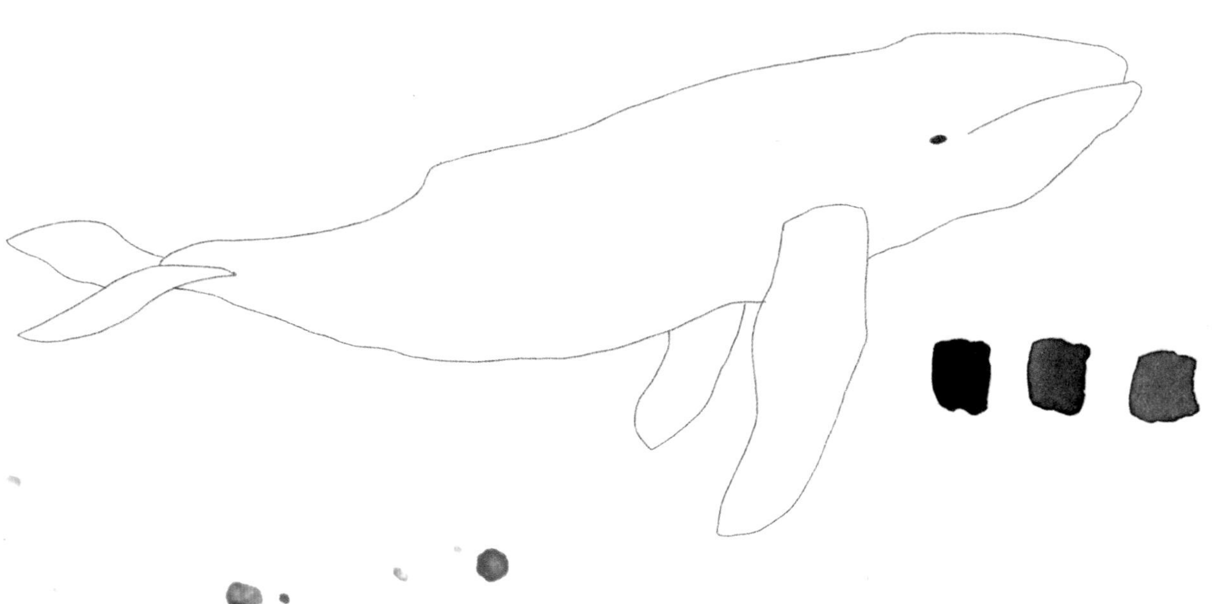

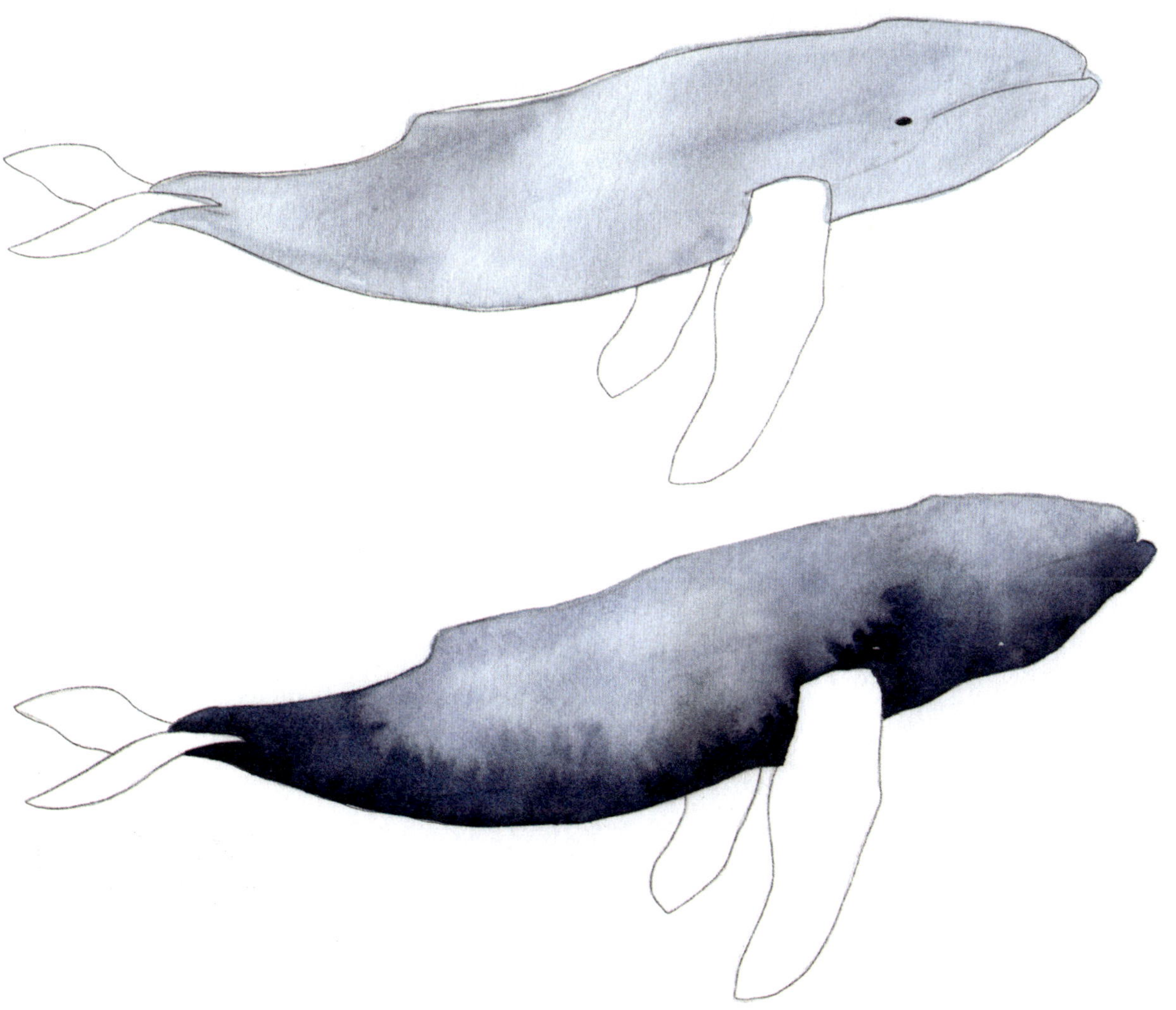

2 After you have mixed up the colours of your choice, wash your brush completely. Then brush the whale's body with clear water, leaving out the fins. Be careful not to use too little water, especially with large motifs, or the paper will dry very quickly and the gradients won't work. Now add the lightest shade and dab it along the edges of the body.

3 If the light colour has spread well across the body, you can move on to a darker tone. Just add it in a few places to create some contrast. We made the lower part of our whale darker so it appears that the body is lit from above.

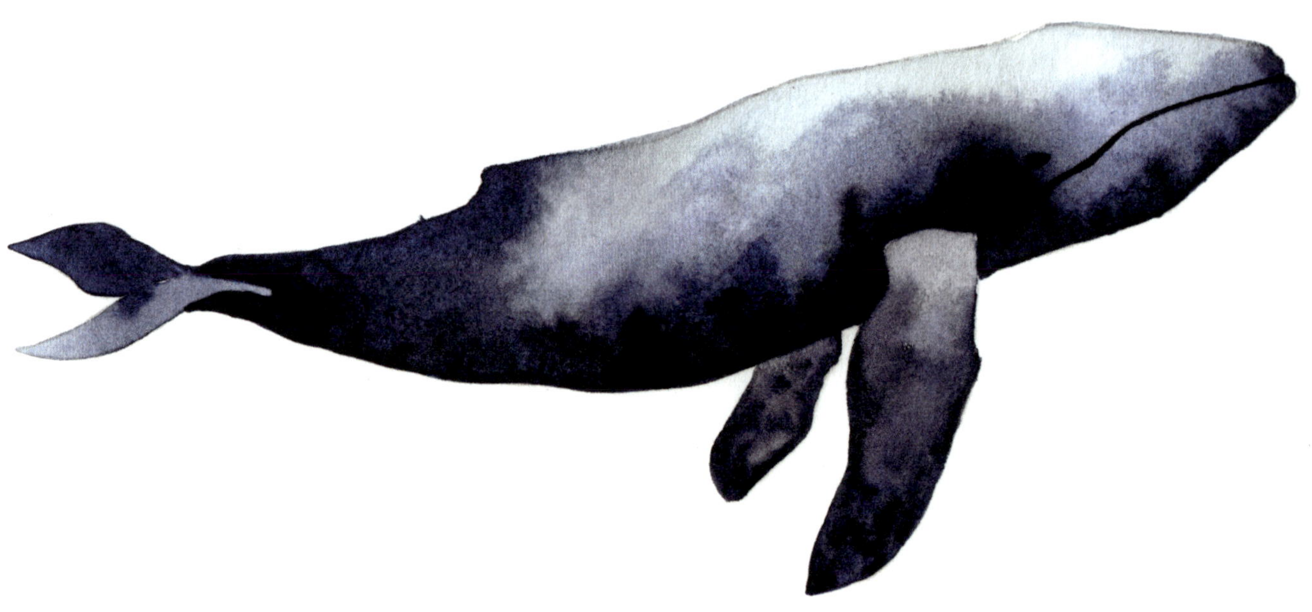

4 So that the fins are clearly separate, you should paint them only when the rest of the body has dried. Follow the same procedure as for the body, priming the fins with water first and then then applying different strengths of paint and working from light to dark. In the last step you can add small details. We have limited ourselves to an eye and the mouth. But you could, for example, add some small dots to indicate the crustaceans that can be found on the skin of a whale.

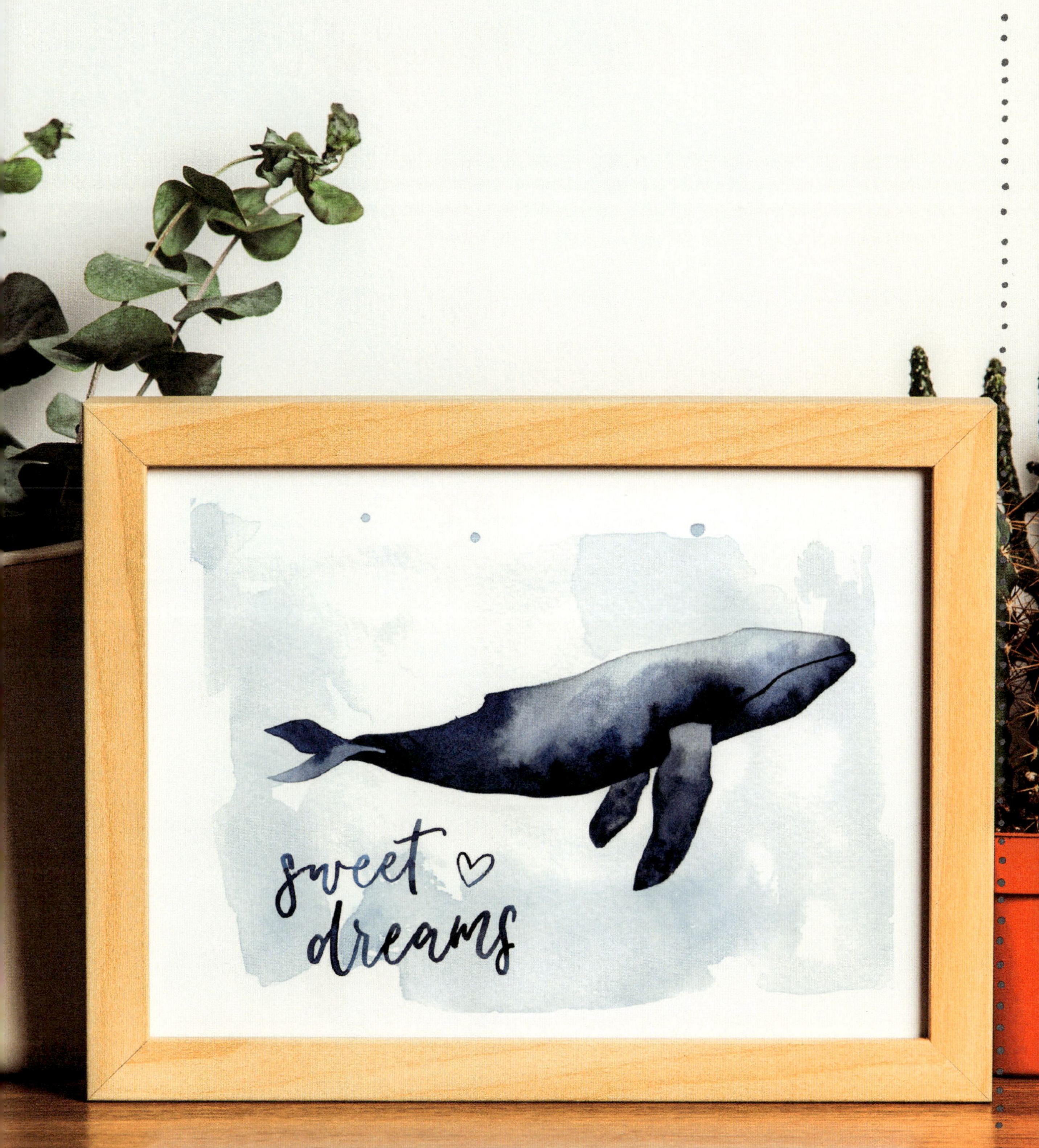

sweet
dreams

Ralf the King Penguin

King penguins have a very distinctive appearance due to the high-contrast colouring of their plumage. Think of black, white and a little orange and the image of this bird already emerges in our mind's eye. The king penguin, therefore, is particularly easy to illustrate. You will need watercolour paper, a size 6 brush, watercolour paints, some water, a pencil and a rubber.

1 First draw a pencil sketch on your paper. Make sure the lines are visible but faint so that you can cover them later with your paint and there are no annoying traces of pencil left.

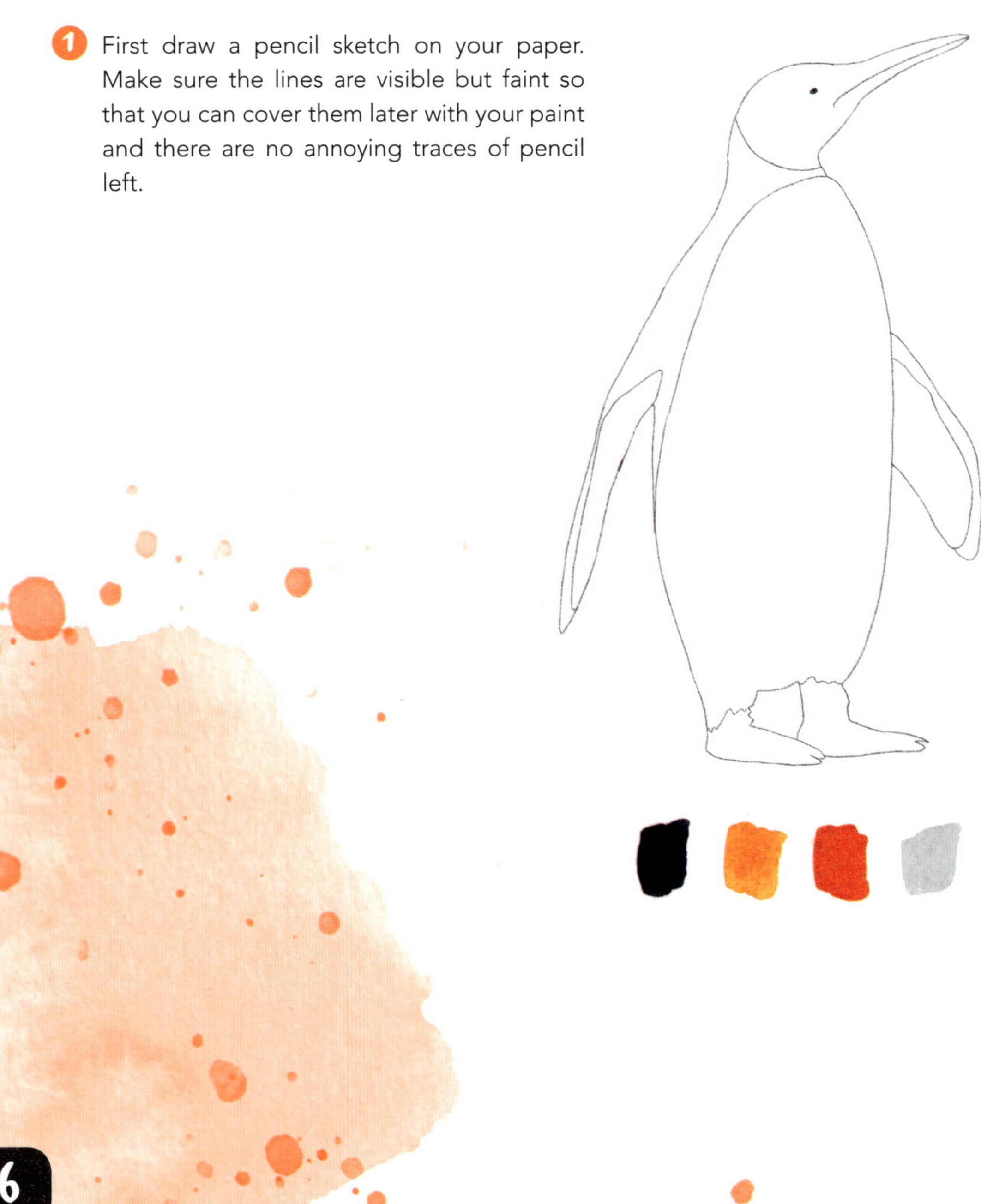

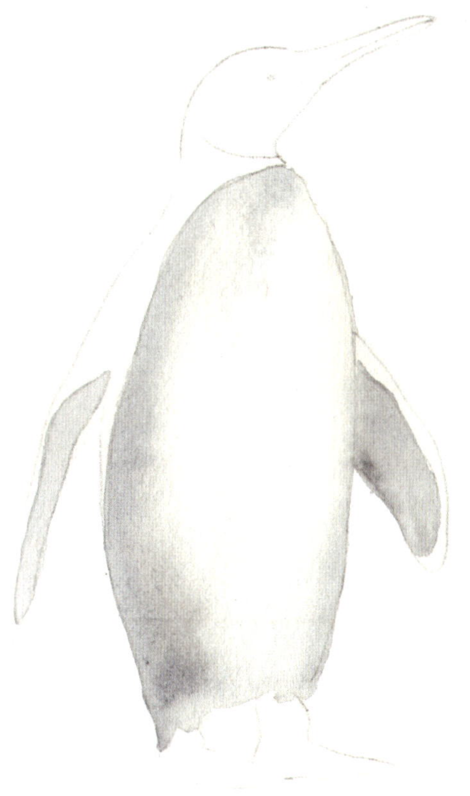

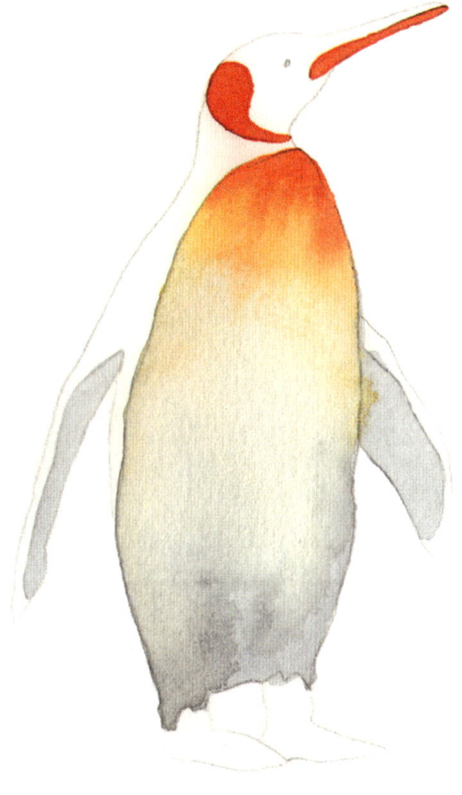

2 Now mix up your colours – we chose black, grey, yellow and orange. The grey should be a very light tone because we want to shade with it only slightly. When you are satisfied with your sketch, first brush the entire surface of the belly and the inside of the wings with water, then add a bit of the light grey at some edges to create shading. In this way, the body looks a little more three dimensional.

3 While the belly is still slightly wet, add a little yellow and orange at the top so they merge into each other and create the typical colouring of the breast plumage. Use a strong tone of orange to paint the spot on the back of the head and the underside of the beak. Leave everything to dry.

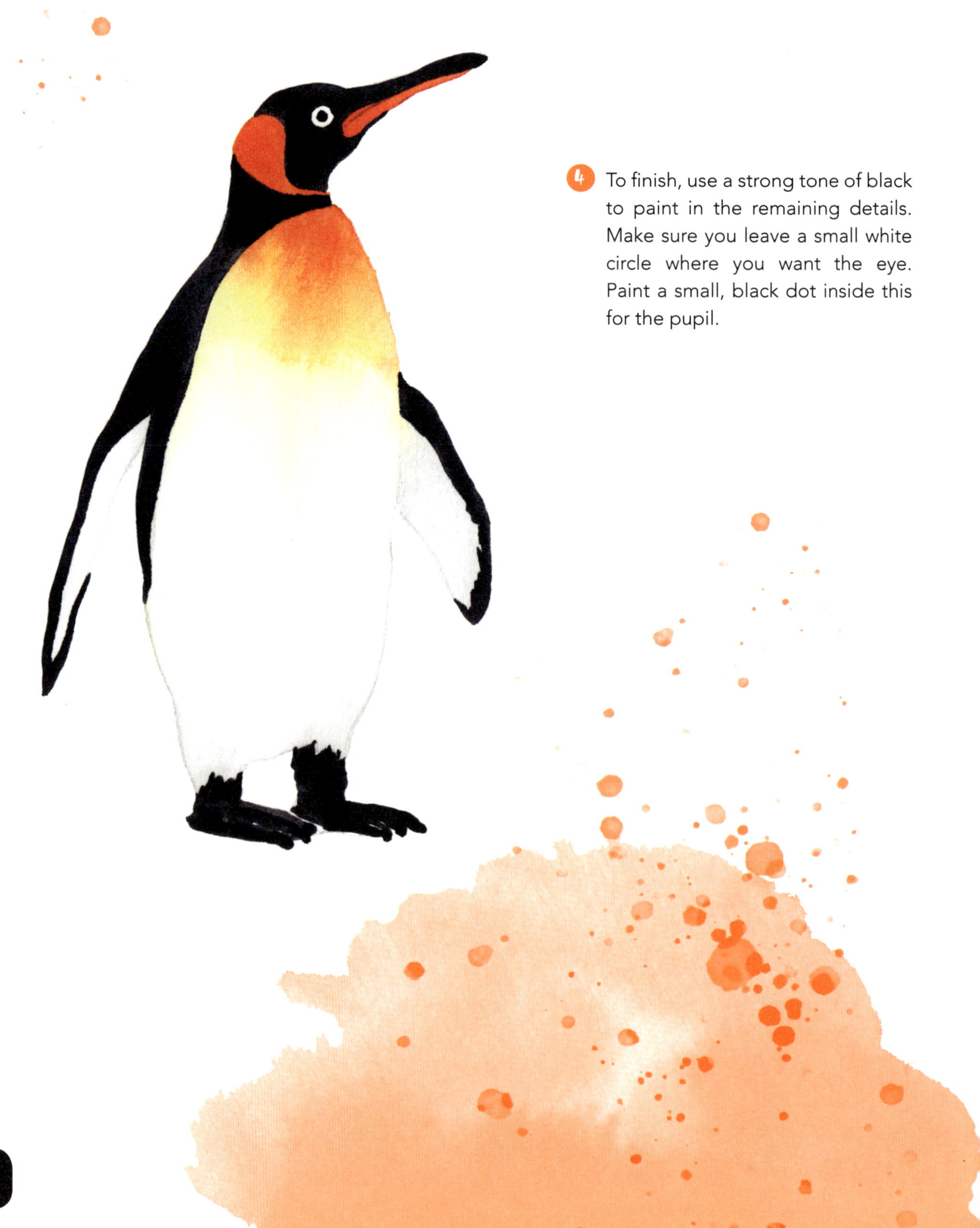

4 To finish, use a strong tone of black to paint in the remaining details. Make sure you leave a small white circle where you want the eye. Paint a small, black dot inside this for the pupil.

Emil the Elephant

At the request of our Instagram followers, we have included Emil the elephant in this book. Elephants are popular animals and are suitable illustrations for many occasions – whether it's a picture for a child's room or a card for grandma. Emil can also be created in watercolour in just a few steps.

All you need is watercolour paper, watercolour paint in shades of grey or blue and a brush suitable for the size of your finished image. If Emil, for example is to be about 15cm wide, then use a size 6 brush. However, if you want to paint the elephant much smaller or larger, it is better to switch to a correspondingly smaller or larger brush.

TIP: Avoid using a brush that is a bit too big. A large brush soaks up a lot of paint and is more difficult to control in a small area.

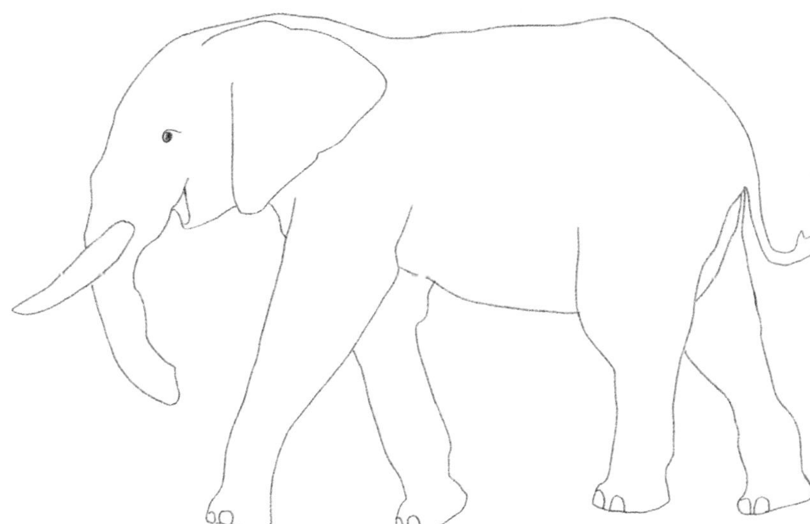

1. Start with a pencil sketch of your elephant. Try not to rub out too many of the lines as this could damage the surface of your watercolour paper. When you're satisfied with your sketch, mix your colours. We worked with a dark and a light grey-blue as this looks more natural that a grey that's mixed from black alone.

2 With a clean brush, go over the whole elephant with water. Then charge your brush with some of the light grey and paint it over the whole elephant. Make sure that the surface is always wet so that the paint can flow. If your design is very large, you can work in steps. For example, first paint the head, then the belly and finally the legs.

To give your illustration more depth, use the darker shade of grey to emphasize the areas on the elephant's body where shadows can be found. These areas are most likely to be, for example, on the lower abdomen, on the left or right side of the legs and under the ear.

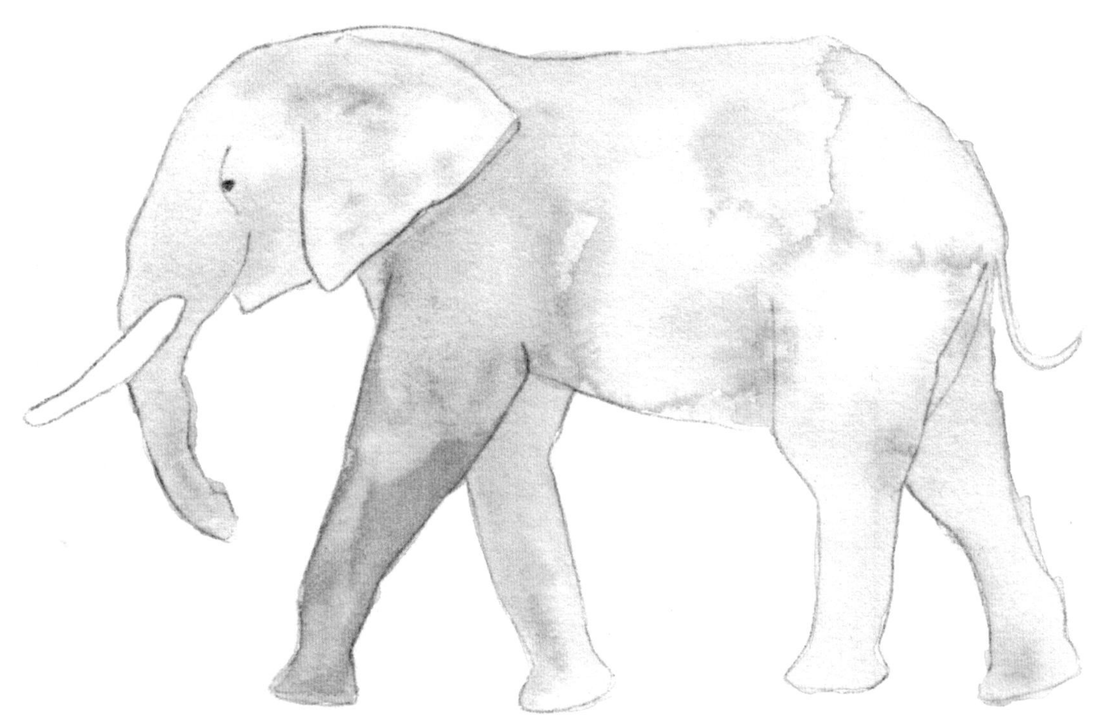

TIP: If you are unsure about adding shading to your illustration, you can look at photos to see where the dark spots are on a real elephant.

3 Once everything has dried, you can paint the legs further away from the viewer with a darker tone to indicate the area where there is less light.

TIP: Watercolour paint will dry to a slightly lighter shade. If you want a high-contrast result, you should paint the darker areas more intensely.

4 Let everything dry thoroughly before painting in any details. In the final step you can add as many little things as you like - here we added only the eyes, toes and a few stripes on the trunk.

TIP: You can find reference images for all these animals on our website **mayandberry.com**

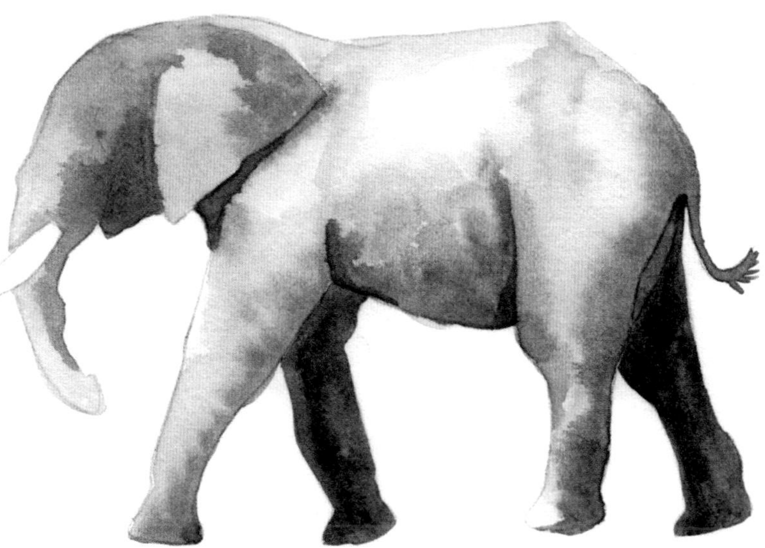

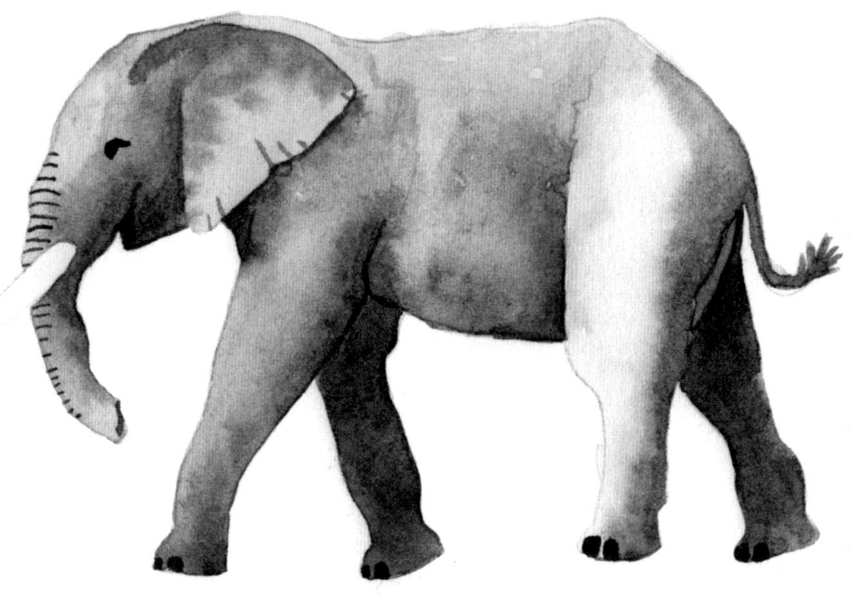

Frederick the Flamingo

Frederick the flamingo is most at home in warmer regions. We think that flamingoes make a fantastic design motif because they can give you that holiday feeling and you also get a chance to work with really bright colours.

As always, you need a round brush in sizes 4 to 6 for this illustration in addition to watercolour paper, water and paints.

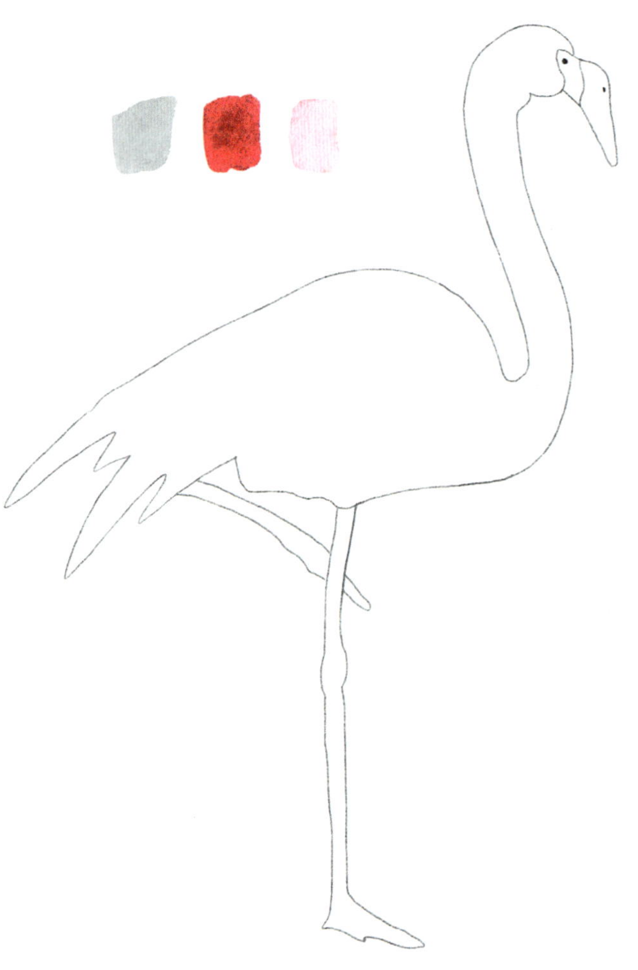

1 Use a pencil to sketch your design. It's best to use a harder HB pencil. A pencil that is too soft leaves too much graphite on the paper and these marks cannot be erased properly later or covered with paint.

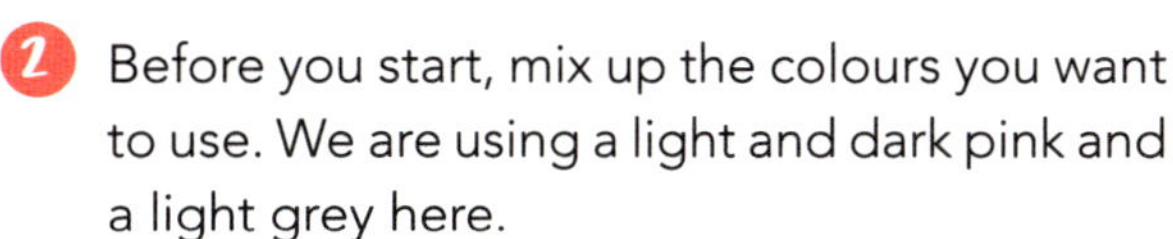

2 Before you start, mix up the colours you want to use. We are using a light and dark pink and a light grey here.

Wash out the brush and prime the body of the flamingo with clear water. Leave the legs and beak for now.

Now apply the lightest shade of pink evenly over the body.

TIP: Pay attention to the amount of water. If you apply too little, the colours will not run and the paper will dry out too quickly. If you use too much water, the colour will pool into a lake on the paper.

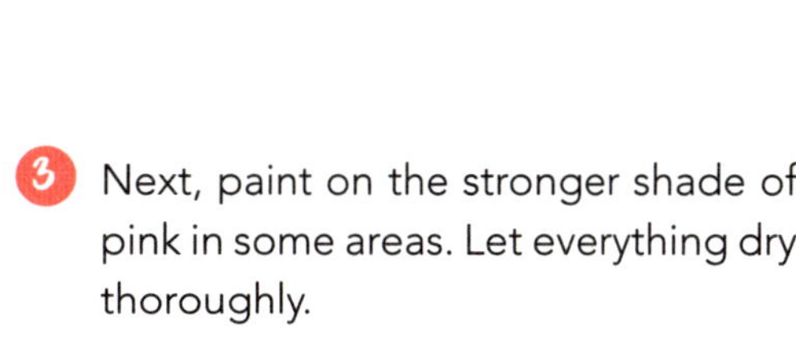

3 Next, paint on the stronger shade of pink in some areas. Let everything dry thoroughly.

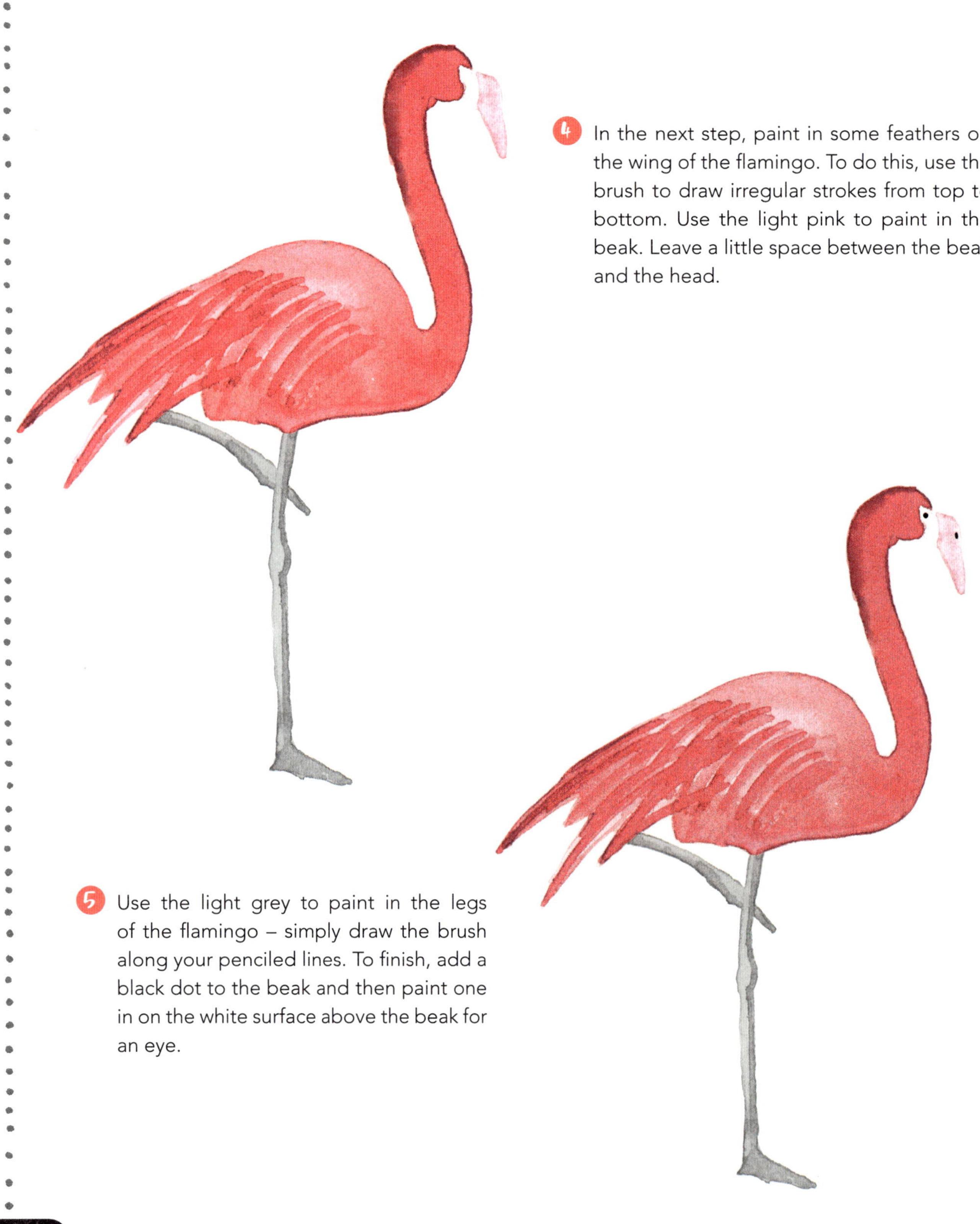

4. In the next step, paint in some feathers on the wing of the flamingo. To do this, use the brush to draw irregular strokes from top to bottom. Use the light pink to paint in the beak. Leave a little space between the beak and the head.

5. Use the light grey to paint in the legs of the flamingo – simply draw the brush along your penciled lines. To finish, add a black dot to the beak and then paint one in on the white surface above the beak for an eye.

Kalli the Raccoon

Kalli the raccoon is a little more difficult to paint because he has a lot of fur, which is also patterned in some places. Again you need watercolour paints, pencil and watercolour paper as well as brushes of the size of your choice. For our raccoon, which is about 10cm high, we used brushes in size 6.

1. First of all, start with the sketch. If you are unsure about what a raccoon looks like, you should try drawing one on a piece of scrap paper. Alternatively, use a photo as a guide.

2. When the sketch is finished, the next step is to add the colour. We used light and dark brown and black. Mix up the appropriate colours before you start painting.

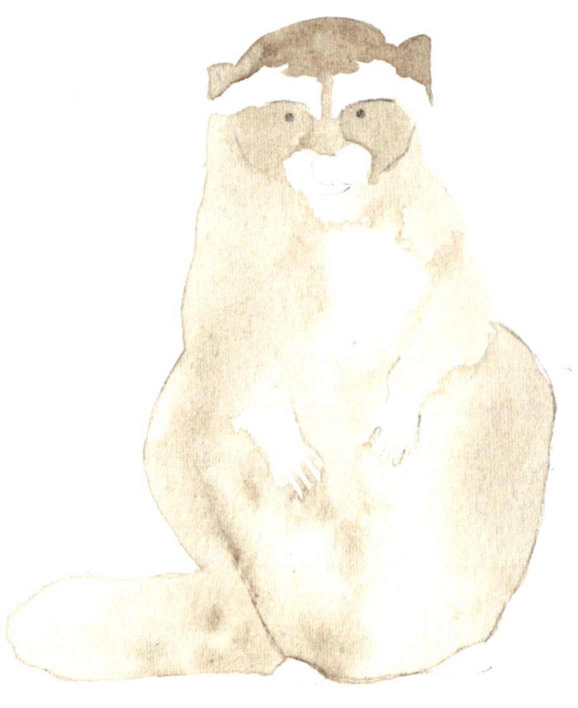

Wash out your brush and then use it to brush over your sketch with water. Leave out the paws, muzzle and the area above the eyes. Paint the light brown shade evenly over the areas where the paper is wet.

TIP: **Since watercolour paints are transparent, you don't have the option to add white highlights afterwards. You need, therefore, to leave blank those areas that you want to be white at the very beginning.**

While the surface is still damp, you can use a slightly darker tone to imitate the fur in the middle of the body. It's easy – just dab the paper irregularly with the brush. Make sure to leave the paws unpainted. You might find it easier to use a smaller brush for this step. Add a few jagged stripes to the tail. Let everything dry well before going on to the next step.

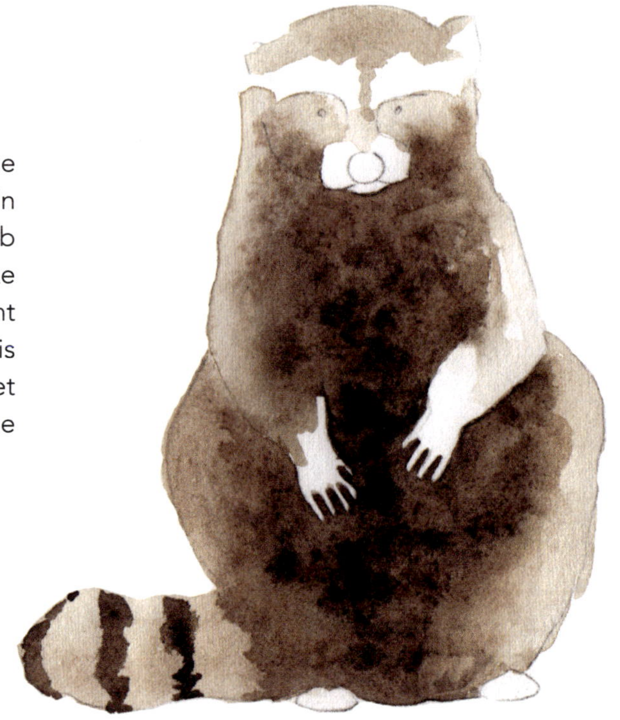

 The special transparent quality of watercolour paint means that you should always work from light to dark. For this reason, it is important with more complex illustrations to think about the individual steps before you start. Because if you paint one part of the image too dark, you cannot brighten it again.

5 Now go over the belly and head of the raccoon with a really strong tone of black. Again, dab with the brush to imitate the texture of the fur.

6 Once everything has dried thoroughly again, add the details to the face such as the nose and eyes.

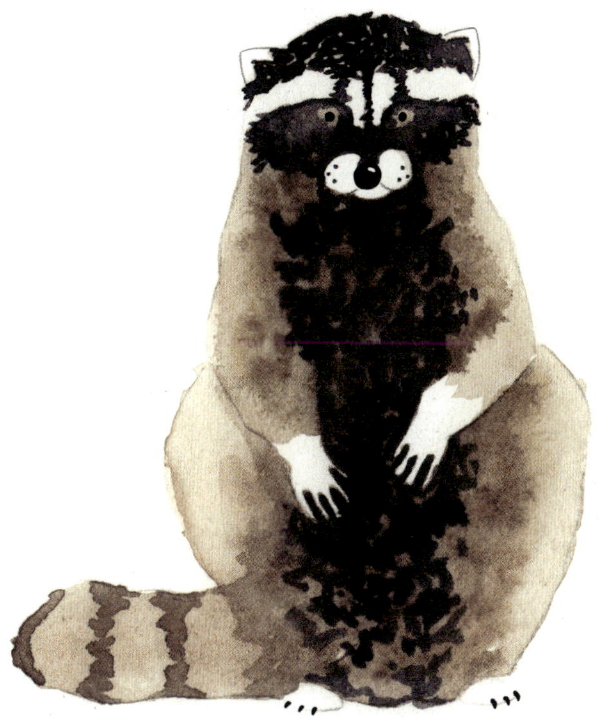

Hubert the Badger

Animals with a lot of fur are often more of a particular challenge when painting. But a badger can also be depicted in just a few steps. You can achieve an impressive result with a few clever details.
For Hubert the badger you will need watercolour paper and colours, pencil and rubber, some water and brushes in sizes 6 and 2.

1 Start again with a simple sketch on your watercolour paper. Then mix up a dark and a light shade of grey paint.

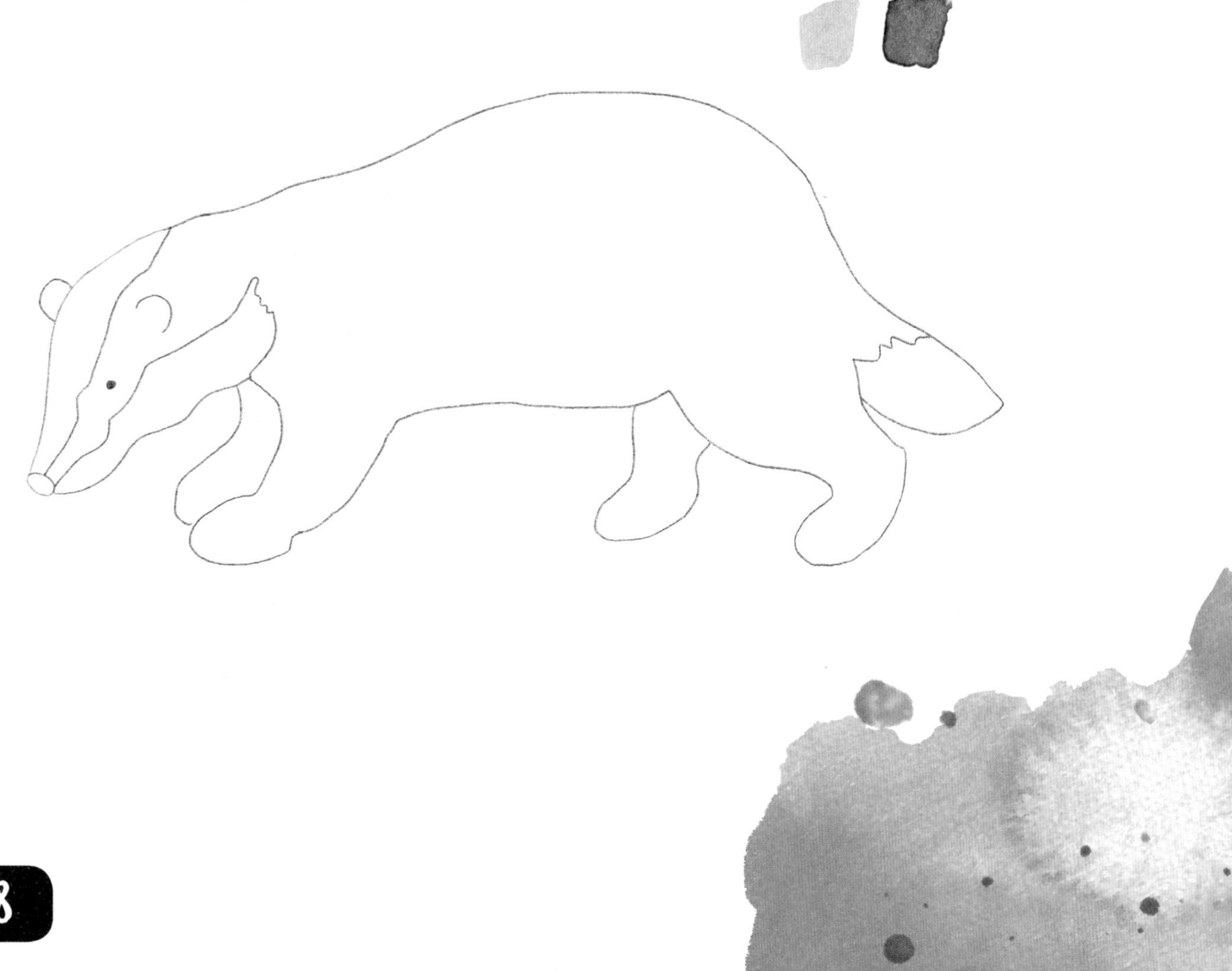

2 Using a size 6 brush, prime the body evenly with the light grey shade. Leave out the right front and rear legs, the tip of the tail and parts of the head.

TIP: **Always work with plenty water when priming! If there is not enough moisture, individual areas will dry out while you are still priming and you'll get edges in the paint. On the other hand, if you work a bit wetter, you get a monochrome finish.**

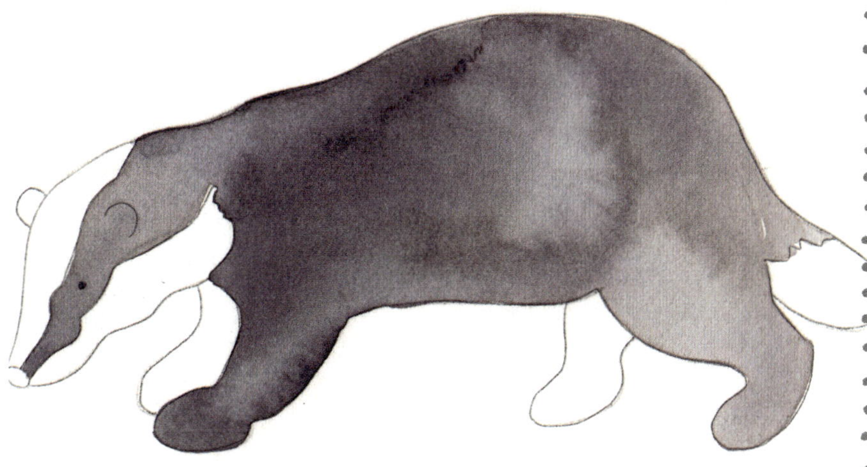

3 When the body is evenly coloured, you can dab a few areas with the dark grey while still wet. For example, the feet and lower belly are ideal for this. The back is left nice and bright so it looks as if it's lit from above.

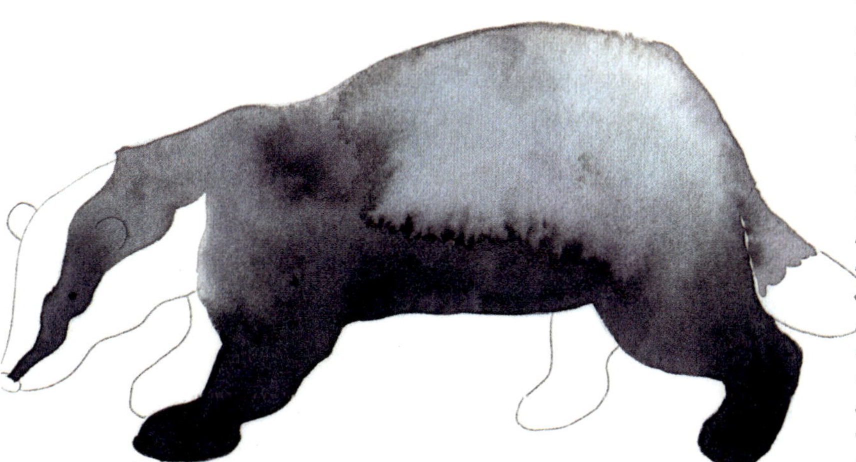

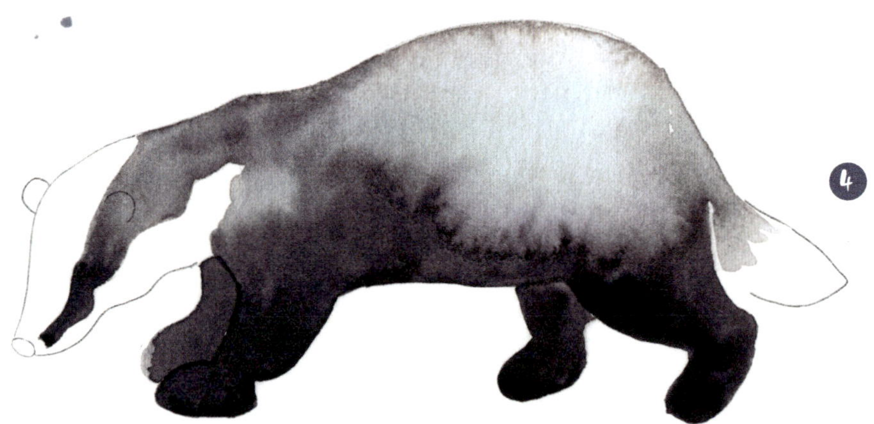

When everything has dried, continue by painting in the right front and rear legs. These should also be relatively dark.

5 In the final step, it's time to add the details. These are particularly important as they help indicate the fur. Use the size 2 brush to paint small, very fine lines in a very light grey on the white areas. You should also add the ears, eyes and nose in a very strong shade of grey. At the very end you can accentuate the paws with small claws.

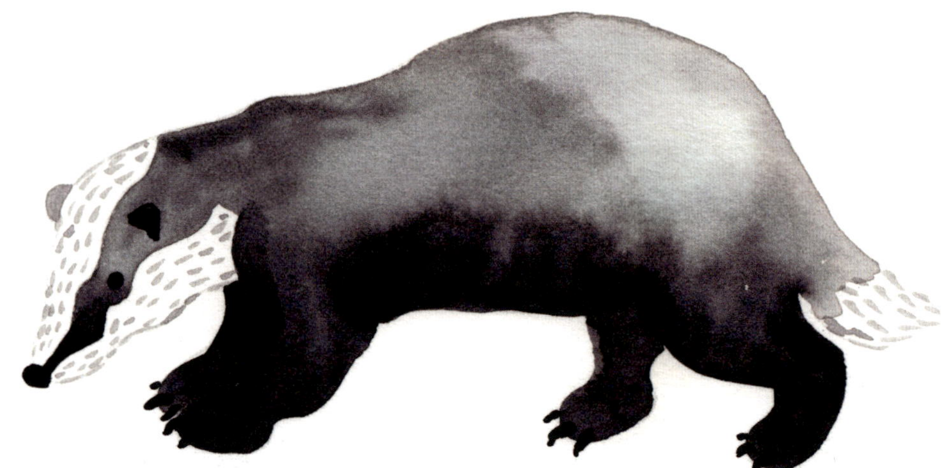

Fred the Budgie

Birds are a little more difficult to illustrate because of their multi-layered plumage. This also applies to Fred the budgerigar, whose feathers are also patterned. However, the complexity of the image can be reduced to a few simple steps.

For Fred you need a size 6 brush in addition to watercolour paper, watercolour paints, water and a pencil. For the small details, such as the beak and eyes, we would recommend using a size 2 brush.

1. For the first step, draw a pencil sketch on your watercolour paper. Try not to press too hard with the pencil because the lines aren't easy to cover well with paint later.

2. If you are satisfied with your sketch, you can mix up your colour. We used a light and a dark blue shade for the plumage, orange for the beak and a light brown for the perch. You can, of course, chose completely different colours for your version of this picture.

3 Wash out your brush and, as with the previous designs, prime the bird's body with water, omitting the beak, perch and part of the wing. Then, using your lightest shade apply the first layer of paint.

TIP: **In our opinion, when it comes to watercolour painting the trickiest thing is to get the balance between too wet and too dry just right. If your paper dries out in one place, wash out the brush completely again and add some more clean water.**

4 While the first layer of paint is still damp you can highlight some areas with a darker tone. Add a few tail feathers by painting in a few lines below the perch. You can also paint in the feet. Use a shade of brown that's slightly darker than the one you will use for the perch. Make sure the feet are dry before going on to paint the perch.

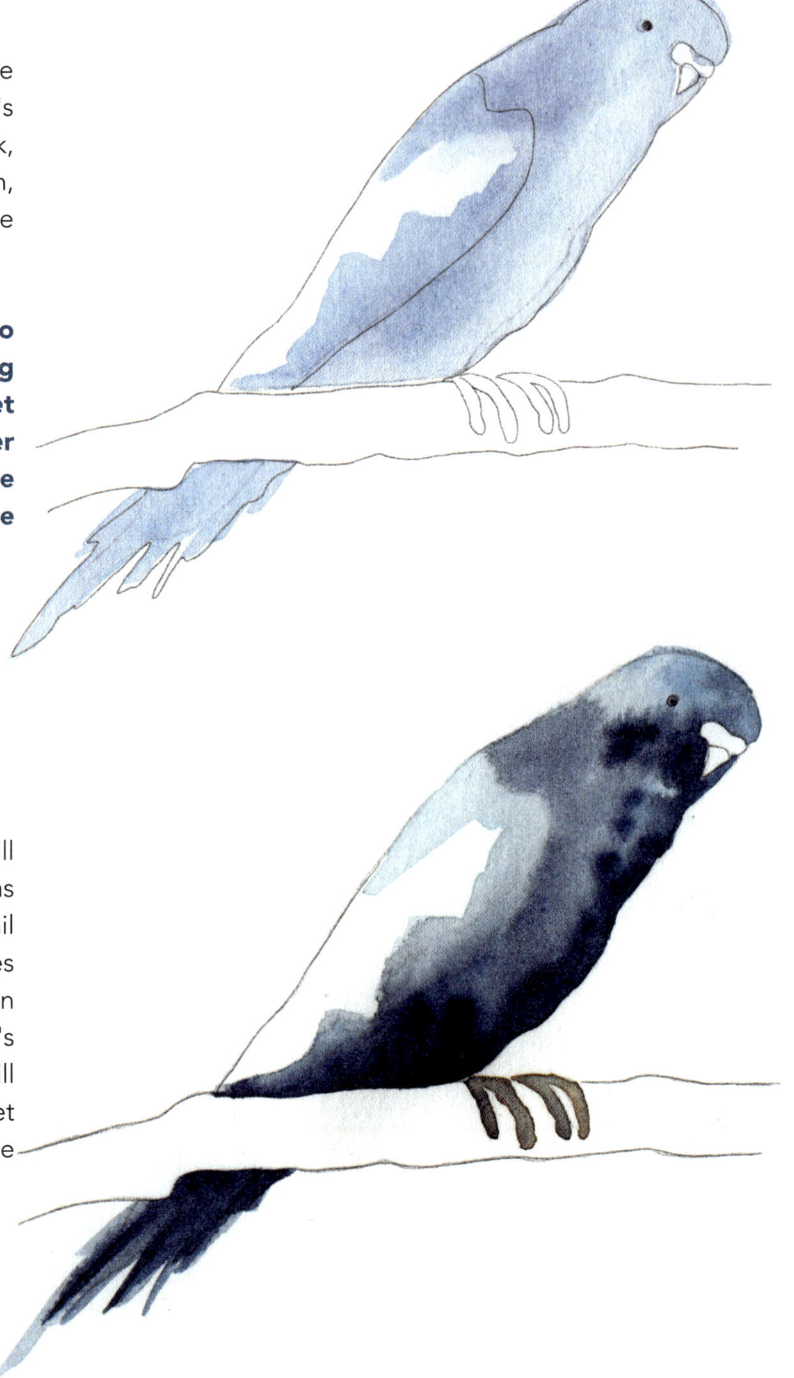

 Make sure your picture is completely dry before moving on to the next step. Using the darkest tone of paint, use your brush to make rough, jagged edged blocks over the birds back. Make these smaller and more delicate towards the head. At the same time, paint in the perch in a light shade of brown. Now add the small details such as eyes, beak and claws, with a size 2 brush.

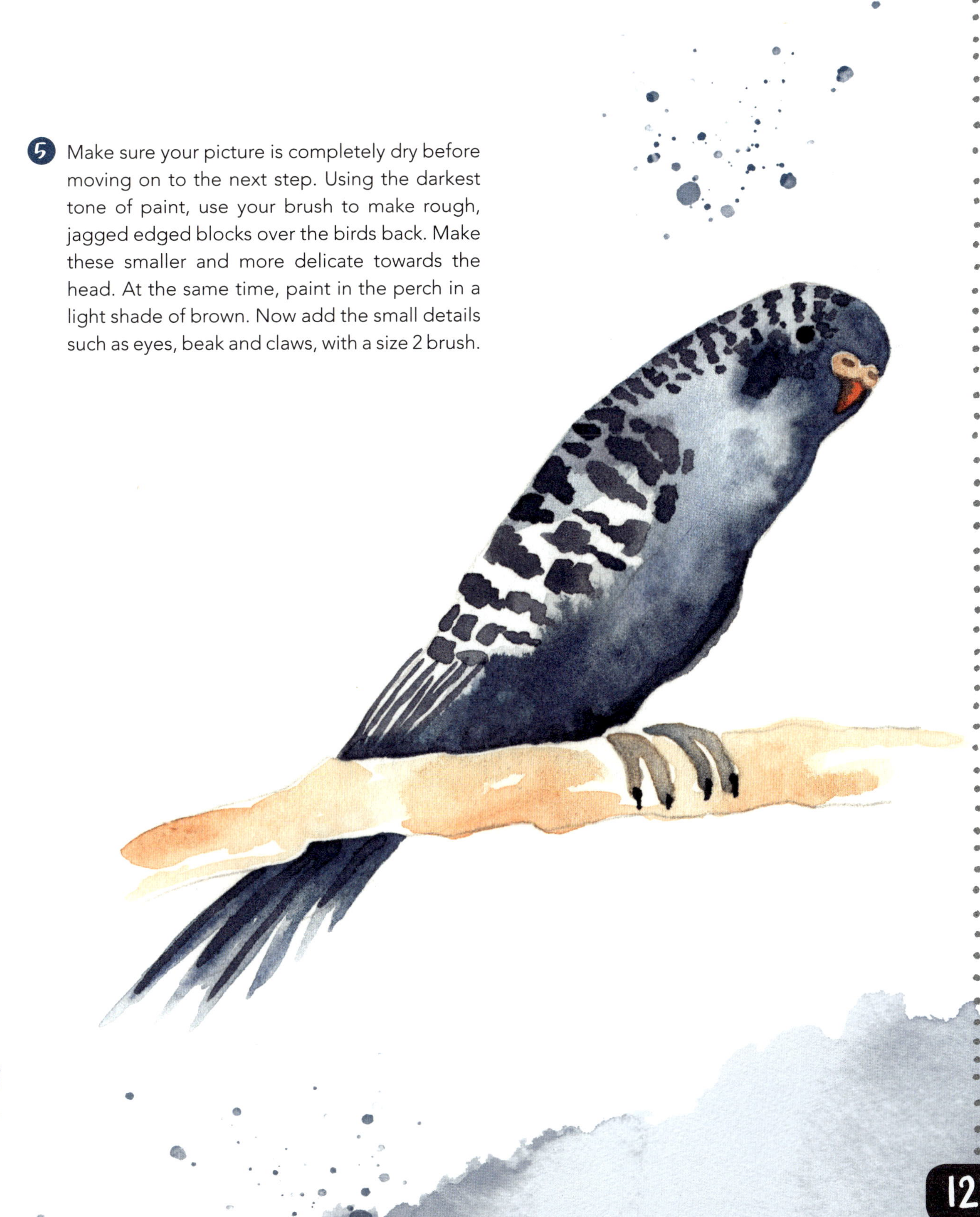

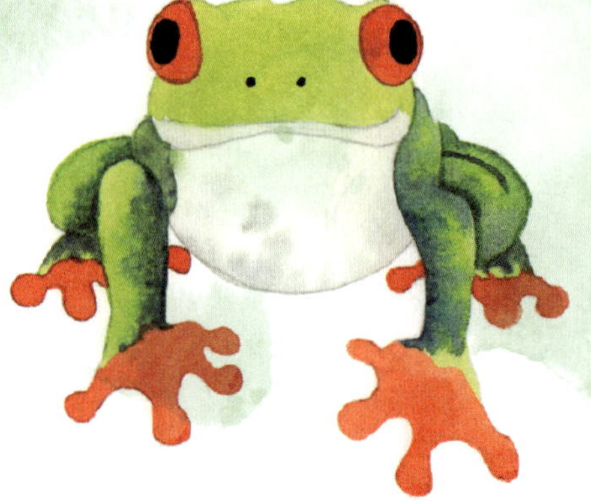

Welcome
TO THE
jungle

Gerd the Frog

This image is one of the more demanding animals that we've included because you need to work in several small stages. However, this little frog is a very nice project to work on because you get to use really bright colours. And since there are frogs in countless colours and shapes, you can also get really creative and choose your own colours. To paint Gerd the frog, you'll need watercolour paper and paints, some water, a pencil and a medium-sized brush.

1. As this is a more complex illustration, start by sketching it out in pencil. If you are not sure about it, you can download a version from our website www.tuvapublishing.com/gerd-the-frog, which you can print out and then copy onto the watercolour paper using graphite transfer paper.

2. It is also important for this project that you prepare all the necessary colours in advance. We opted for a grass green, an indigo blue, a light grey and black as well as an intense orange.

TIP: **With illustrations that really depend on the choice of colours, it's a good idea to think about them beforehand. This is very easy to do if you create a colour scheme. Simply paint small squares of colour side by side on a piece of paper. That way, you can see straight away whether the colours harmonize with each other.**

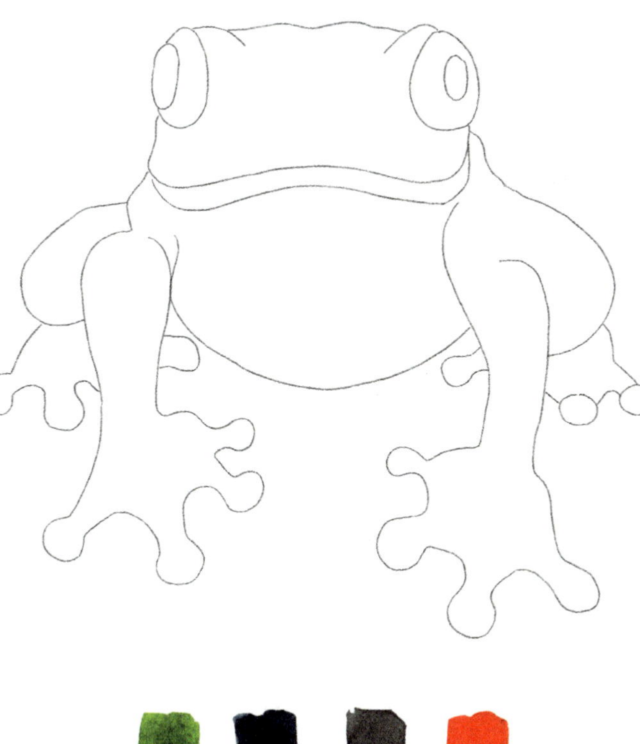

3. For this frog, we will progress in several small steps, because we want to avoid the colours running into each other at the points where the different sections meet. Start by painting the head evenly in a light shade of green. Then follow with the left hind leg, painting over the top section of the leg. Work carefully and try to avoide any paint going on to the front leg.

Dab a little blue on the inner side of the leg, close to the body, while the first paint is still wet. Repeat the process with the right hind leg. Leave everything to dry thoroughly.

4. Now paint the front legs with the light shade of green and a little blue in the same way as the hind legs. Allow everything to dry well in between each stage so that the colours in each section do not run into each other.

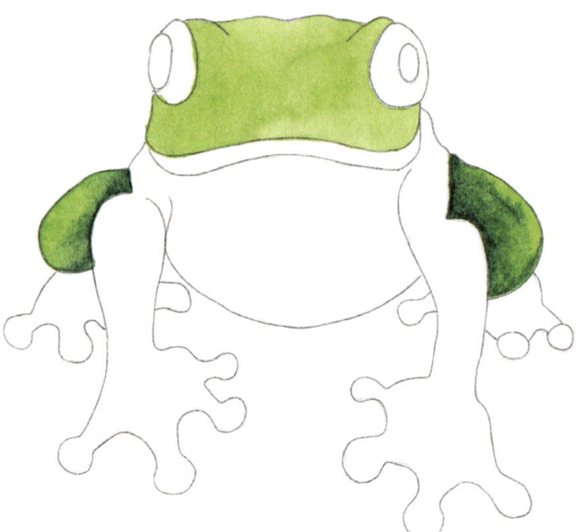

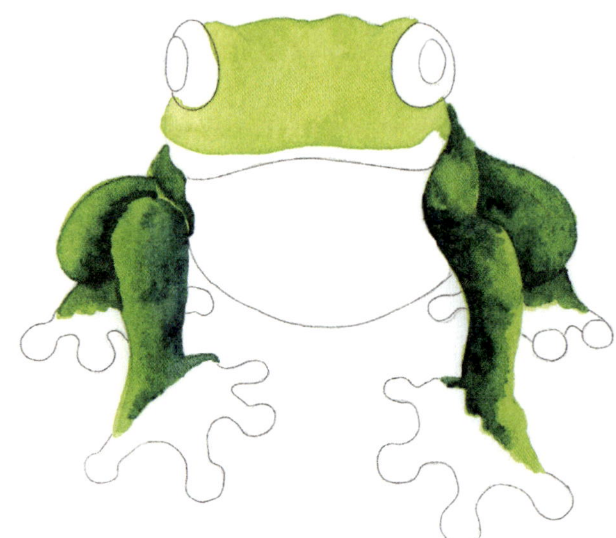

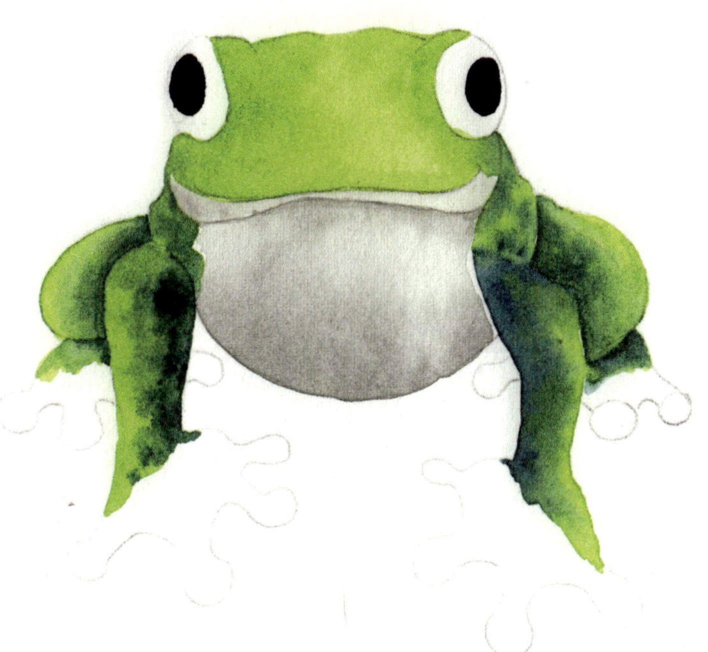

In the next step, paint the belly in a light shade of grey. It's also a good idea to make the lower part is a little darker so the belly appears more three dimensional. Then colour the lower part of the mouth a light grey. Paint in the two pupils using a very strong shade of black.

6 Finally, colour the frog's feet with an intense tone of orange. Then follow with the eyeballs, which can be an even darker shade. Finish off by adding two nostrils in black. Use a smaller brush to paint these more delicate areas.

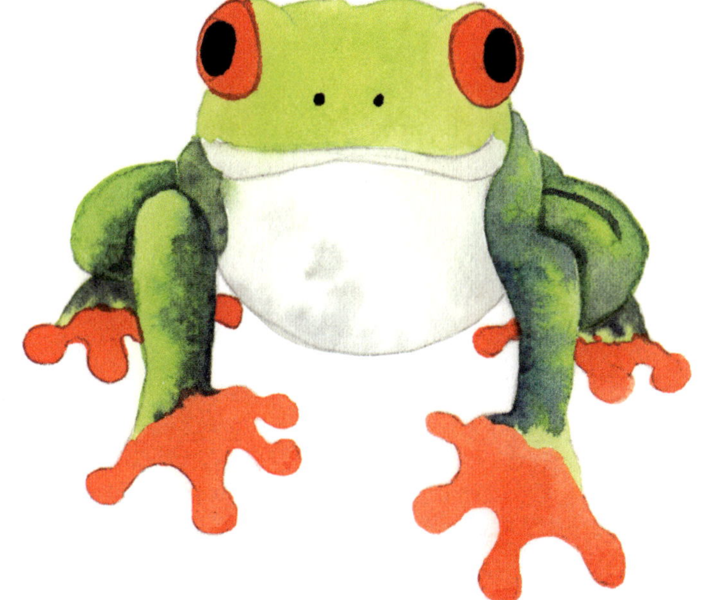

Andi the Alpaca

The alpaca comes originally from the Andes where it is traditionally equipped with colourful blankets and bridles. The many details, bright colours and patterns that you might find are a great opportunity to paint a slightly more unusual design. As always, you'll need watercolour paper and colours, some water, a pencil and rubber and brushes in sizes 2 and 6.

1 First draw the outline of the alpaca on your watercolour paper in pencil. Try not to press too hard to avoid damaging the paper.

2 When you are satisfied with your sketch, you can choose the colours for the design. We kept the alpaca itself in grey and grey-brown, but chose yellow, red and magenta for the blanket. Of course, you can always try other colour combinations for your alpaca.

3 Start by painting the animal's upper body in grey using a size 6 brush. Leave the left legs and the lower parts of both right legs free of paint. Don't paint the face or blanket area.

TIP: Your painting doesn't have to be that neat. By not painting the body too evenly, areas of light and shade appear. If you leave small spots completely unpainted, these points of light provide even more interest in your illustration.

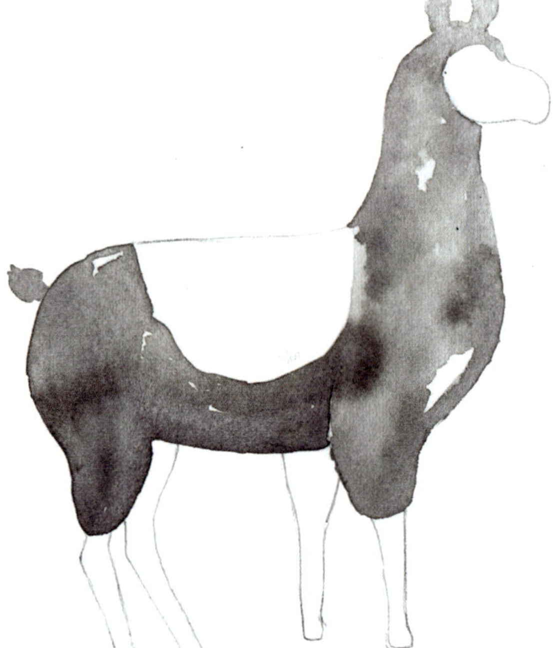

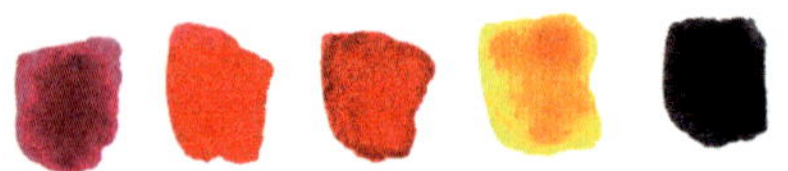

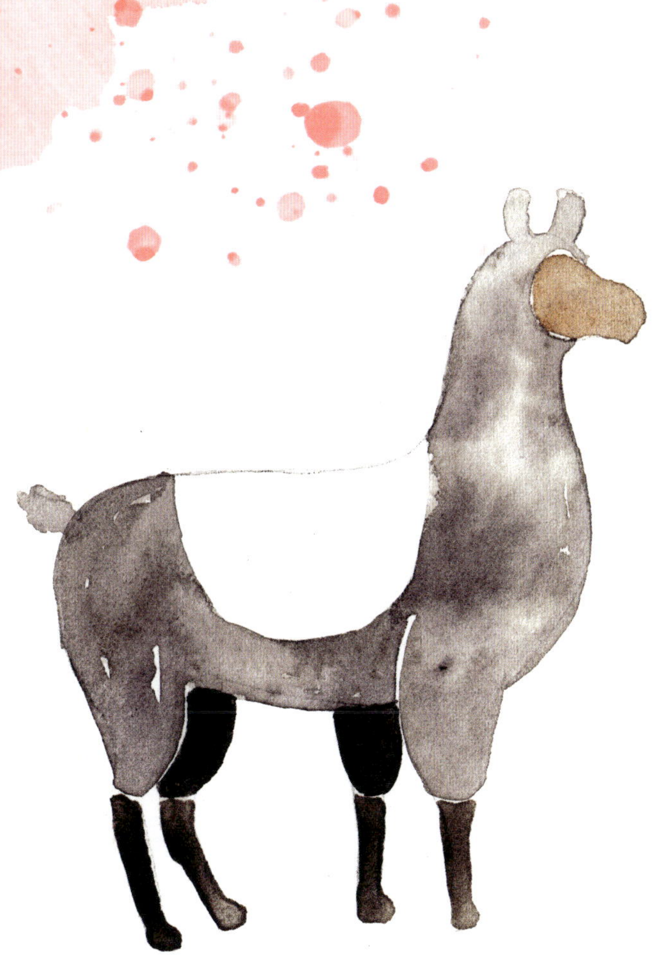

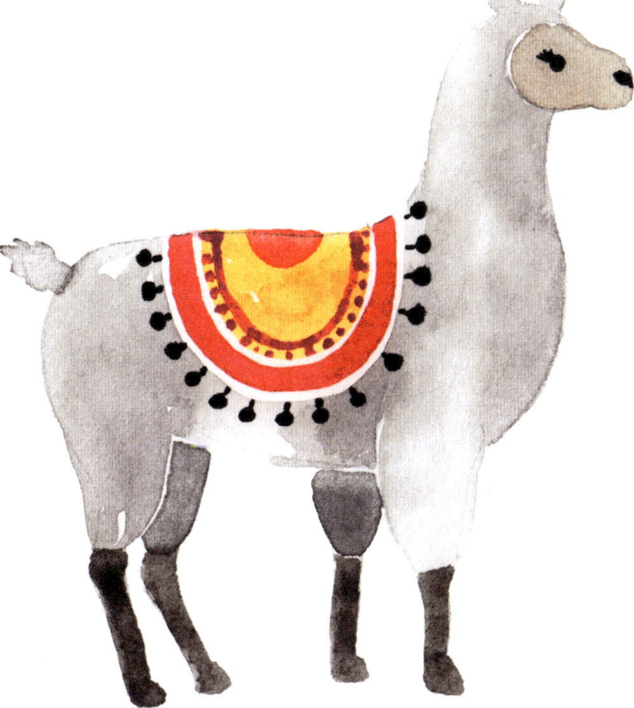

4. In the next step, paint the top part of the left legs in a slightly darker grey. Since these are further from the viewer, they should recede into the background. Paint the lower parts of all the legs with a grey-brown and the face with a lighter brown. Let everything dry really well.

5. Now it's time to add the bright colours and the details. You can create any pattern for the blanket – the more colourful, the better. If you want to put different layers of paint on top of each other, make sure to let each one dry. Otherwise the colours flow into each other and the pattern is no longer recognizable. In the last step you can give your alpaca a face. Use a size 2 brush to paint in a mouth and nose.

Brush Lettering for your Alpaca

If alpacas could talk, they would certainly be speaking Spanish. They make their home in the Andes mountains, in South America. That is why we have added is a happy greeting from this sweet alpaca in Spanish!

FOR THE BRUSH LETTERING YOU NEED:

- a pencil

- a round brush, size 4

- black watercolour paint or ink

1. Sketch out your lettering on a scrap of paper, then transfer it to the watercolour paper. The words should fall approximately half-way between the alpaca and the top edge of the paper.

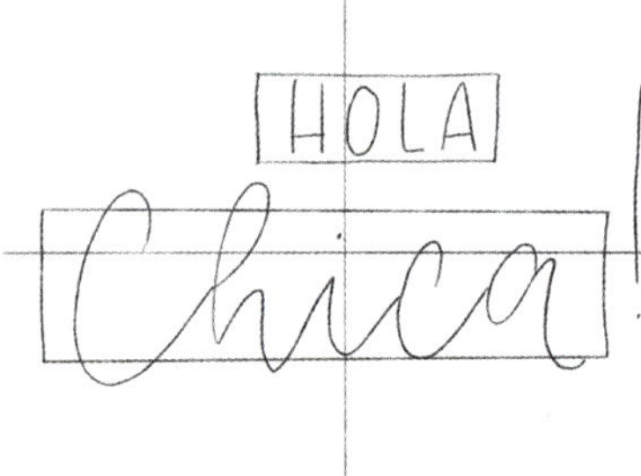

2. Now it's time to use brush and paint. When mixing the colour, it is important to find the right consistency. If it is too thick, the lettering will be too dark and the brush quickly becomes too dry. With a little water, the paint will flow much better.

3. Take some diluted paint onto a dampened brush. Starting with the second word 'Chica', write the C in one swing. At the beginning the line will be a little thinner because you are using an upward stroke. As you go down, you put a little more pressure on the brush and the line automatically becomes stronger as it leads up to the next letter. When writing with the brush, it is important not to take too much time or the paint may dry out in the process.

4. When the word 'Chica is dry, continue with the first word 'HOLA' in simple block capitals. 'HOLA' is smaller than 'Chica' but we will still use the same brush. Apply less pressure for this word – this will make the strokes even and thin.

5. At the end there is only the exclamation mark to add. You can also apply a little more pressure here so that it isn't too thin.

Now the matching brush lettering for your alpaca picture is complete. Adiós!

HOLA
Chica!

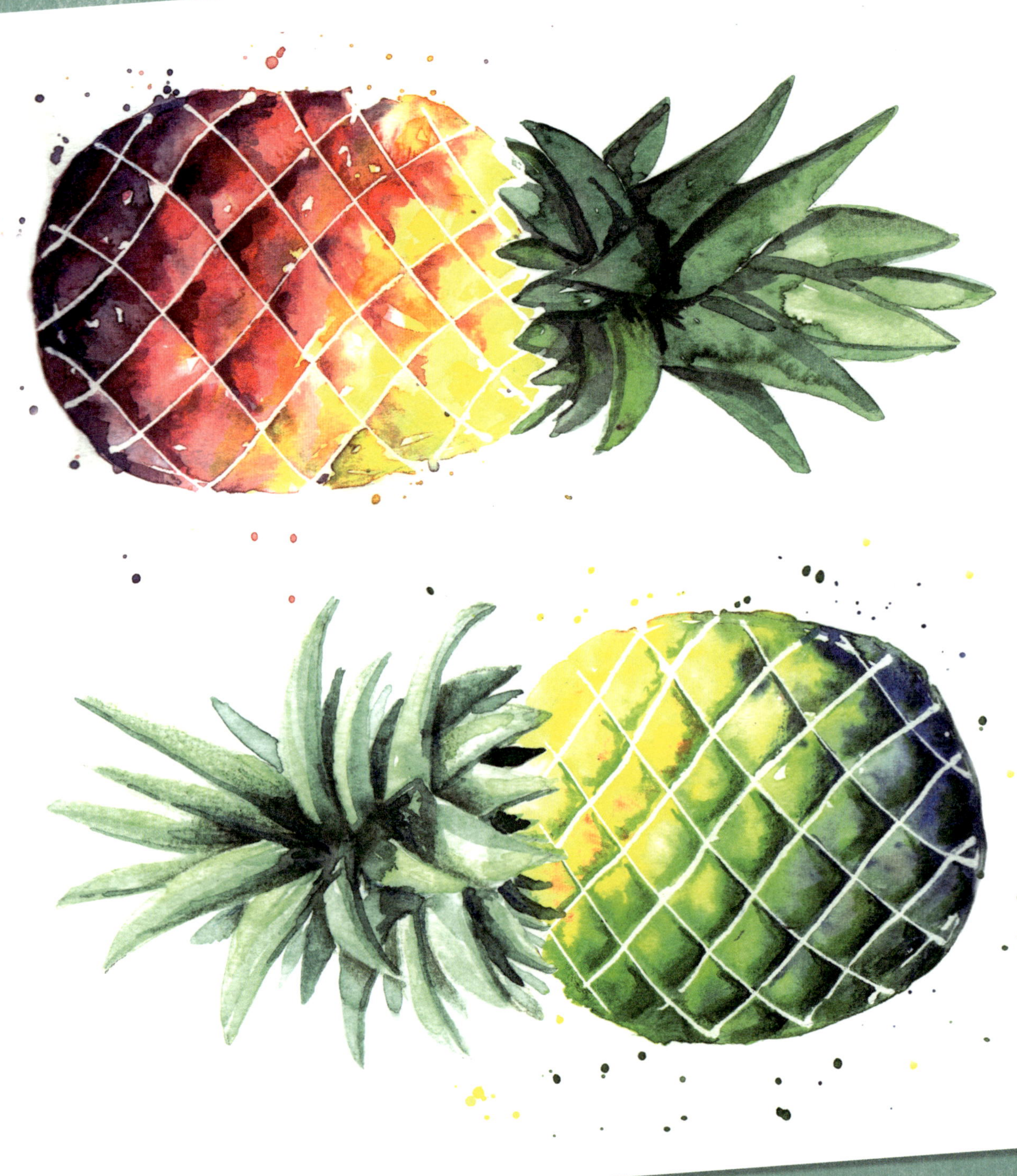

Sweet Small Fruits

I have a passion for hand lettering, but above all, I love brush lettering done with watercolour paint and a brush. In this chapter, I've created some fruit designs that are really eye-catching and you can have a lot of fun with them and with hand lettering.

In this chapter, we look at how to create some painted healthy treats, step by step. Using colour-coordinated brush lettering rounds off the illustrations and at the same time adds a bit of humour to your picture.

We'll start simply with some basic shapes. Start small and begin by trying these different shapes and colour combinations first. We'll then continue with the ideal entry-level fruits – a cherry and a grape – and then get a bit more complex with a pear and a pineapple. Patterns, structures and accents can be applied layer by layer – the transparency of the colours makes it possible. I will also show, step by step, how you can paint a realistic strawberry using a special technique.

Individual fruits look good on their own, but there are many other great ways to present them. You can add them to wreaths or incorporate them into a hand-written recipe. In my chapter you will even find letters that are made up of fruit and lettering that fit inside fruit. So, what are you waiting for? Let's get painting these sweet small fruits!

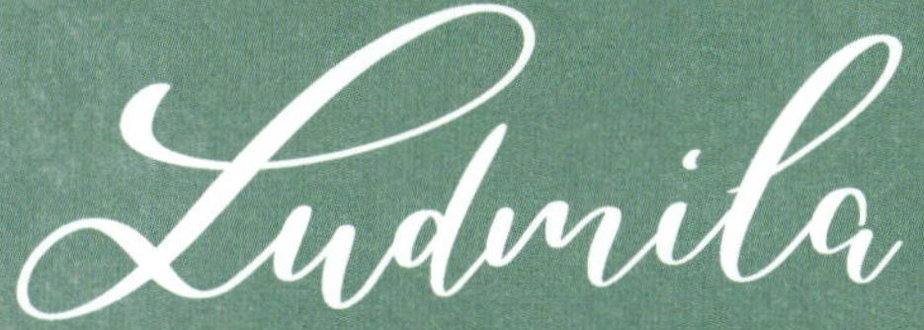

Practice pieces

The nice thing about watercolour is that you can use it to paint completely uncomplicated, small illustrations. Depending on which style you prefer, a less realistic depiction of small pieces of fruit may be even more appealing to you at first.

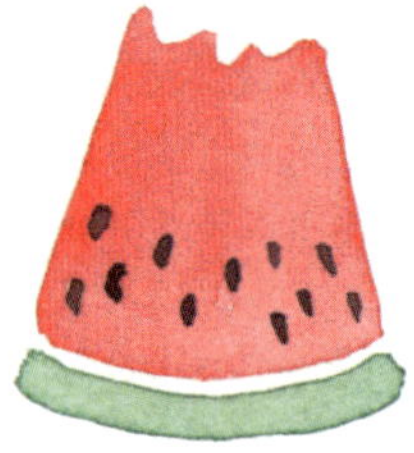 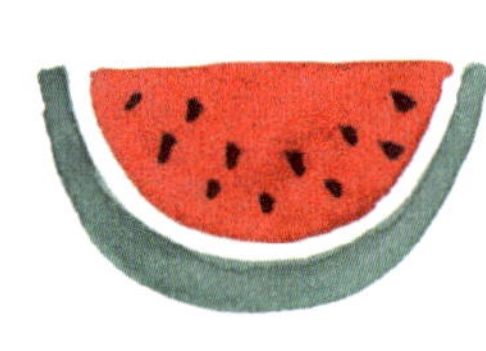 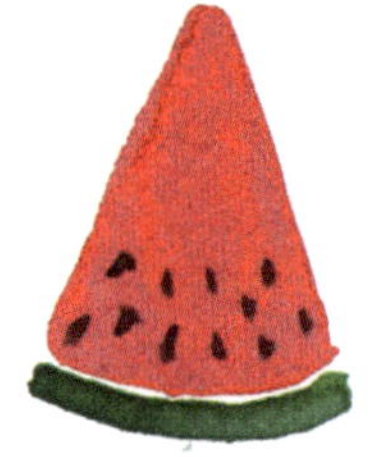 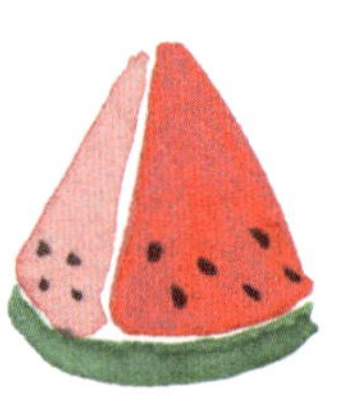

I recommend painting these small fruits as a quick and easy warm-up. The small images will help you deal with the basic shape of the respective fruits and to explore the right colour combinations.

Maybe you'll come up with some completely new ideas. How about, for example, showing your fruit nibbled? Or maybe insert some lettering in the fruit?

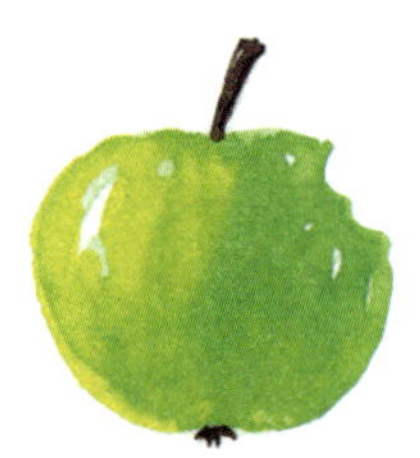 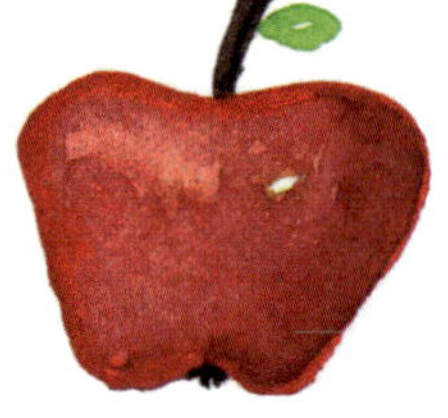

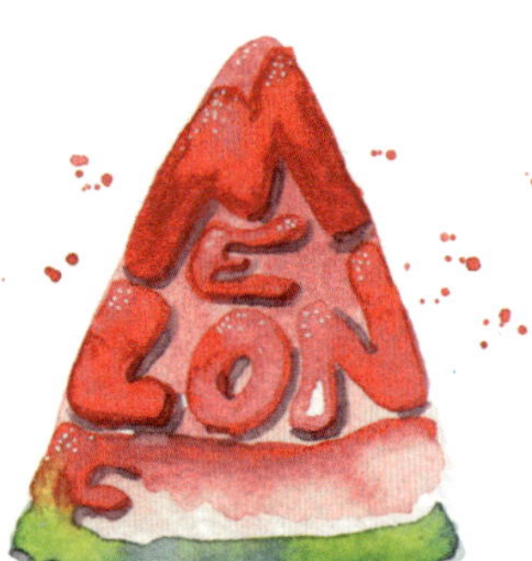

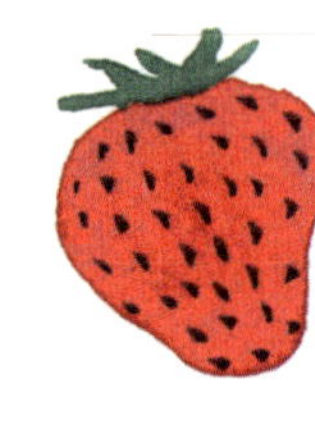

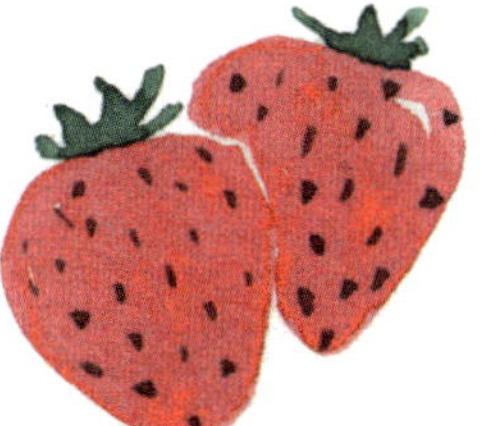
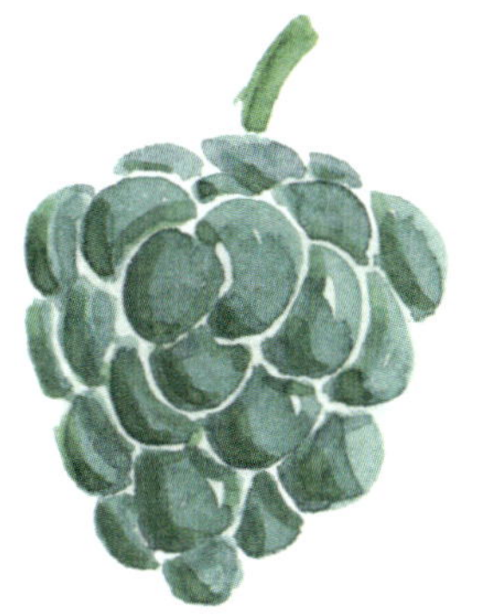
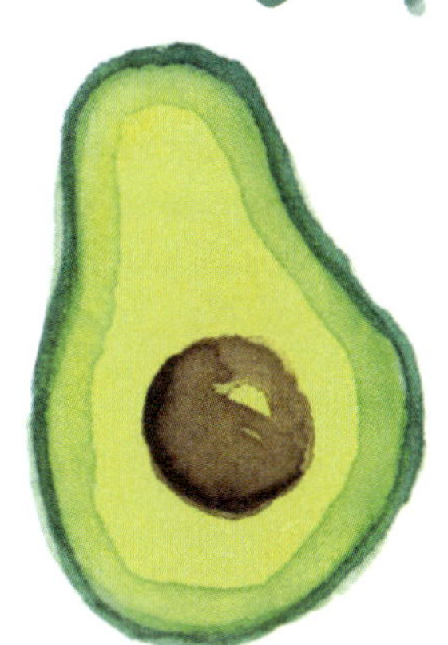

If you paint more complex structures like bunches of grapes or berries with leaves in a small format you can understand how the individual elements go together and also practise effects such shading.

To represent a piece of fruit in three dimensions, painting a small watercolour picture will give you a chance to explore the effects of light and shadow.

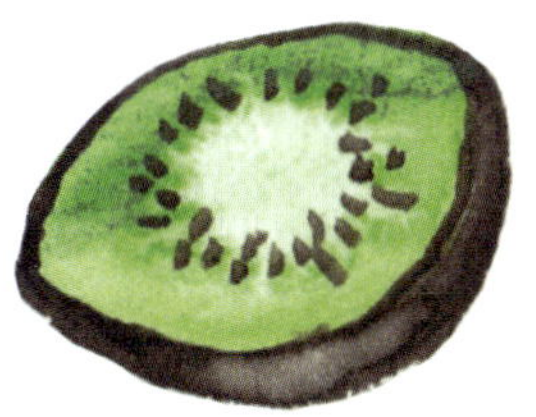

Even if you find painting these simple, small fruits addictive you should definitely try one of the other designs that I will introduce you to on the following pages. At first glance, some may seem more complicated than they really are. But don't worry, each design is explained step by step.

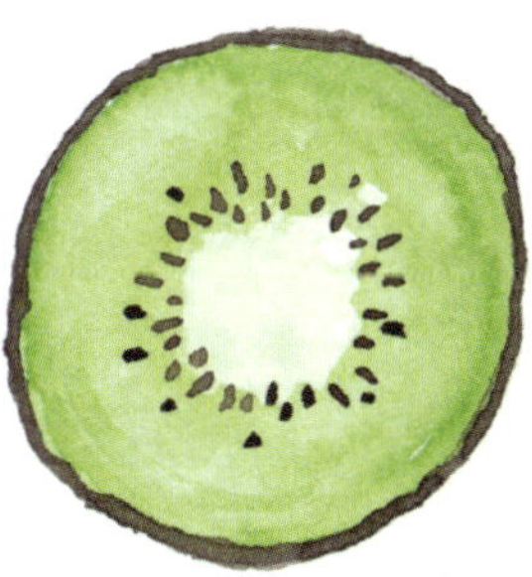
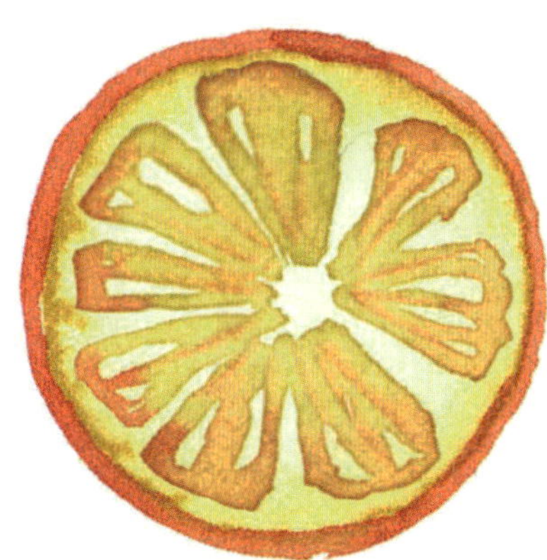

Watermelon

A piece of watermelon not only tastes great but also makes a wonderful motif for a summer-themed piece of lettering. Before you start, have all your colours ready because we will be working wet-on-wet here. Mix three or four different shades of red and two shades of green. You'll also need yellow and brown.

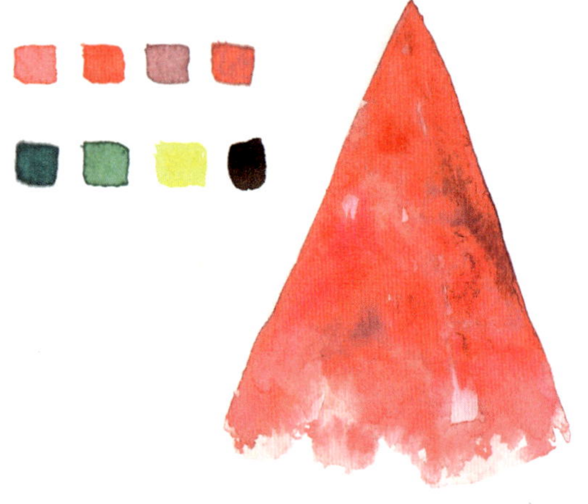

1 Start your melon by forming a triangle with a brush that is soaked in clear water. The bottom edge of the triangle should be slightly rounded.

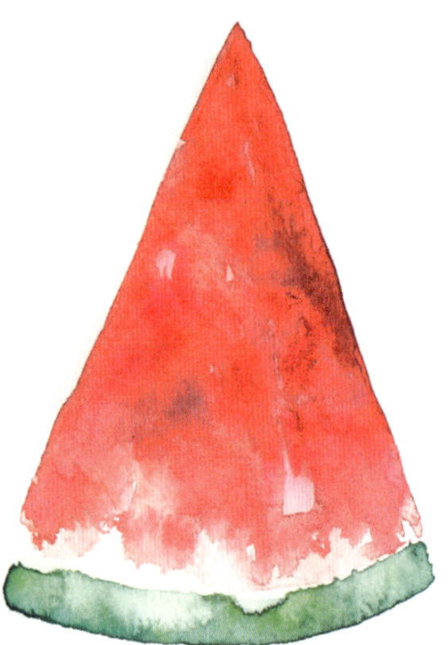

2 Now pick up the first shade of red and dab some colour into the damp triangle at various points. Wash out the brush and repeat this step with the other red shades. Make sure to keep the bottom of the triangle light. You can remove excess paint with some kitchen paper. Let everything dry well. For the green rind of the melon, use clear water to paint a border at the base of the triangle and then dab on different shades of green and yellow.

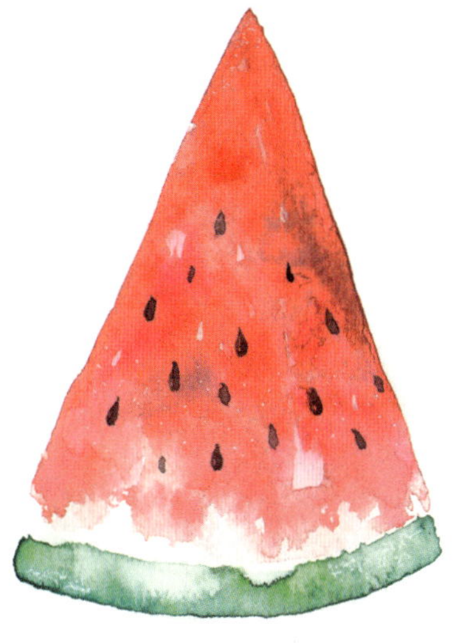

3 When everything is dry you can paint in the pips with a dark shade of brown. A white gel pen is can be used to add white pips or small highlights.

Frauen und Wassermelonen sind GLÜCKSSACHE

Grapes

For these grapes you will need light, medium and darker tones of your desired colour. Grapes don't only have to be green or blue – you can try new colours. Red, purple and pink, for example, look great in combination.

1 Practise on a single grape before you go to the whole bunch. First paint an oval in a light shade and leave a small area white. This should be the area where the most light falls – in this case, from the top right. Apply a darker shade to the wet paint opposite the highlight. Leave to dry and then repeat the step to increase the intensity of the colours.

2 If you want to paint a whole bunch, paint several ovals in a light tone next to each other. Make sure that the ovals overlap in some places.

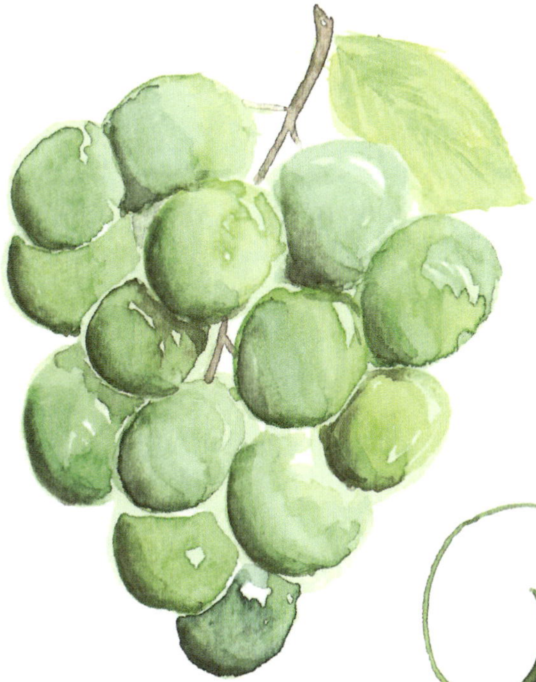

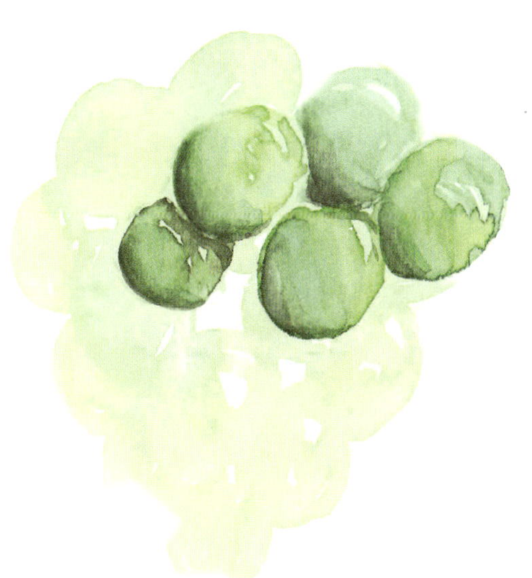

Oh, it's Wine o'clock

3 Once your bunch of grapes has dried, paint in the individual fruit as you practised at the beginning. Where the individual grapes partially cover each other you don't need to paint the whole oval in these places. Experiment with lighter and darker tones and feel free to add more colours. Finally, if you like, add some stems and leaves.

Cherry

This cherry is easy to paint. You can also paint several cherries together and add as many leaves as you like. You'll need to mix just a single shade of red for the fruit but you will also need some brown for the stem and one or two shades of green for the leaf.

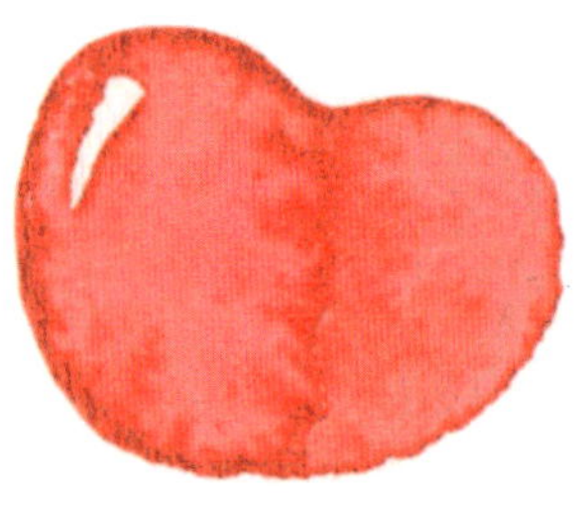

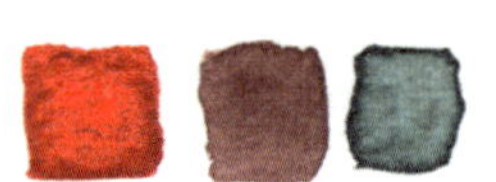

1 Using the red, paint a squat, slightly rounded heart. Leave a small spot white as a highlight. Dab a little clear water onto the still damp colour with your brush to help give the cherry a bit more structure.

2 Leave to dry before adding more paint to intensify the shade of red. A little brown on one side makes the cherry look more three dimensional – dab the darker shade into the still damp colour. After the cherry has dried, paint in a small, brown stem.

3 Now place the brush soaked with green lightly on the stem and draw a curved line away from the stem. This is the first half of the leaf. Press the brush a little harder in the middle of the leaf to make the line a little wider at this point. Repeat this step for the second half of the leaf. Leave some space between the two halves to create a bright centre of the leaf.

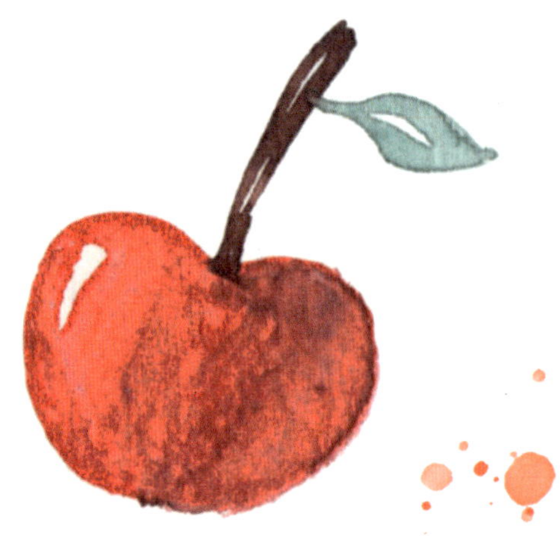

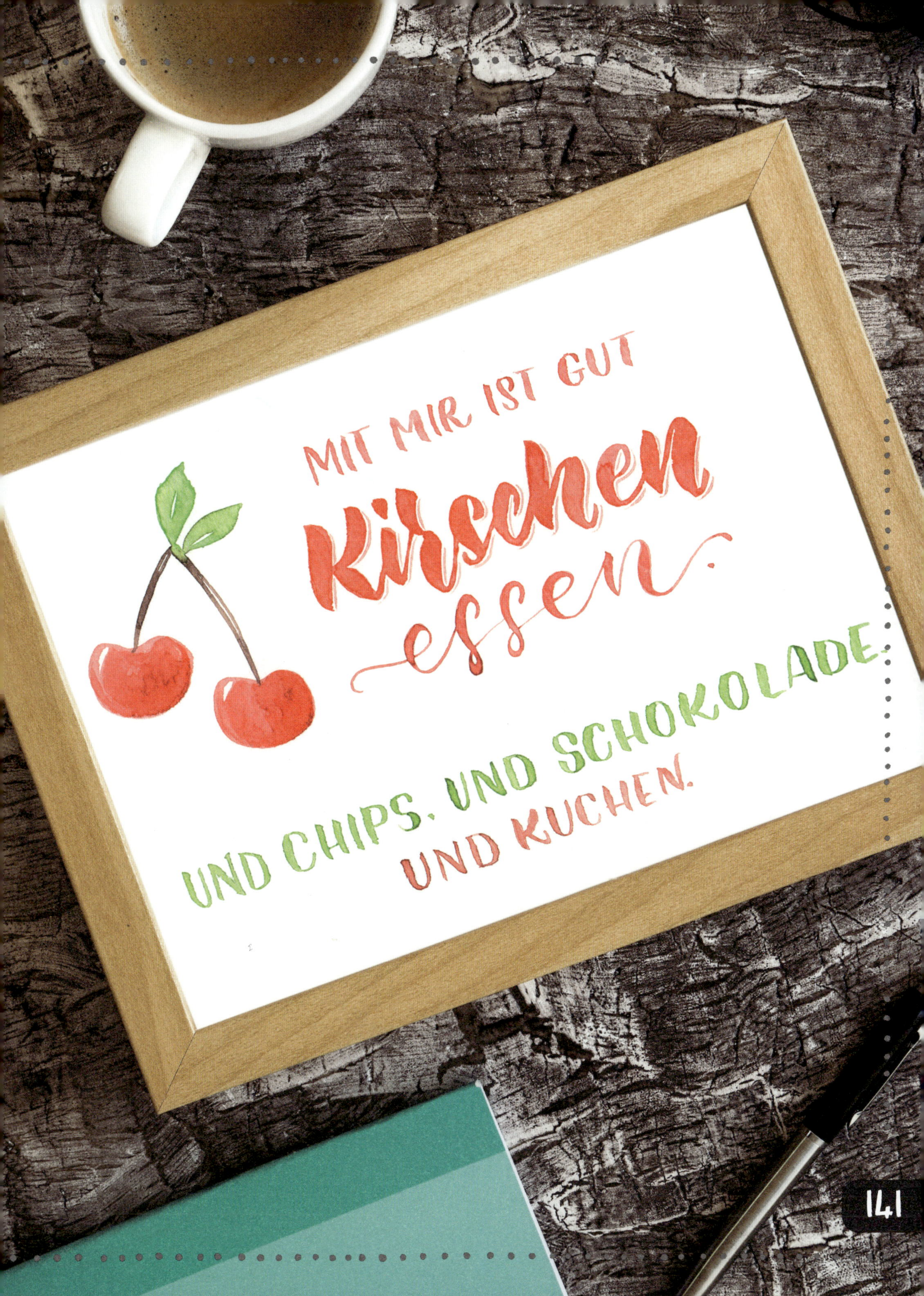

MIT MIR IST GUT
Kirschen
essen.
UND CHIPS. UND SCHOKOLADE.
UND KUCHEN.

NOBODY
IS
PEARfect

Pear

To paint this pear, we'll combine different techniques – we'll paint wet on wet and wet on dry. Start by mixing up a shade of beige and of green as well as a brown and a yellow on your palette.

1. First paint a pear shape in beige. While the surface is still damp dab a little more paint in some places and clear water in others, to create structure. Leave to dry thoroughly.

2. Working quickly, add a pale shade of green to one side of the pear. Add some yellow on the other side, then let everything dry.

3. Finally, there are the details to add using the wet-on-dry technique. As well as the stem, you can add the small, brown dots that are found on many types of pear.

Use the shade of brown to give the pear even more structure. Dilute the colour heavily and apply it to individual areas of your pear.

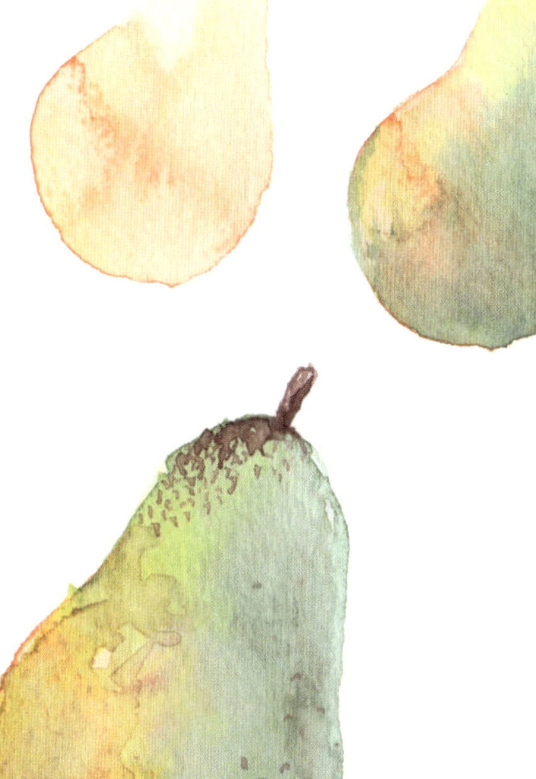

Pineapple

The skin of a pineapple has a rather complex structure, but it's not necessary to try and reproduce it exactly when painting. A uniform pattern, for example, made up of checks or small V-shapes, can remind you of the pineapple's characteristic skin without trying to reproduce it faithfully.

In this project, you'll be using masking fluid. This liquid is applied to those areas in the image that you want to remain white before you begin painting. It is applied with a cocktail stick or silicone brush and then removed when the painting is dry by rubbing it gently with a clean fingertip.

1 Draw an oval shape in pencil. Using masking fluid, fill it with a pattern of V-shapes. The paper will remain white where you've applied the masking fluid. Make sure you let the masking fluid dry really well before moving on to the next step.

2 Mix up a combination of two to three different colours for the pineapple, as well as green for the leaves. Here, I've used shades of yellow, orange and red.

Colour your pineapple with the lightest colour first, then add more colours to the base of the fruit.
Finally, paint a spiky crown of leaves on top of the fruit.

3 Add more layers of colour and extra details if you like. After everything has dried thoroughly, you can gently rub off the masking fluid.

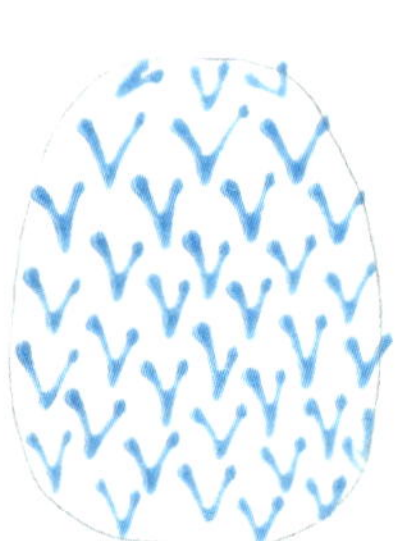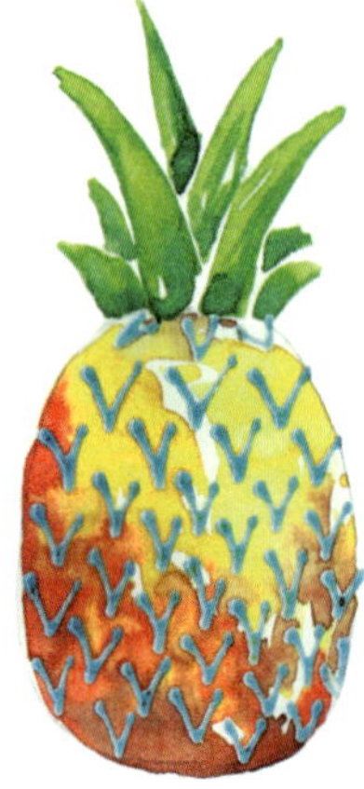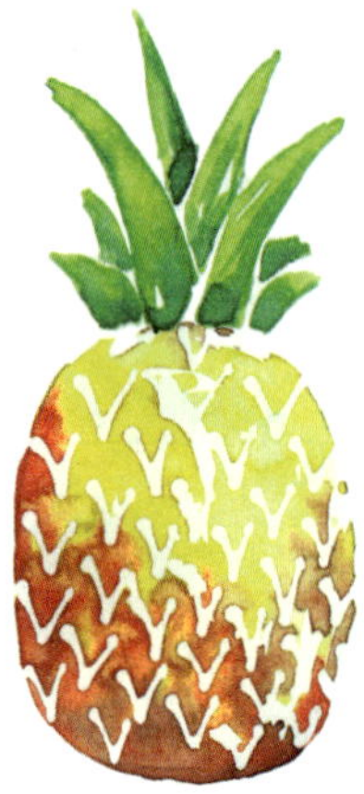

TIP: You don't need to stick to natural colours with your pineapple. Try out bright colours and unusual combinations. Anything is allowed!

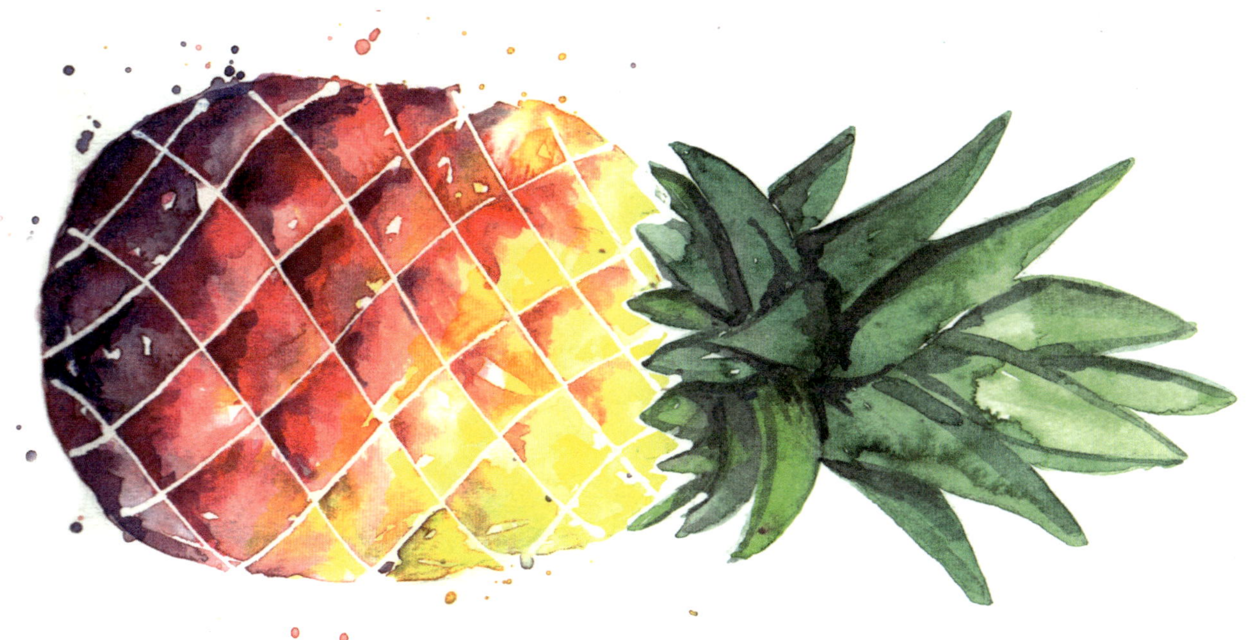

tropical

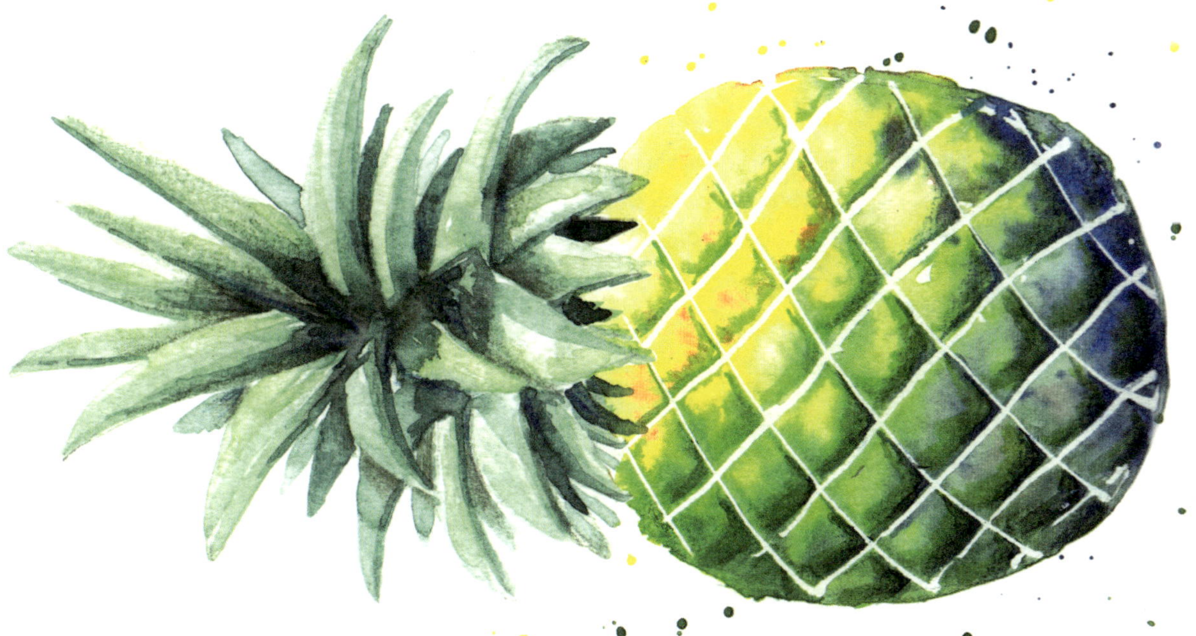

Strawberry

I have developed a technique for painting a strawberry that helps give it a very realistic appearance with little effort. As with the pineapple on the previous pages, we will be use masking fluid here.

1. First draw the outline of a strawberry in pencil – a rough heart shape is about right. Then add some small droplets of masking liquid over the surface. These will be the seeds of the strawberry, which you will colour in yellow later.

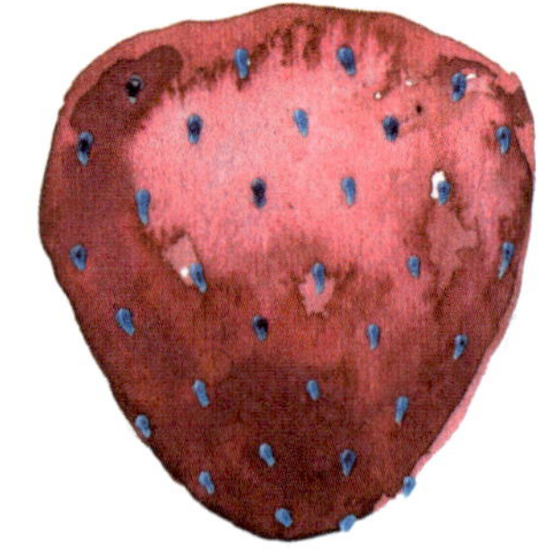

2. When the masking liquid has dried, paint the strawberry in a strong shade of red. Leave a light area in the upper third of the strawberry shape to indicate the place where most of the light hits the fruit. When the first layer of colour has dried, you may notice that the strawberry still looks a little pale. If this is the case, paint it again in red, shading the lower area with a darker tone. This works best when using the wet-on-wet technique.

3. Once the second coat of paint has dried, add shade around the seeds by painting a ring around each drop of masking liquid with a darker tone of red. Let everything dry thoroughly before rubbing off the masking fluid with your finger or an eraser.

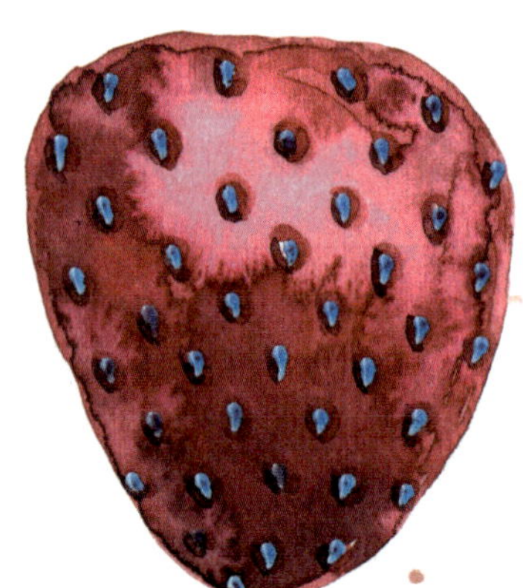

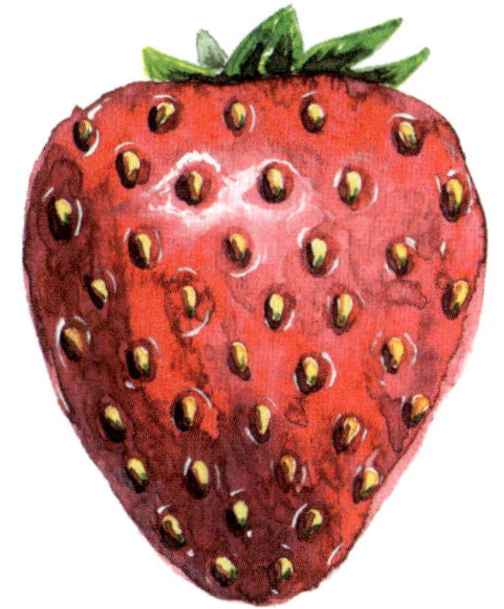

4 Colour in the seeds with a bright yellow. The seeds will look even more realistic if you add a little shading to each one. Dab a tiny dot of ochre on one side of each seed to achieve this. You can also use a white gel pen or some white gouache paint to add white highlights around the seeds.

Finally, add some leaves to the top of the strawberry.

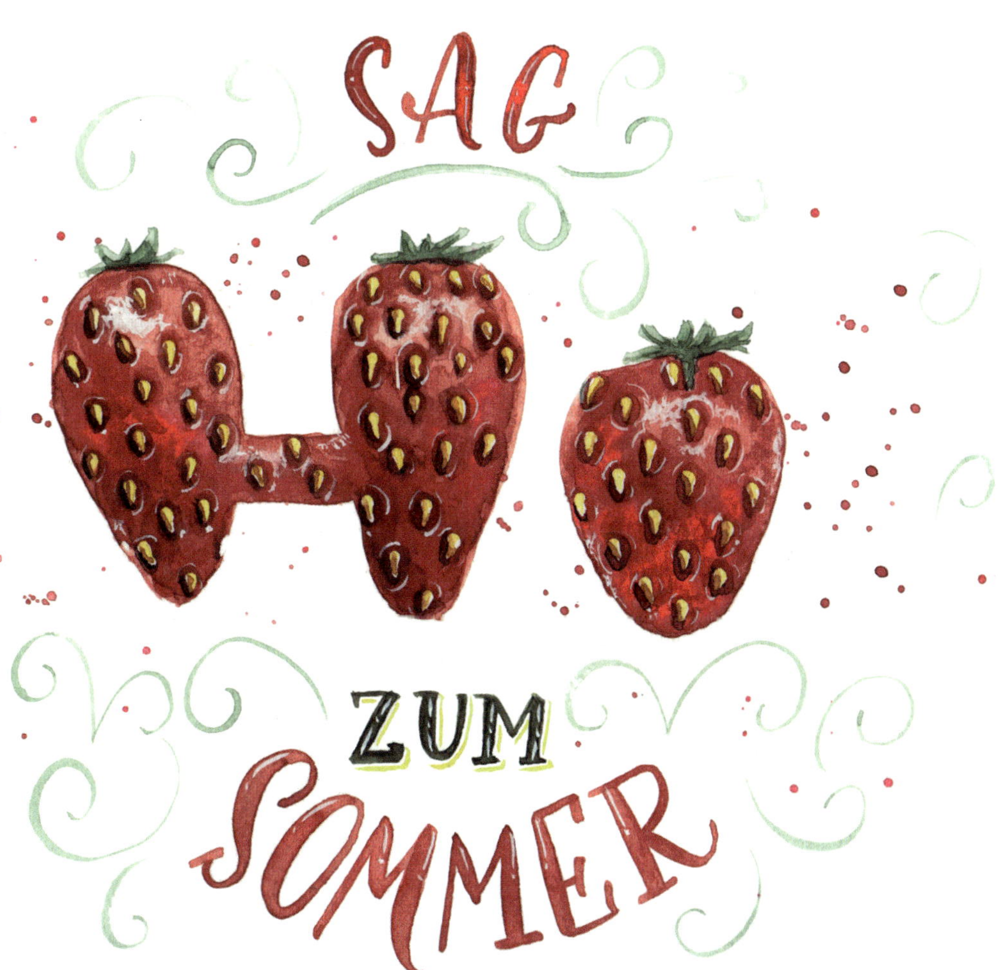

Blueberries

When you see blueberries in the shop, they're neatly presented in punnets. In nature, they're found growing on bushes. These pretty berries are easier to paint if you don't arrange them too tightly together.

1. Mix up a nice violet-blue. Divide the colour between two wells in your mixing palette and thin one of them so you have two shades of the same colour available.

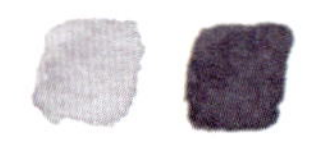

2. To paint a single blueberry, first use the lighter shade to paint a small disc, leaving a small spot white as a highlight. Shade the opposite side to the highlight with the darker colour to give the berry shape.
   When the paint has dried, you can repeat the last step to intensify the effect. Then paint a small, dark spot on your blueberry.

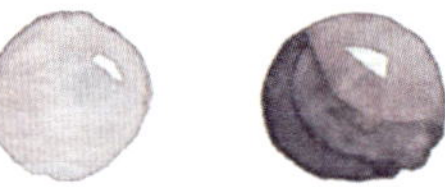

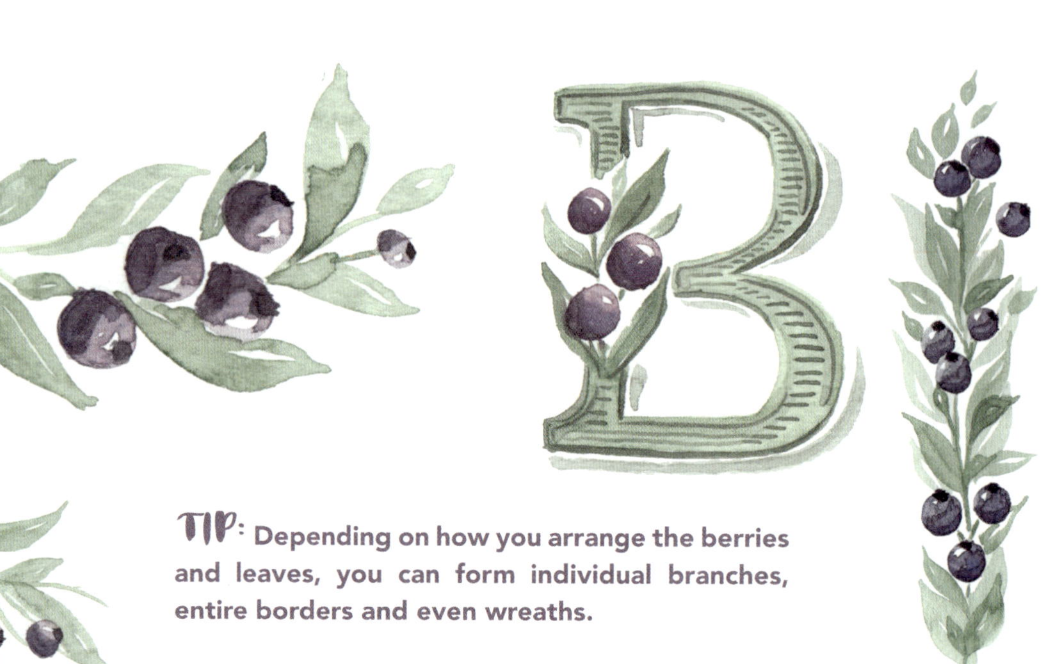

TIP: Depending on how you arrange the berries and leaves, you can form individual branches, entire borders and even wreaths.

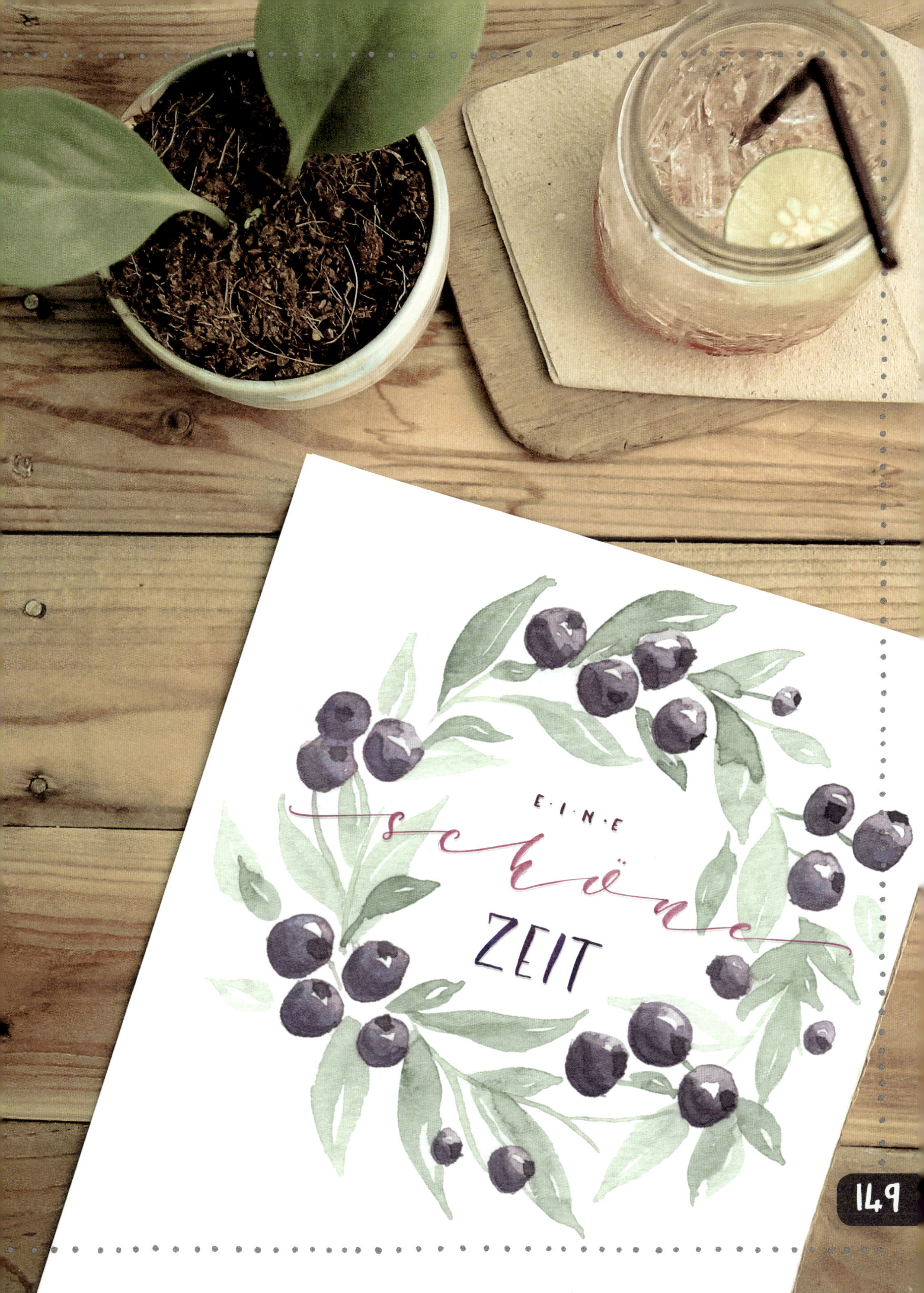

E·I·N·E
schöne
ZEIT

guacamole

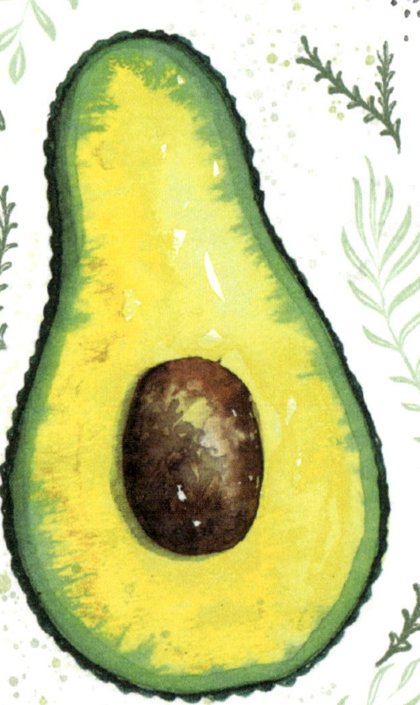

Salz
UND
Pfeffer

Zitrone

Knoblauch

AVOCADO

Avocado

An avocado is easier to recognize when you paint it if it's cut open and with the stone still in place. This beautiful motif works well when combined with lettering, especially if it's illustrating a recipes

1 The basic form of an avocado is pear-shaped. Paint one on your paper in a shade of yellow and leave a blank oval in the middle for the stone. Drip some water on here and there so that interesting effects are created where runs form in the pigment.
Apply a shade of green to the edge of the still-damp shape so that it runs nicely into the yellow area.

2 To intensify the colours of the avocado, you can repeat the first step. Then, when everything is dry add a thin border of a darker green.
To give your picture more detail, you can make the edge of the border slightly wavy. This help remind you of the pitted surface of the fruit.

3 Finally, add the avocado stone. Use different shades of brown to get a rich final colour. It is important to leave a light area on the stone to achieve a three-dimensional effect. You can enhance this by adding a darker area opposite the bright one.

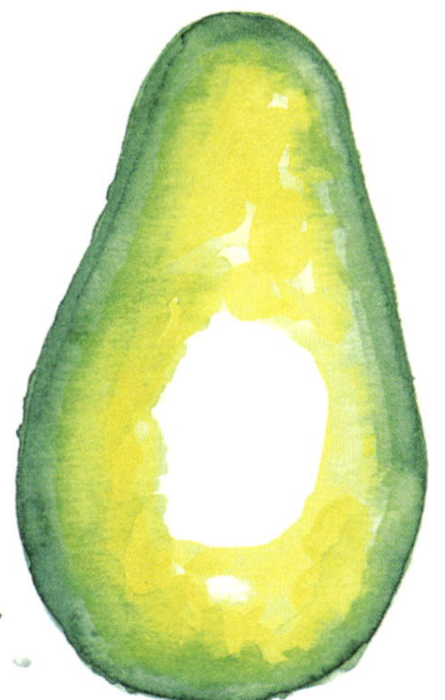 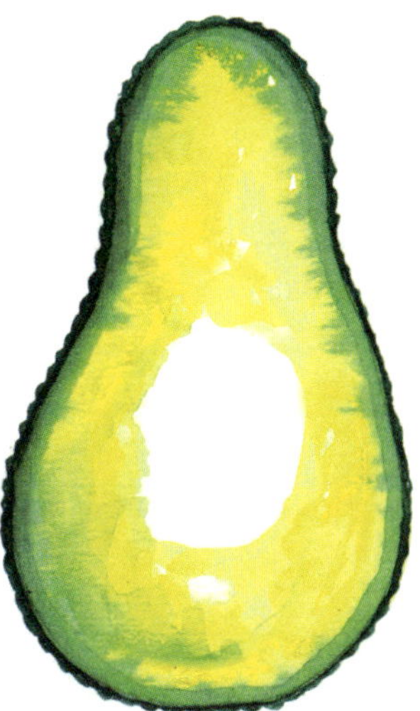 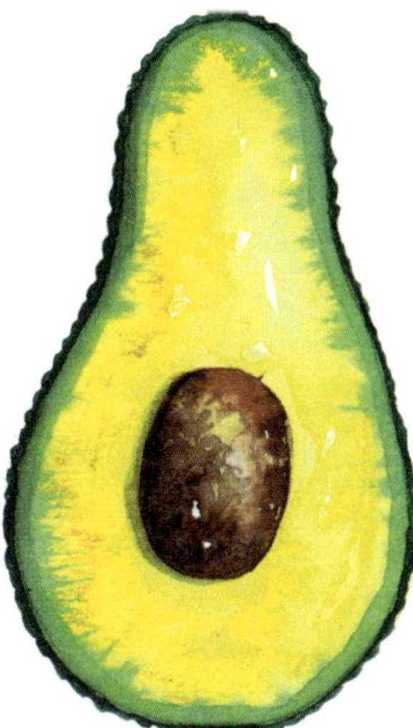

Kiwi

A sliced kiwi, with its green flesh and black seeds, is really distinctive. That's why you can transform the basic kiwi into letters and designs that are instantly recognizable as such.

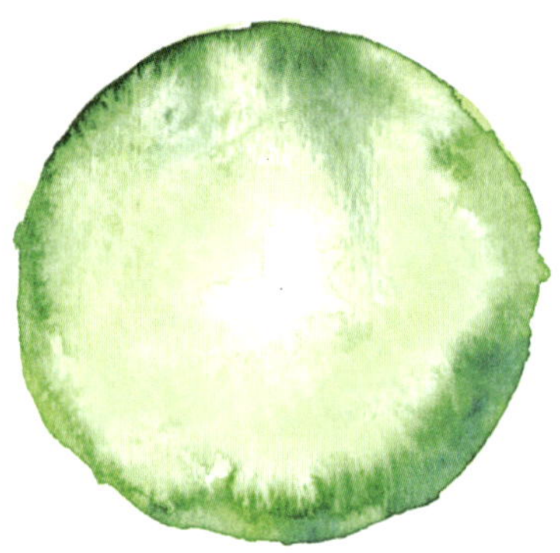

1. For a sliced kiwi, first paint a circular shape with a bright green. Leave the centre unpainted and dry. Apply darker shades of green to the edge.

2. Then use a watery green to paint short lines radiating out from the centre in a shape that looks like a flower.

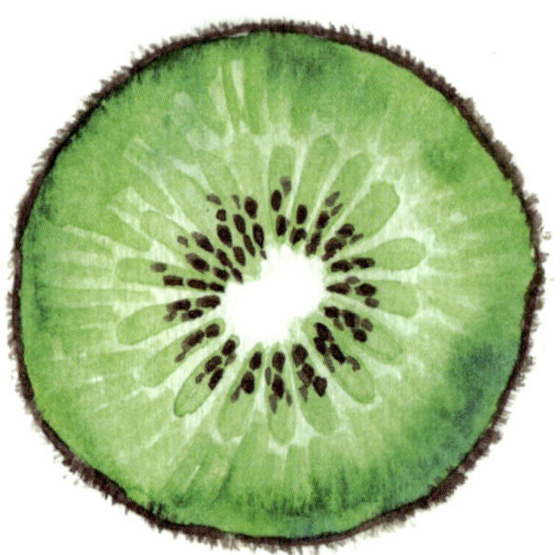

3. Use a dark brown and a very fine brush to paint a border of tiny dabs around the edge to resemble the furry skin of the fruit. Paint small dots around the centre for the seeds.

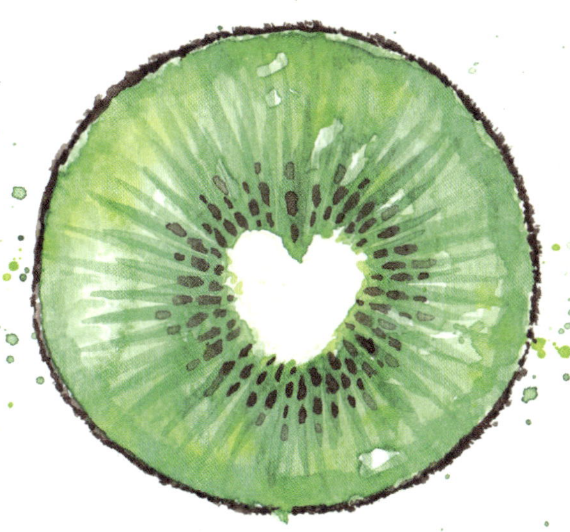

Even in nature, the bright centre of a kiwi can resemble a heart – so why not leave a white heart shape in the centre of your fruit? You can also take the basic design of the kiwi and turn it into letters – as in the 'LOVE' shown here.

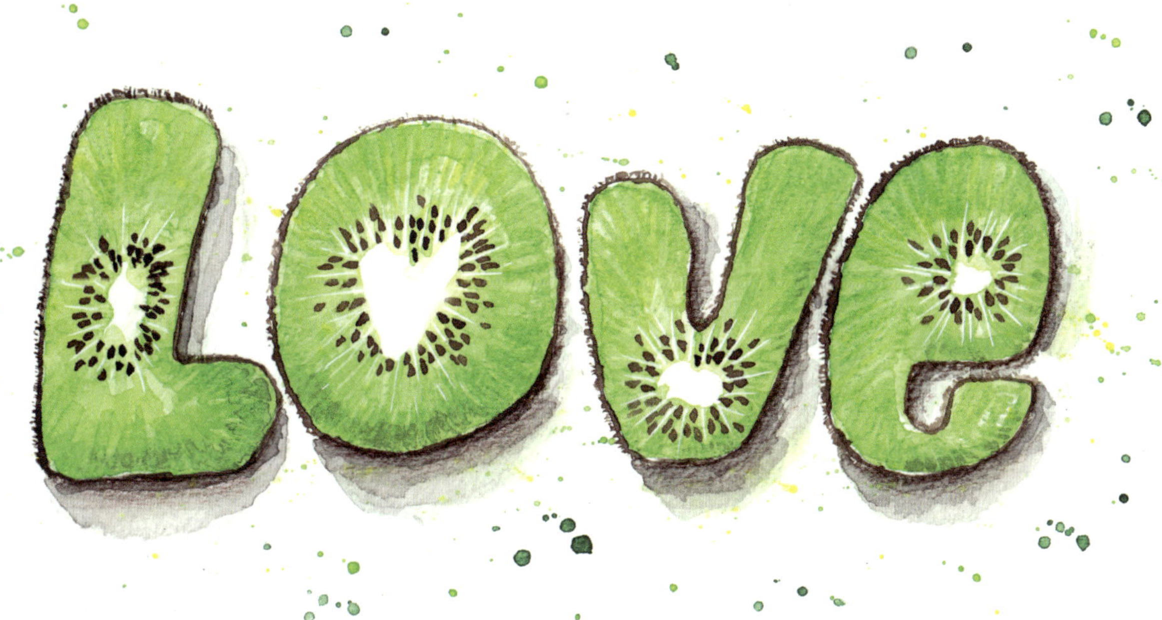

Fruity Lettering

For the fruit paintings that I've shown you so far, I have largely tried to copy nature. So at the end of this chapt[er]
want to be a little more abstract with my designs. Here, I've retained the shapes and colours of the different typ[es]
of fruit but I'm now using them as a background for lettering.

PEAR

This pear is made in three simple steps. In addition
to watercolour paint, brushes, water and watercolour
paper, you also need masking liquid.

1 Use the masking liquid to apply your lettering –
here 'mmh' – to your paper. If you want a longer
piece of text, you should draw the pear shape
and the letters with a bright coloured pencil first.

2 After the masking liquid has dried, paint a pear
shape around your lettering with clear water.
Then dab it with paint in shades of red, yellow
and green.
Keep in mind that green and orange quickly
mix to a brown tone. If you want to avoid this,
have a yellow area between the red and green.

3 Once everything is thoroughly dry, remove the
masking liquid by rubbing it gently with your
finger or an eraser. Your fruity lettering will be
even more lively if you add a few splashes of
strong colour.

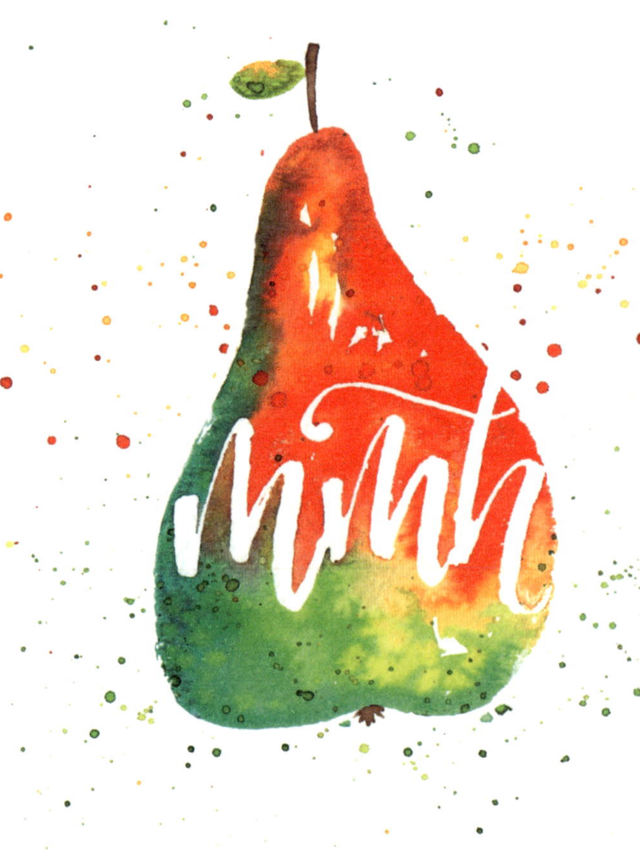

APPLE

The apple is also created with the help of masking fluid. This time, however, the lettering is not painted with it; use masking fluid to paint the outline of the apple, its stem and the leaf.

1 Use the wet-on-wet technique for the lettering within the shape of the apple. First paint the letters with a wet brush. Then quickly drip in yellow, blue and green paint. Don't forget to colour the leaf and the stem.

2 To highlight the outline of the apple, dab and spray on red and yellow paint in splatters and sprinkles around the edge. Protect your lettering with a piece of paper that has been cut to size.

3 Finally, remove the masking liquid by rubbing it gently with your finger or an eraser.

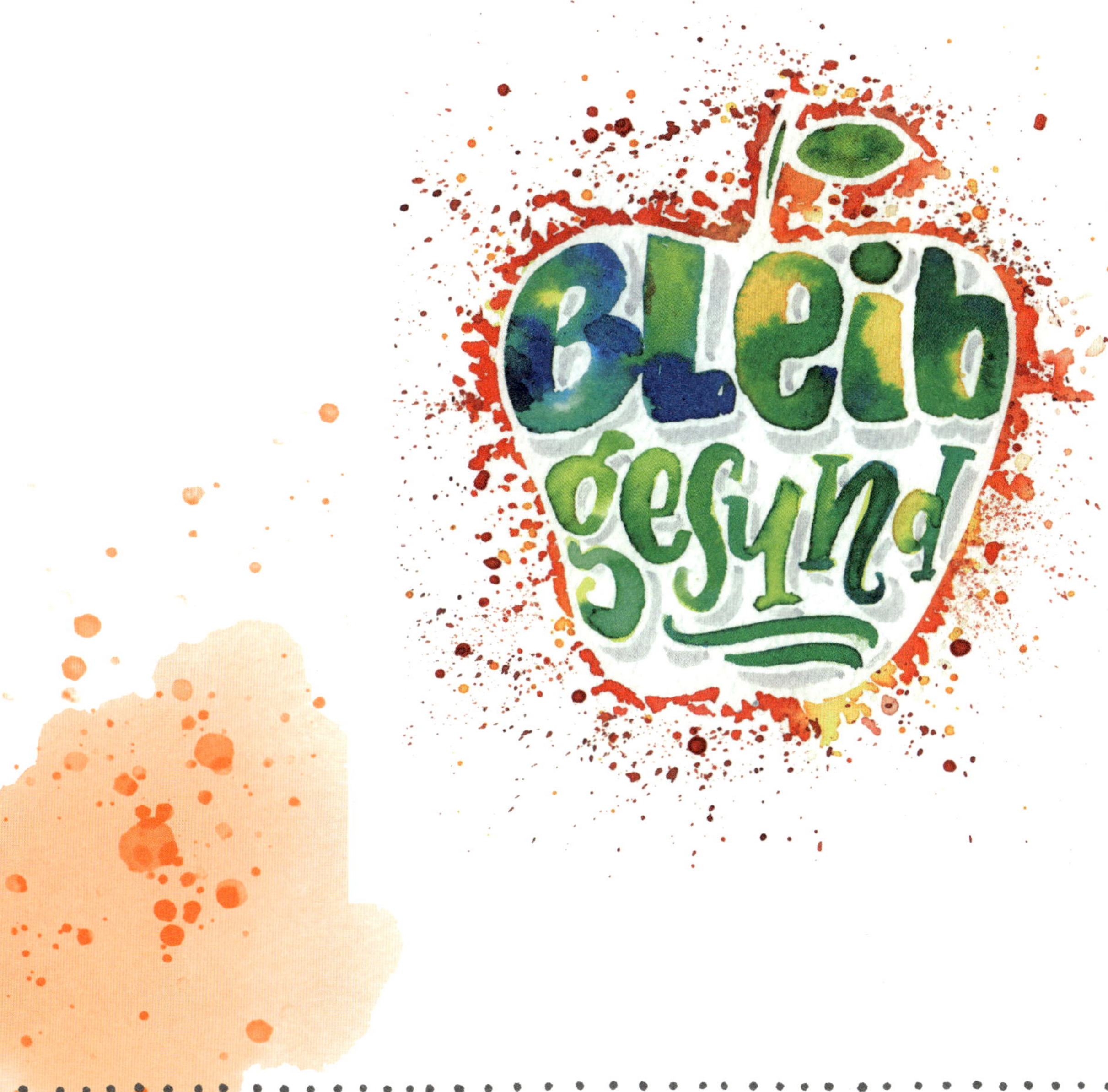

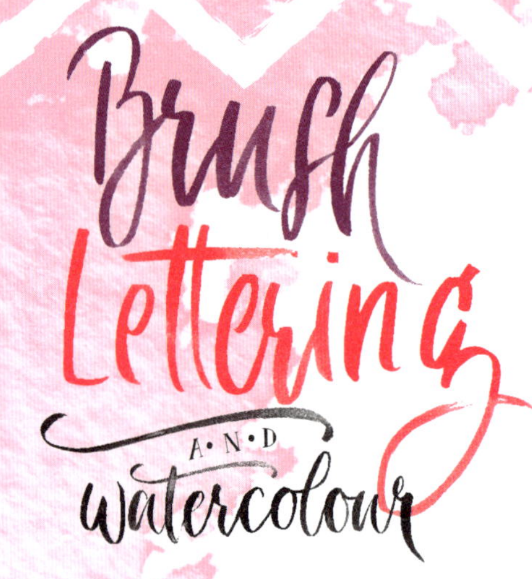

Brush lettering - hand lettering with brush pens - and creating designs with watercolour paints guarantees you plenty of colourful creative fun! The combination of beautiful lettering with a colourful gloss and the delicacy of watercolours open up a range of new design possibilities. Katja Haas presents various types of lettering and concentrates in particular on the special features of writing and decorating with brush pens.

Ideas for feather-light blossoms, tendrils and decorative elements and suggestions for special occasions make this the perfect companion to lettering. Happy lettering!

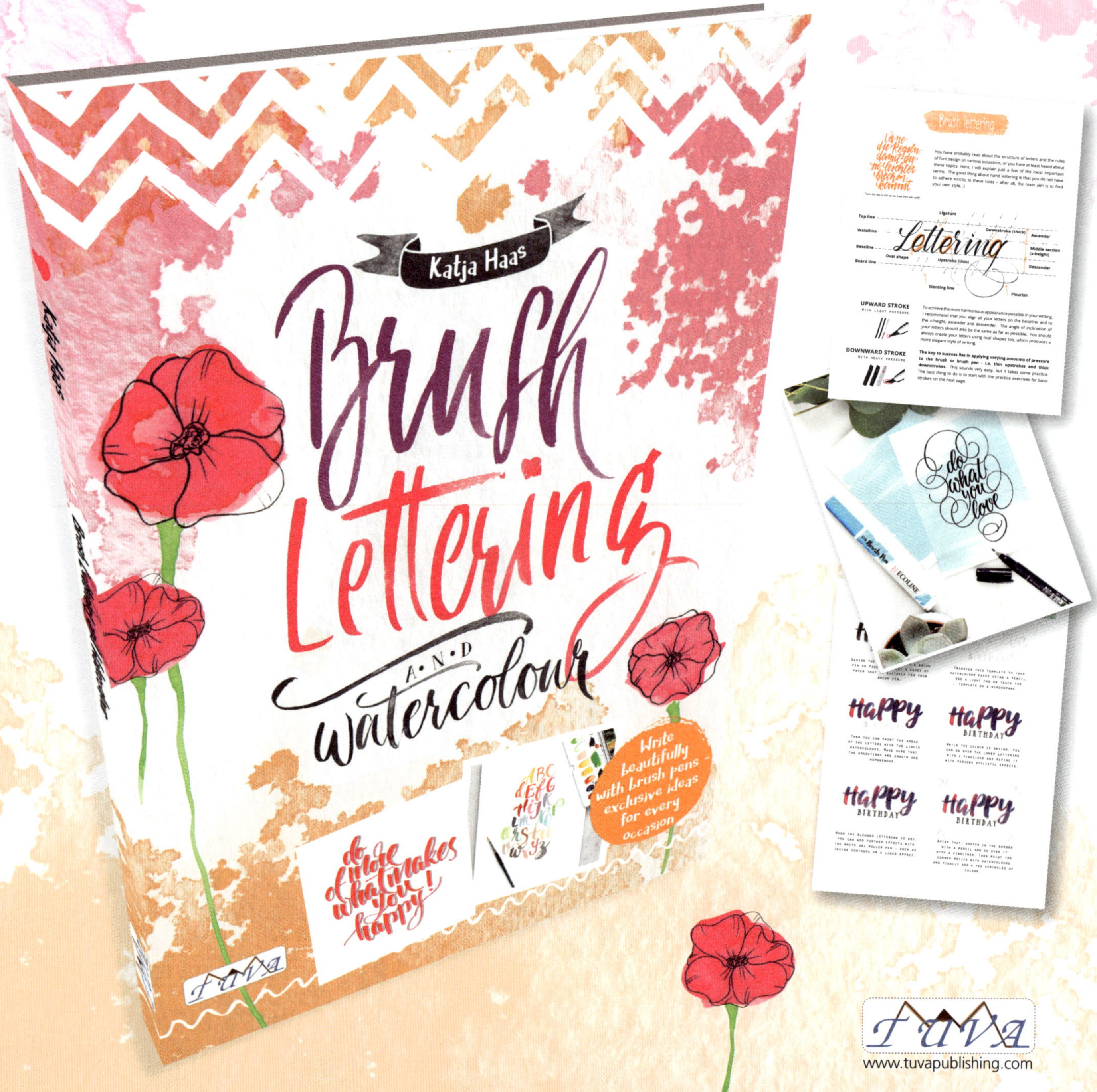

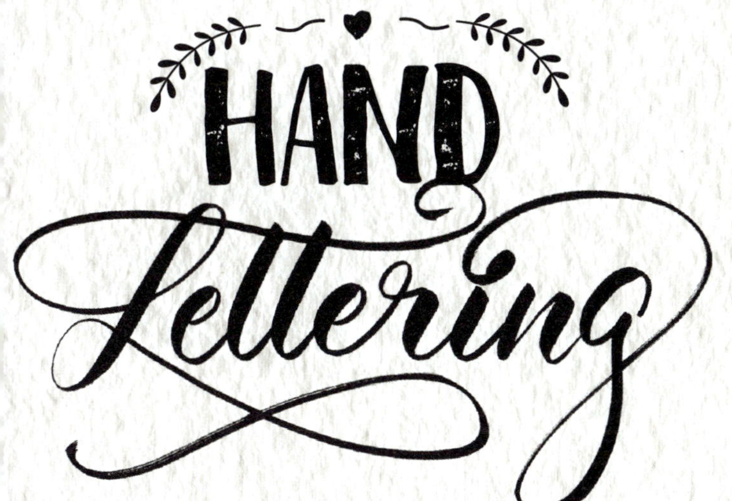

Small works of art created from letters and words - written and drawn by hand with love. Hand lettering gives you a little time for relaxation with pen and paper. Katja Haas introduces the art of beautiful writing, presenting the different types of lettering, materials, all the basics principles and practical tips and tricks for your own designs.

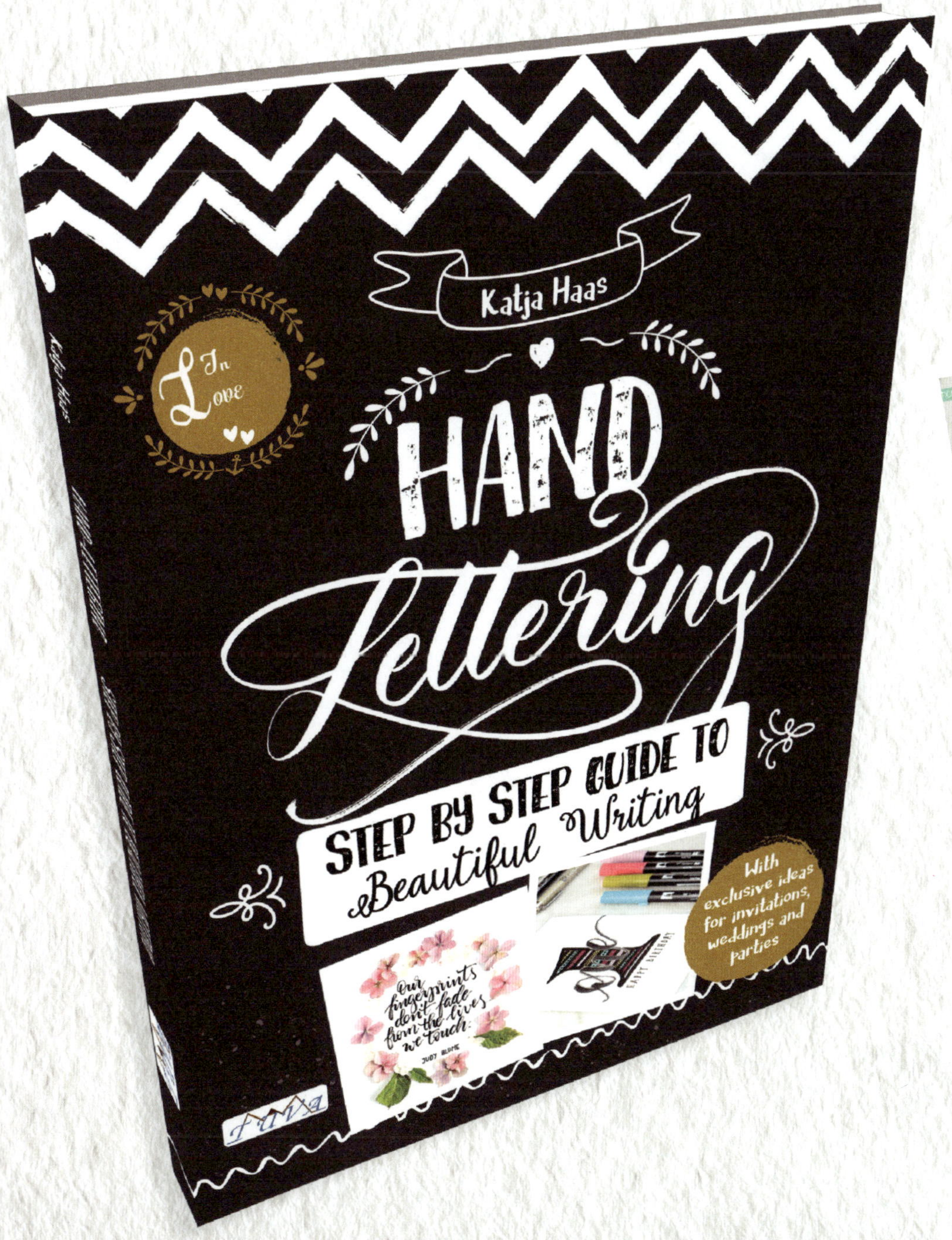

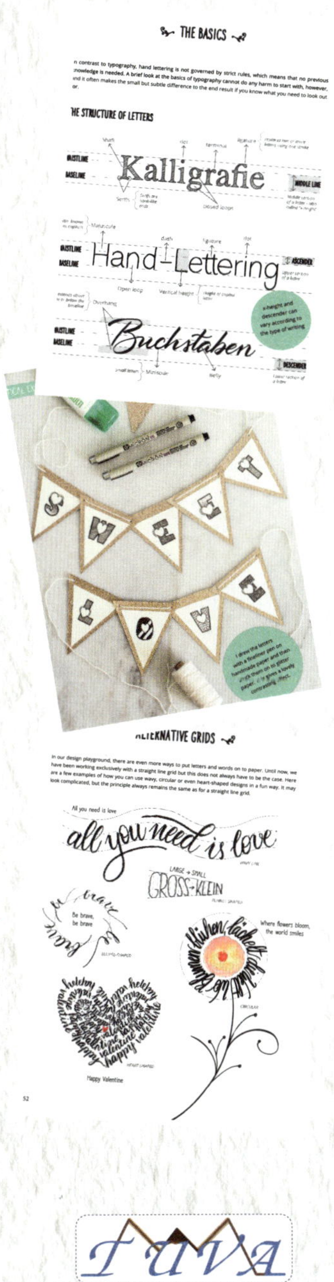

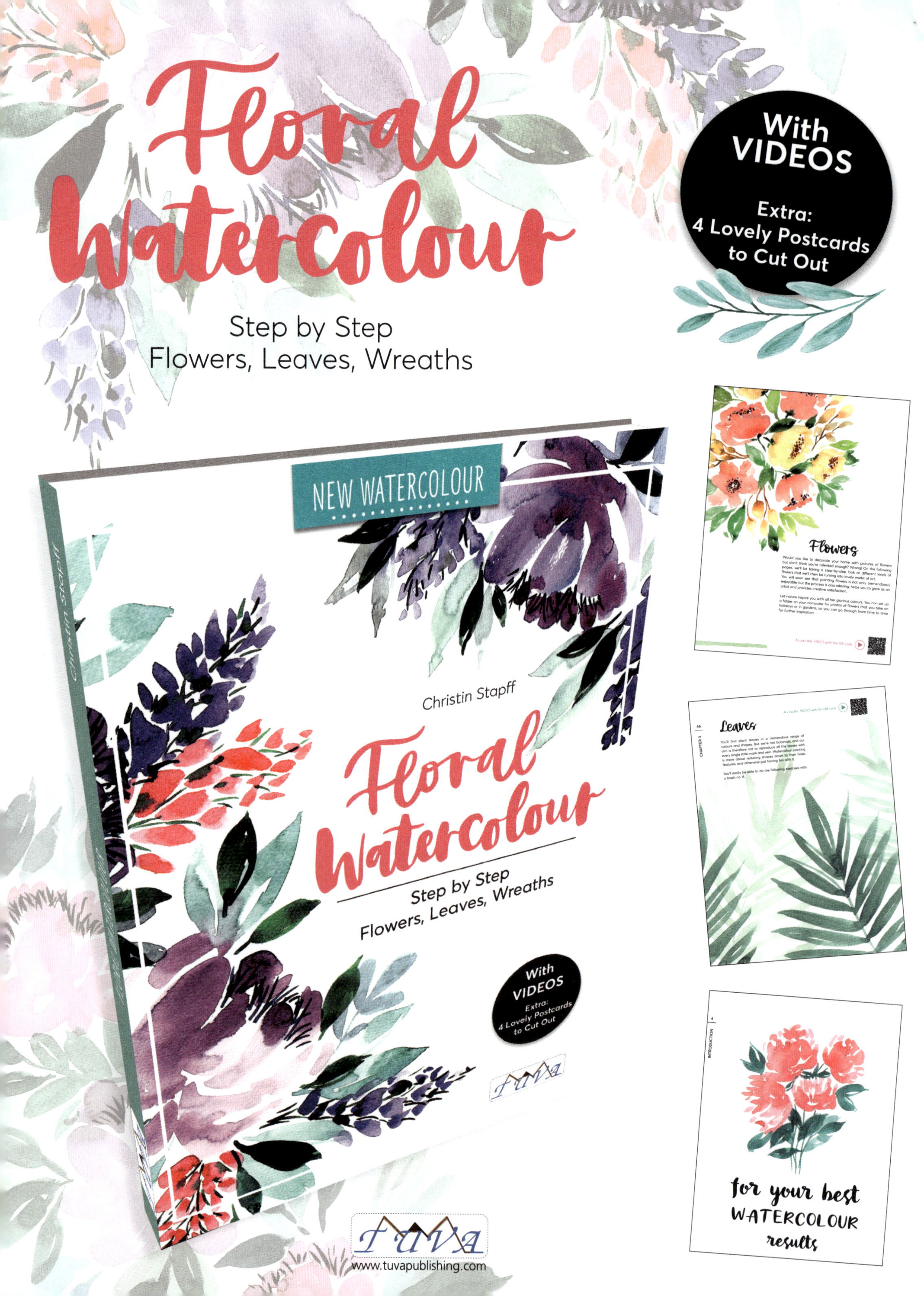

Floral Watercolour

Step by Step
Flowers, Leaves, Wreaths

Christin Stapff

Floral Watercolour

Step by Step
Flowers, Leaves, Wreaths

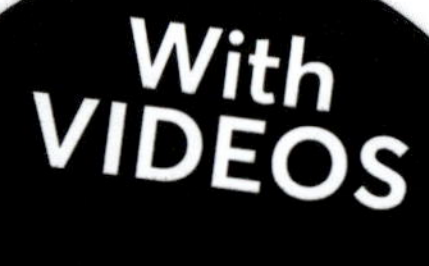

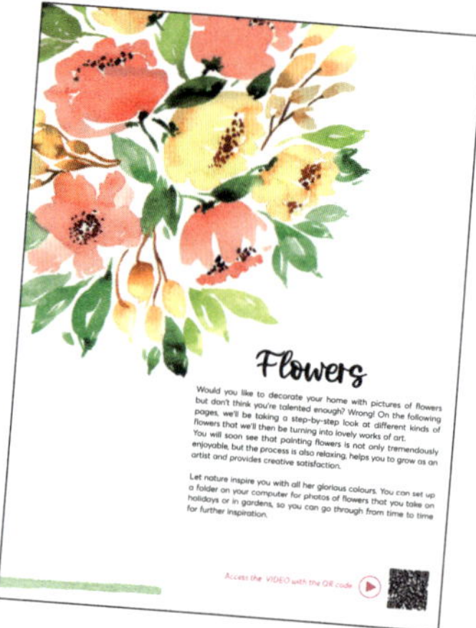

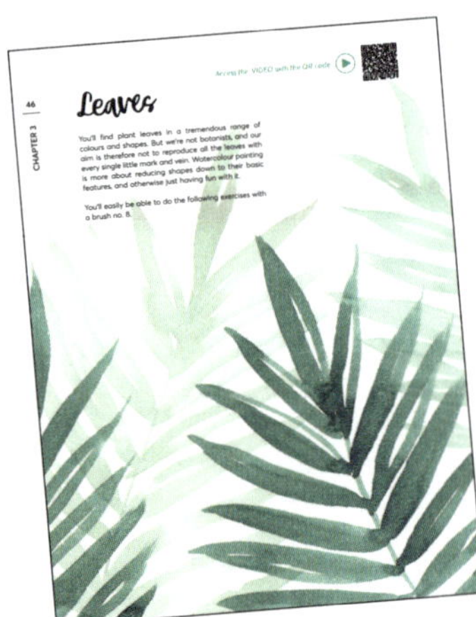

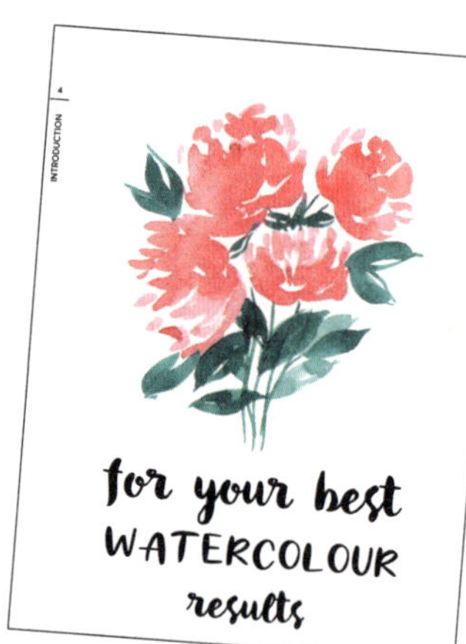

TuVa
www.tuvapublishing.com

Brush Lettering And Watercolour
My Workbook

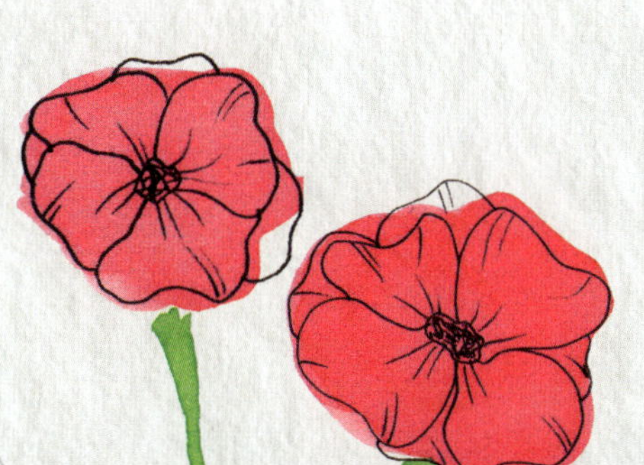

Katja Haas introduces the exercise book to her Brush Lettering and Watercolour. This workbook offers plenty of space for your own letterings and watercolour creations as well as compact overview of the brush lettering basics and instructions for writing and decorating with brushes. Lots of space to practice and try out.

Hand Lettering
My Workbook

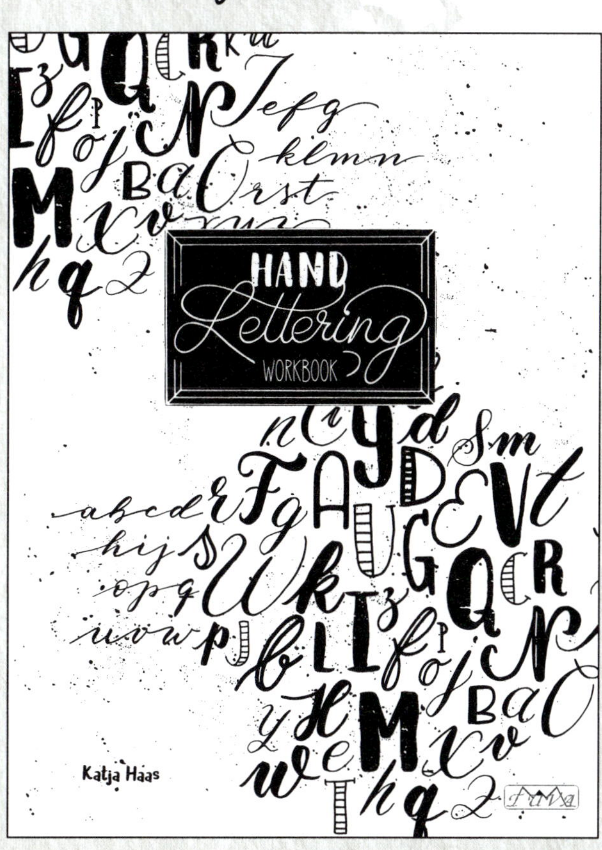

You will find in this workbook lots of examples with plenty of space for you to write. You can learn the basics of hand lettering step by step and get started straight away. You will find a number of sayings, which you can use according to the motto "copy and learn", first tracing the letters and then drawing them yourself. There is also plenty of blank space for creating your own letters and, of course, an A-Z guide of letters. Naturally, the more you practise, the faster you will perfect your hand lettering.

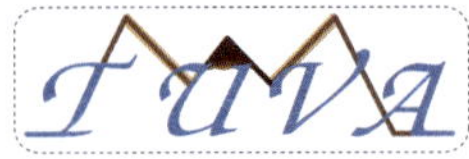

Tuva Publishing

www.tuvapublishing.com

Address

Merkez Mah. Cavusbasi Cad. No:71
Cekmekoy - Istanbul 34782 / Turkey
Tel: +90 216 642 62 62

Watercolour Meets Hand Lettering

The original German edition was published as
Watercolor Meets Handlettering
Copyright © 2019 frechverlag GmbH, Stuttgart,
Germany (www.topp-kreativ.de)
This edition is published by arrangement with
Claudia Böhme Rights & Literary Agency, Hannover,
Germany (www.agency-boehme.com).

First Print

2020 / September

All Global Copyrights Belong To
Tuva Tekstil ve Yayıncılık Ltd.

Content

Watercolour

Editor in Chief

Ayhan DEMİRPEHLİVAN

Project Editor

Kader DEMİRPEHLİVAN

Text & Illustrations

Bunte Galerie, Geliebtes Chaos
Mädchenkunst May & Berry

Graphic Designers

Ömer ALP, Abdullah BAYRAKÇI, Tarık TOKGÖZ

ISBN

978-605-7834-14-0

 TuvaYayincilik   TuvaPublishing
 TuvaYayincilik   TuvaPublishing